SUPERMAN
FIRST THUNDER
SHAZAM!

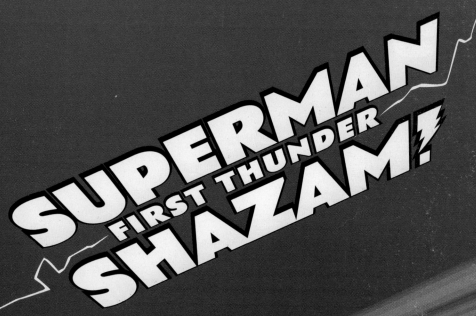

SUPERMAN

FIRST THUNDER

SHAZAM!

JUDD WINICK *WRITER* **JOSHUA MIDDLETON** *ARTIST*

NICK J. NAPOLITANO *LETTERER*

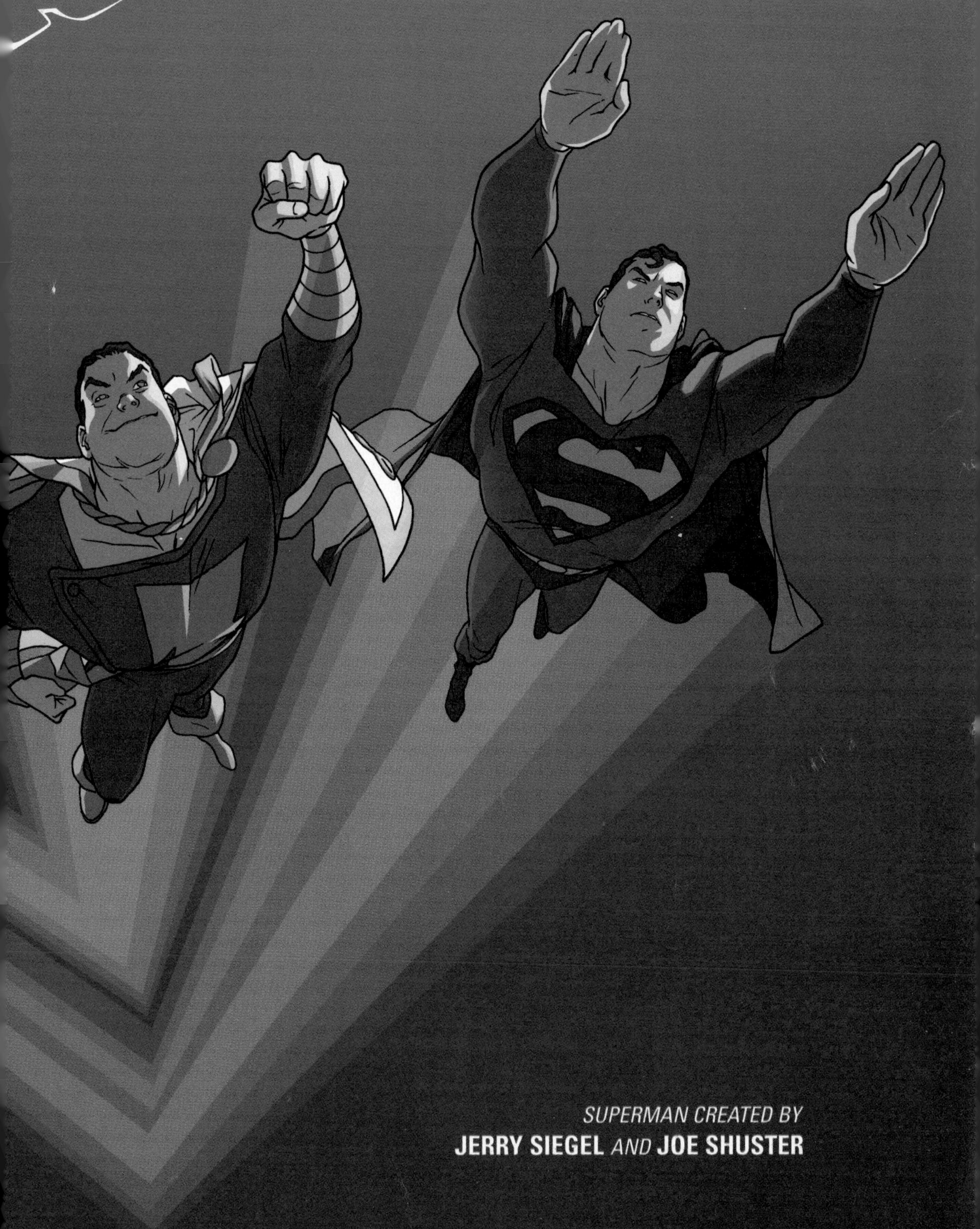

SUPERMAN CREATED BY

JERRY SIEGEL *AND* **JOE SHUSTER**

SUPERMAN/SHAZAM: FIRST THUNDER
Published by DC Comics. Cover and
compilation copyright © 2006 DC
Comics. All Rights Reserved. Originally
published in single magazine form as:
SUPERMAN/SHAZAM: FIRST THUNDER
1-4. Copyright © 2005, 2006 DC Comics.
All Rights Reserved. All characters, their
distinctive likenesses and related elements
featured in this publication are trademarks
of DC Comics. The stories, characters and
incidents featured in this publication are
entirely fictional. DC Comics does not read
or accept unsolicited submissions of ideas,
stories or artwork. DC Comics, 1700
Broadway, New York, NY 10019. A Warner
Bros. Entertainment Company. Printed in
Canada. First Printing.
ISBN: 1-4012-0923-8
ISBN 13: 978-1-4012-0923-0
Cover art by Joshua Middleton
Publication design by John J. Hill

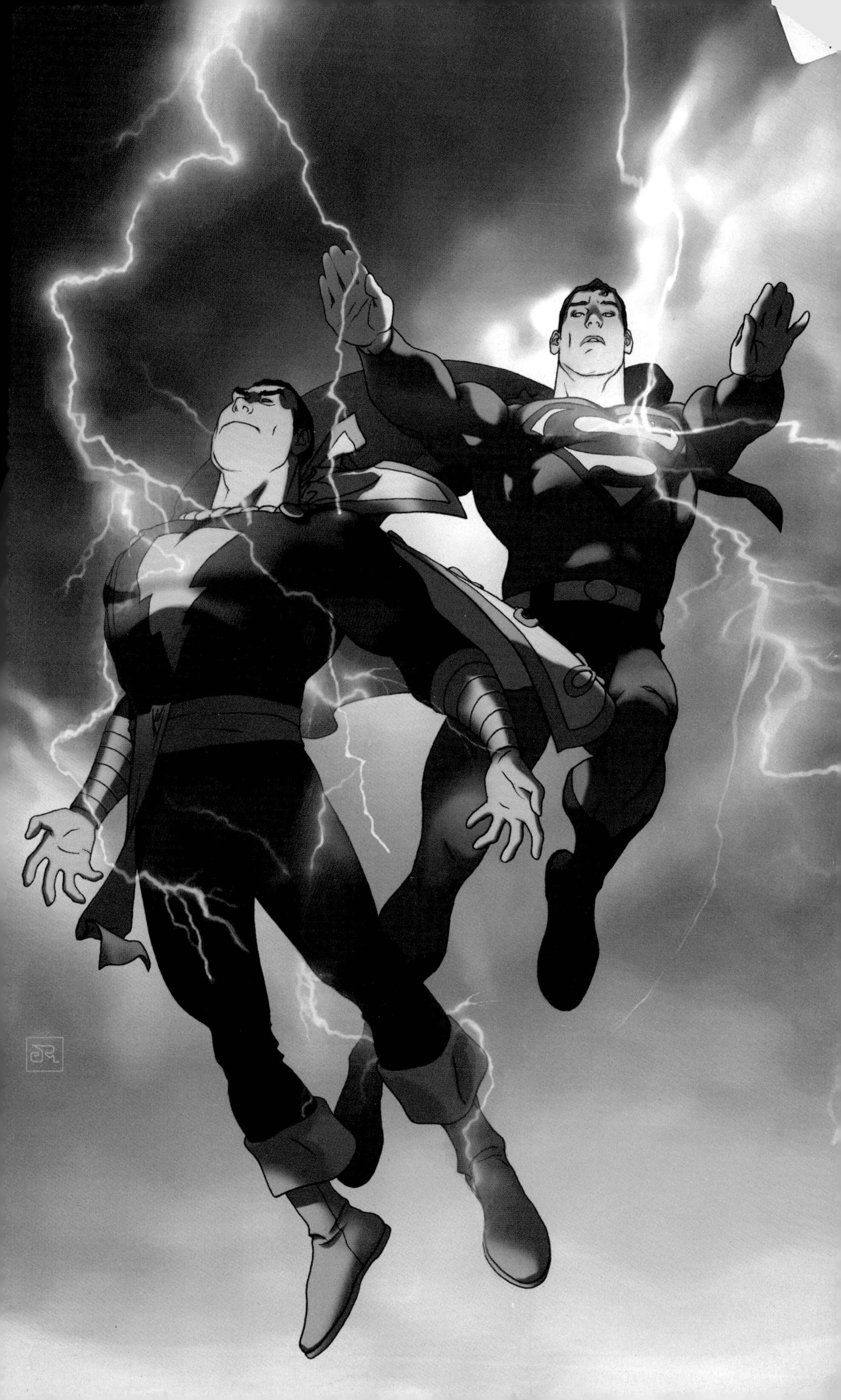

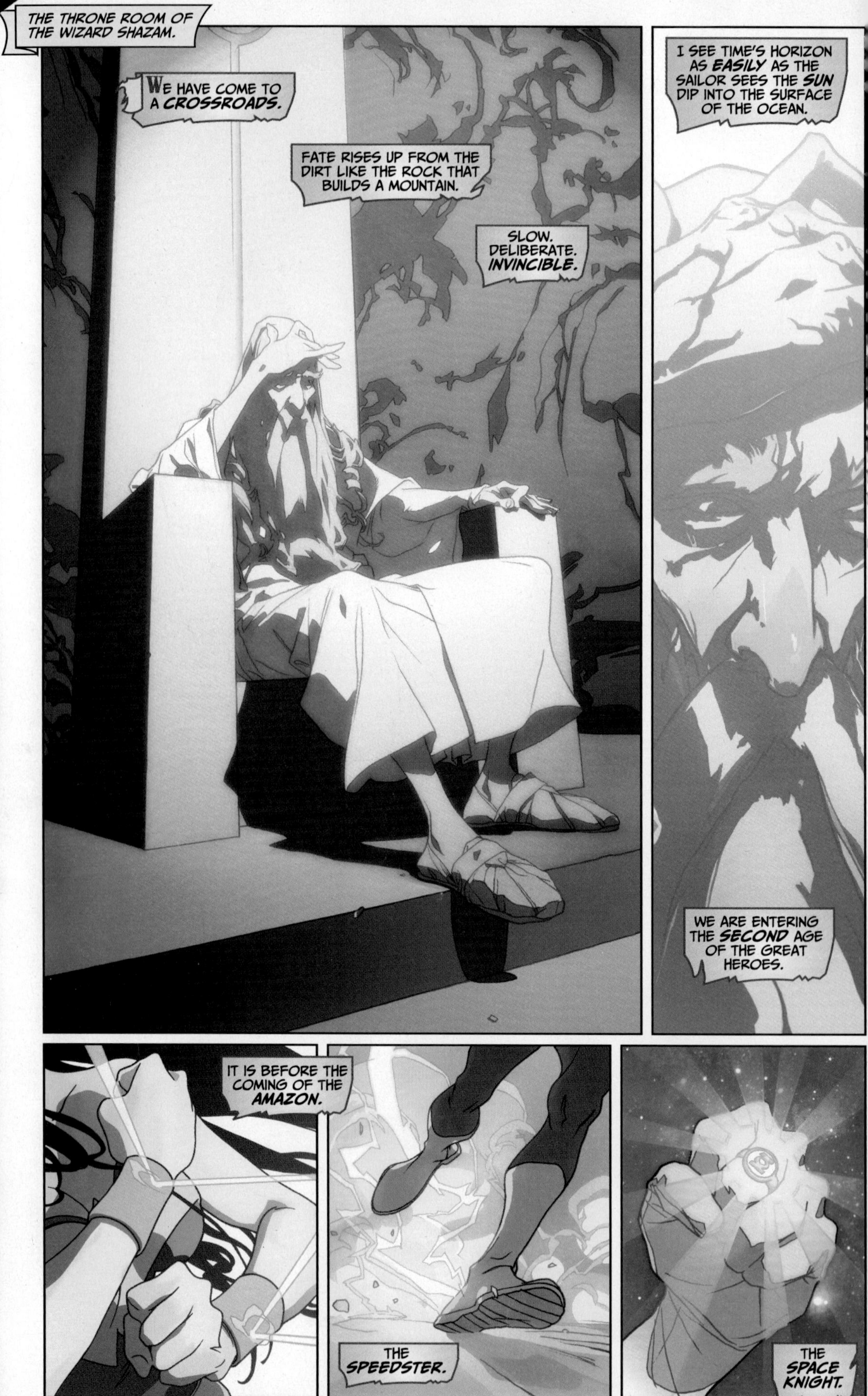
THE THRONE ROOM OF THE WIZARD SHAZAM.
WE HAVE COME TO A CROSSROADS.
FATE RISES UP FROM THE DIRT LIKE THE ROCK THAT BUILDS A MOUNTAIN.
SLOW. DELIBERATE. INVINCIBLE.
I SEE TIME'S HORIZON AS EASILY AS THE SAILOR SEES THE SUN DIP INTO THE SURFACE OF THE OCEAN.
WE ARE ENTERING THE SECOND AGE OF THE GREAT HEROES.
IT IS BEFORE THE COMING OF THE AMAZON.
THE SPEEDSTER.
THE SPACE KNIGHT.

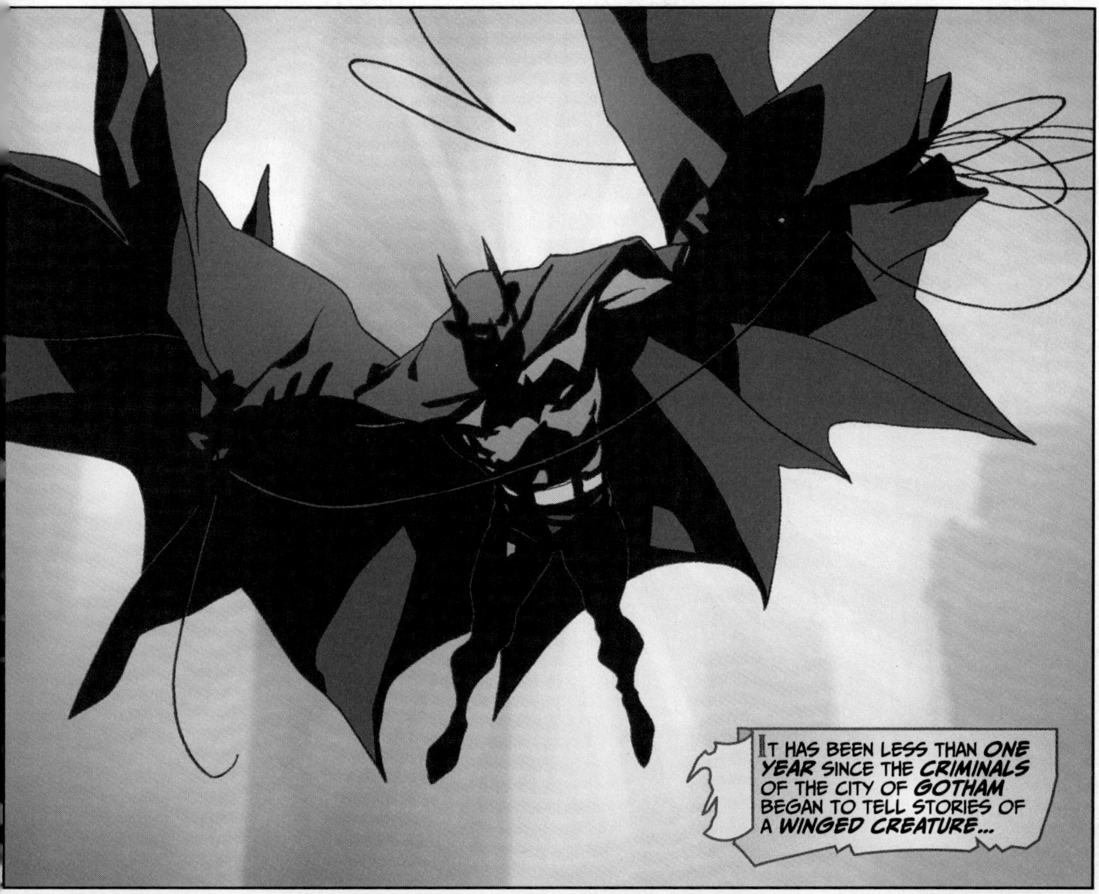
IT HAS BEEN LESS THAN ONE YEAR SINCE THE CRIMINALS OF THE CITY OF GOTHAM BEGAN TO TELL STORIES OF A WINGED CREATURE...

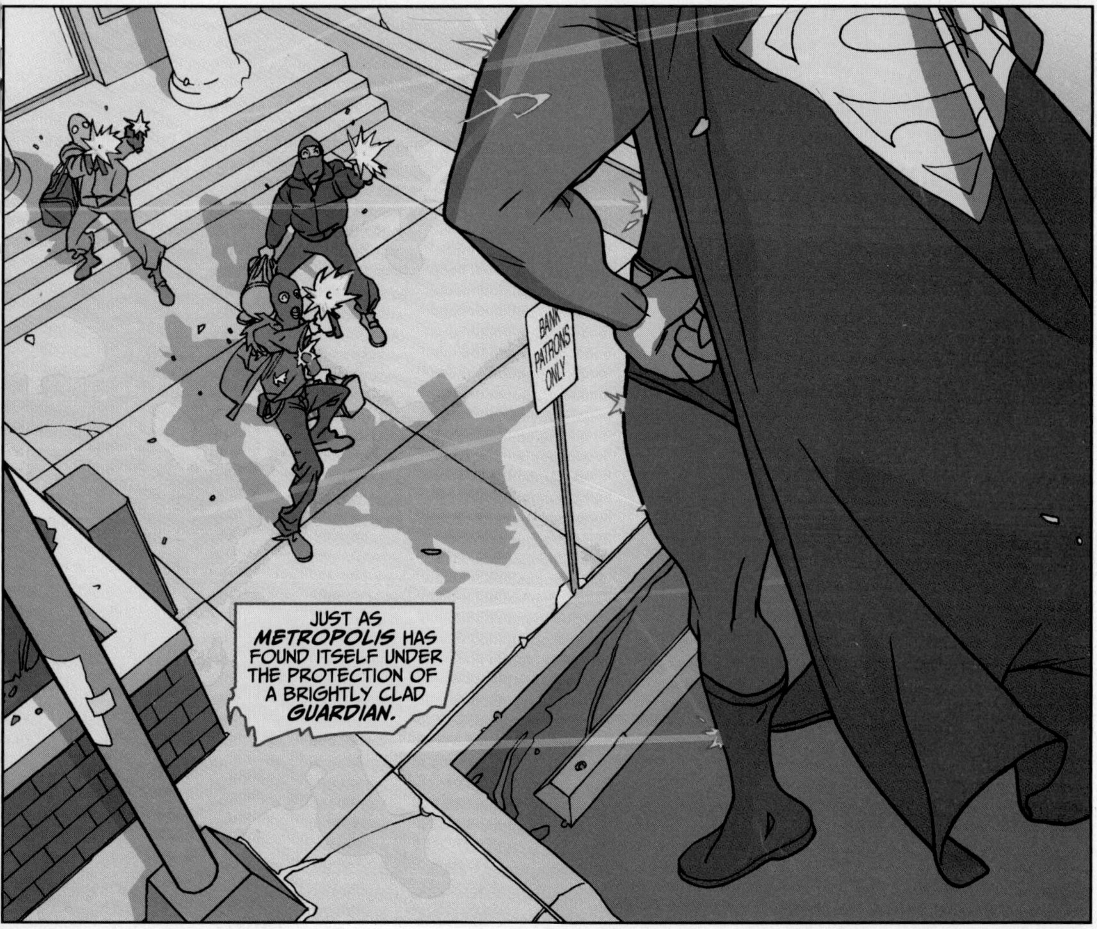
BANK PATRONS ONLY
JUST AS METROPOLIS HAS FOUND ITSELF UNDER THE PROTECTION OF A BRIGHTLY CLAD GUARDIAN.

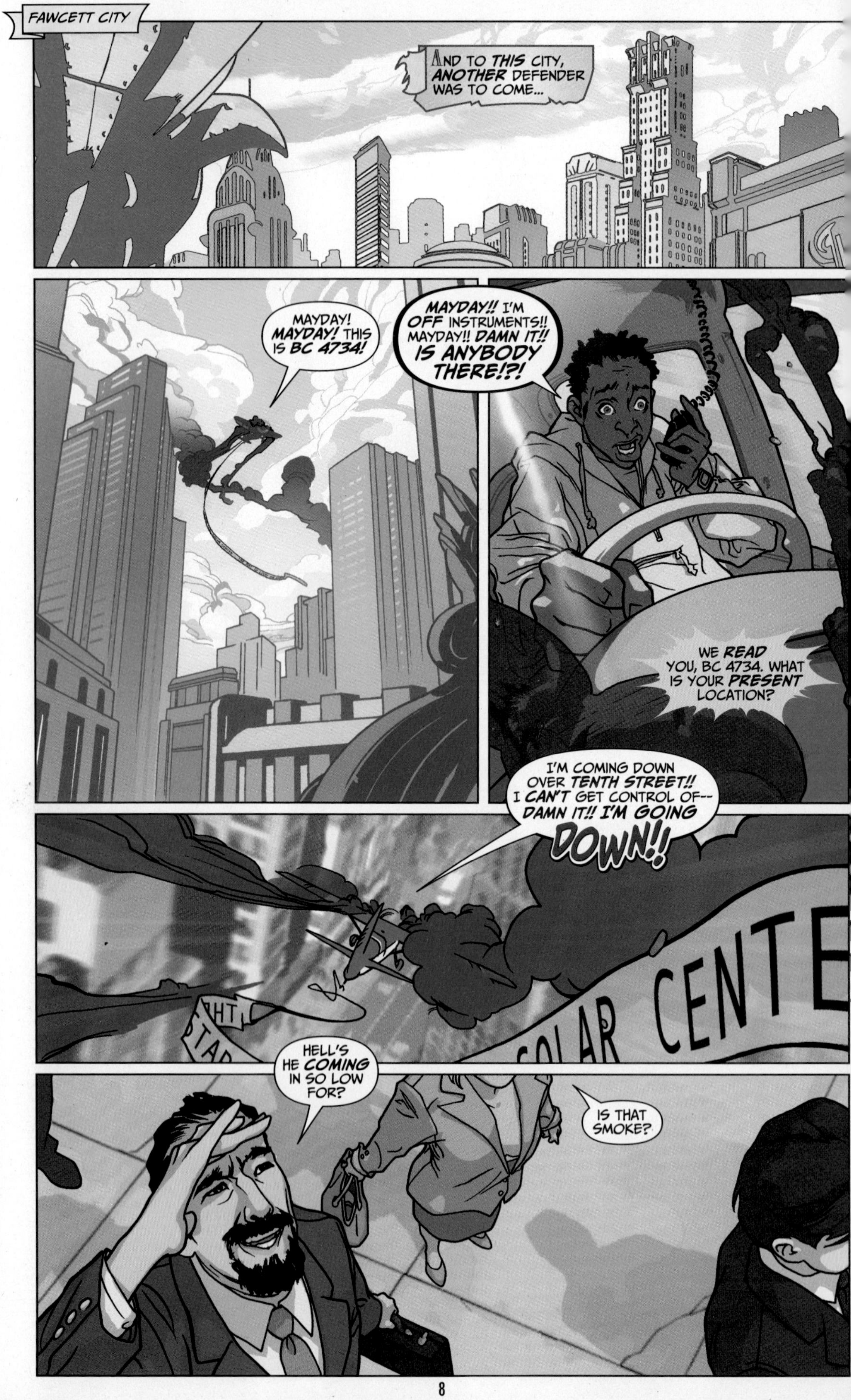
FAWCETT CITY
AND TO THIS CITY, ANOTHER DEFENDER WAS TO COME...
MAYDAY! MAYDAY! THIS IS BC 4734!
MAYDAY!! I'M OFF INSTRUMENTS!! MAYDAY!! DAMN IT!! IS ANYBODY THERE!?!
WE READ YOU, BC 4734. WHAT IS YOUR PRESENT LOCATION?
I'M COMING DOWN OVER TENTH STREET!! I CAN'T GET CONTROL OF-- DAMN IT!! I'M GOING DOWN!!
SOLAR CENTE
HELL'S HE COMING IN SO LOW FOR?
IS THAT SMOKE?

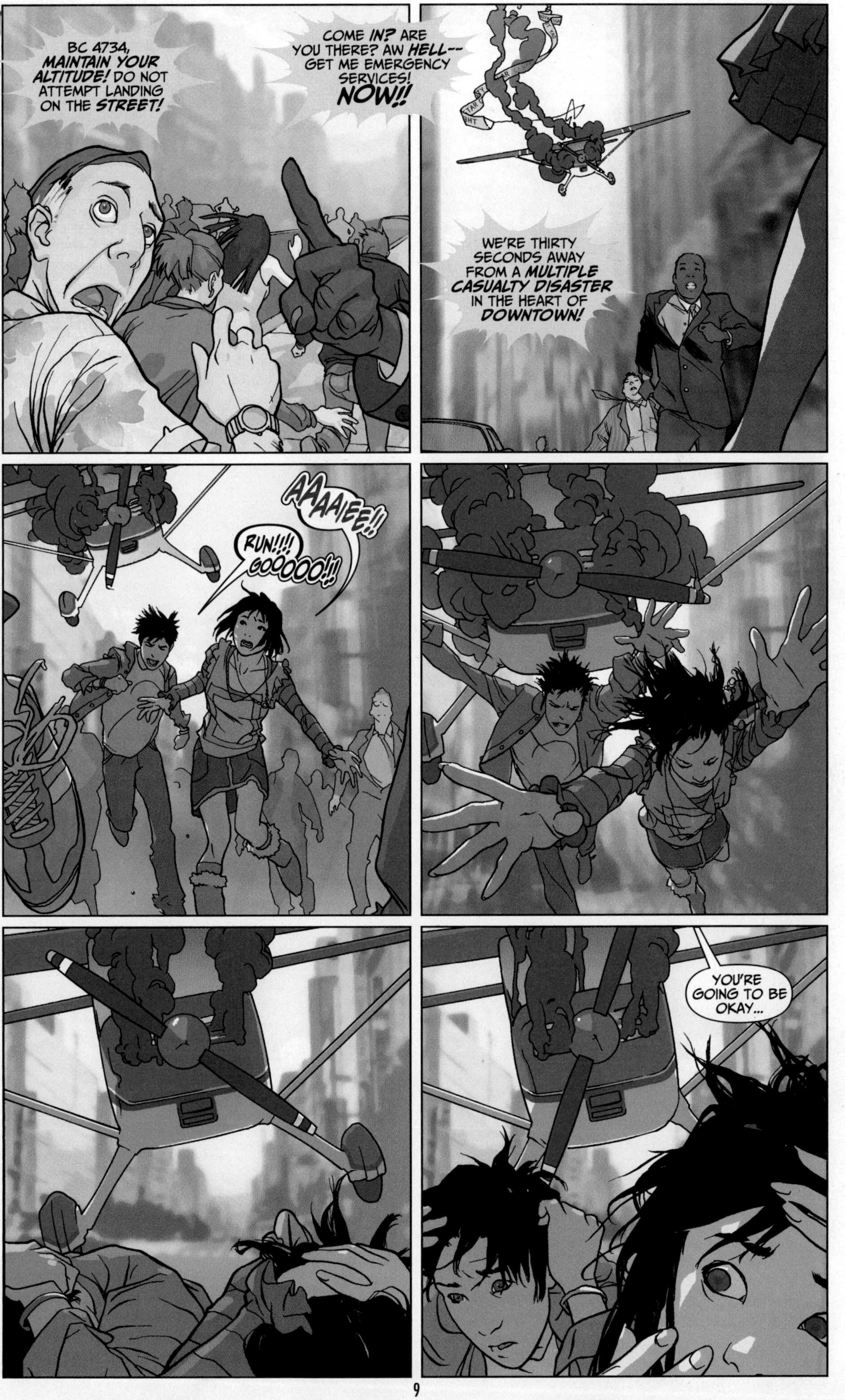
BC 4734, MAINTAIN YOUR ALTITUDE! DO NOT ATTEMPT LANDING ON THE STREET!
COME IN? ARE YOU THERE? AW HELL-- GET ME EMERGENCY SERVICES! NOW!!
WE'RE THIRTY SECONDS AWAY FROM A MULTIPLE CASUALTY DISASTER IN THE HEART OF DOWNTOWN!
AAAAIEE!!
RUN!!!! GOOOOO!!!
YOU'RE GOING TO BE OKAY...

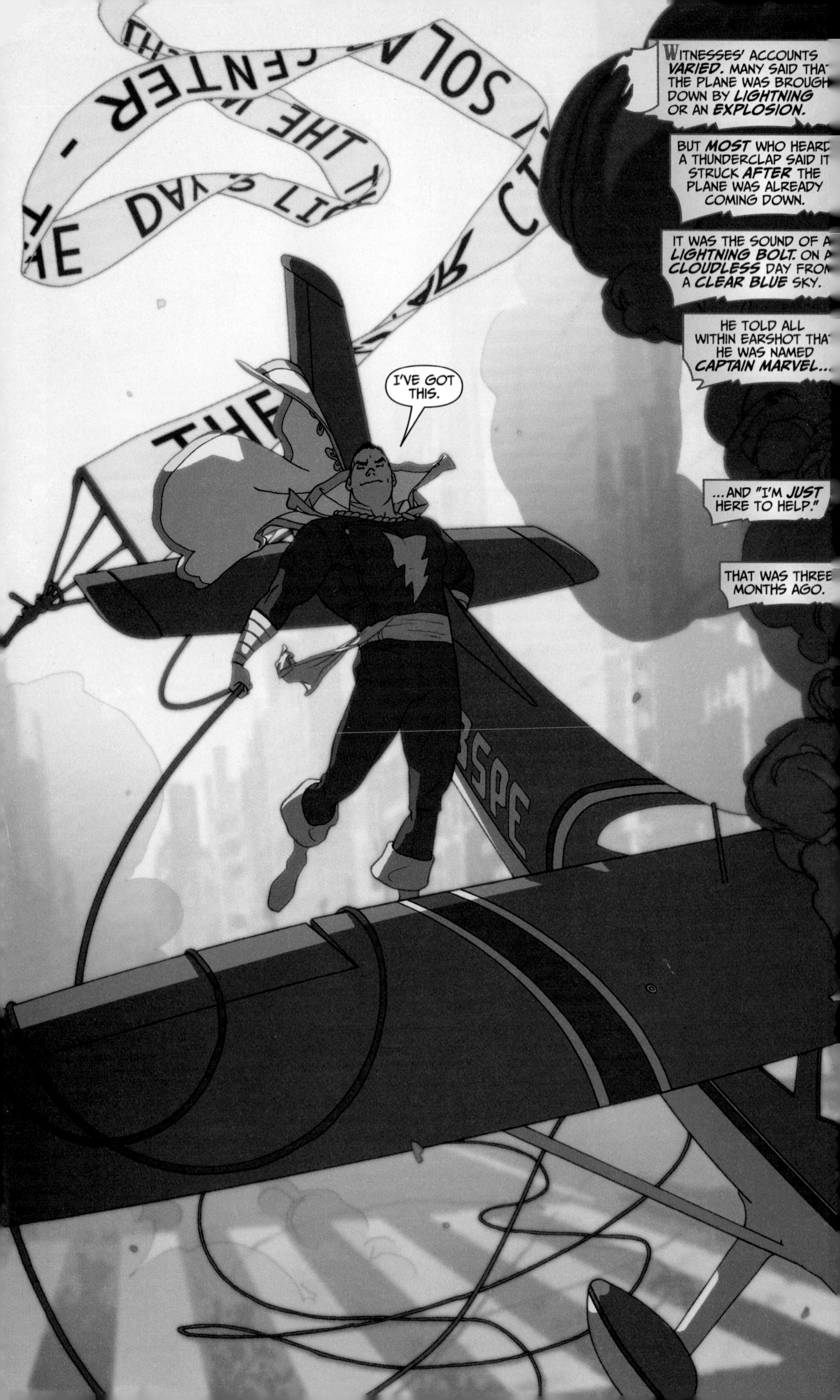
WITNESSES' ACCOUNTS VARIED. MANY SAID THA THE PLANE WAS BROUGH DOWN BY LIGHTNING OR AN EXPLOSION.
BUT MOST WHO HEARD A THUNDERCLAP SAID IT STRUCK AFTER THE PLANE WAS ALREADY COMING DOWN.
IT WAS THE SOUND OF A LIGHTNING BOLT. ON A CLOUDLESS DAY FROM A CLEAR BLUE SKY.
HE TOLD ALL WITHIN EARSHOT THAT HE WAS NAMED CAPTAIN MARVEL...
I'VE GOT THIS.
...AND "I'M JUST HERE TO HELP."
THAT WAS THREE MONTHS AGO.

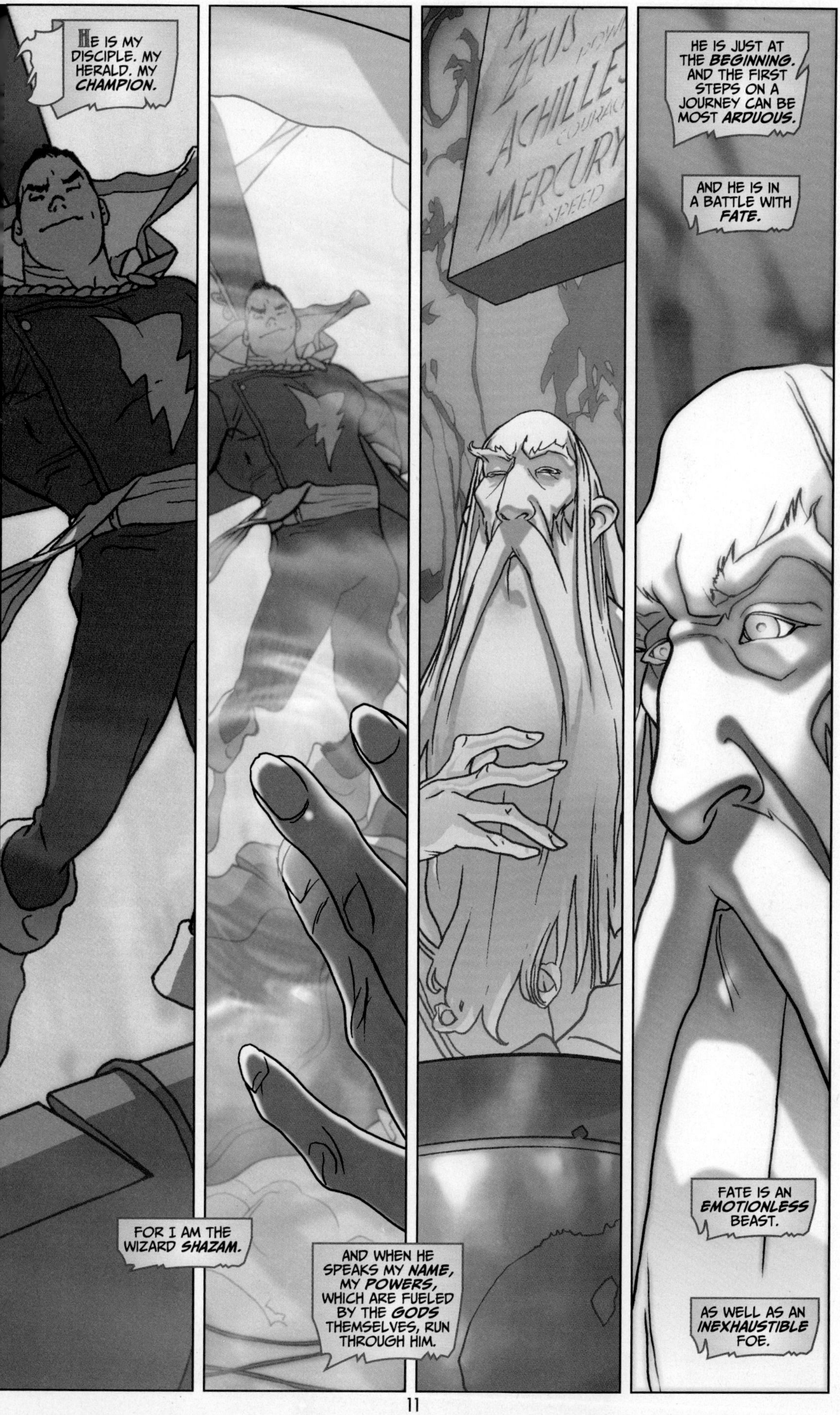
HE IS MY DISCIPLE. MY HERALD. MY CHAMPION.
FOR I AM THE WIZARD SHAZAM.
AND WHEN HE SPEAKS MY NAME, MY POWERS, WHICH ARE FUELED BY THE GODS THEMSELVES, RUN THROUGH HIM.
ZEUS
ACHILLES
MERCURY
SPEED
HE IS JUST AT THE BEGINNING. AND THE FIRST STEPS ON A JOURNEY CAN BE MOST ARDUOUS.
AND HE IS IN A BATTLE WITH FATE.
FATE IS AN EMOTIONLESS BEAST.
AS WELL AS AN INEXHAUSTIBLE FOE.

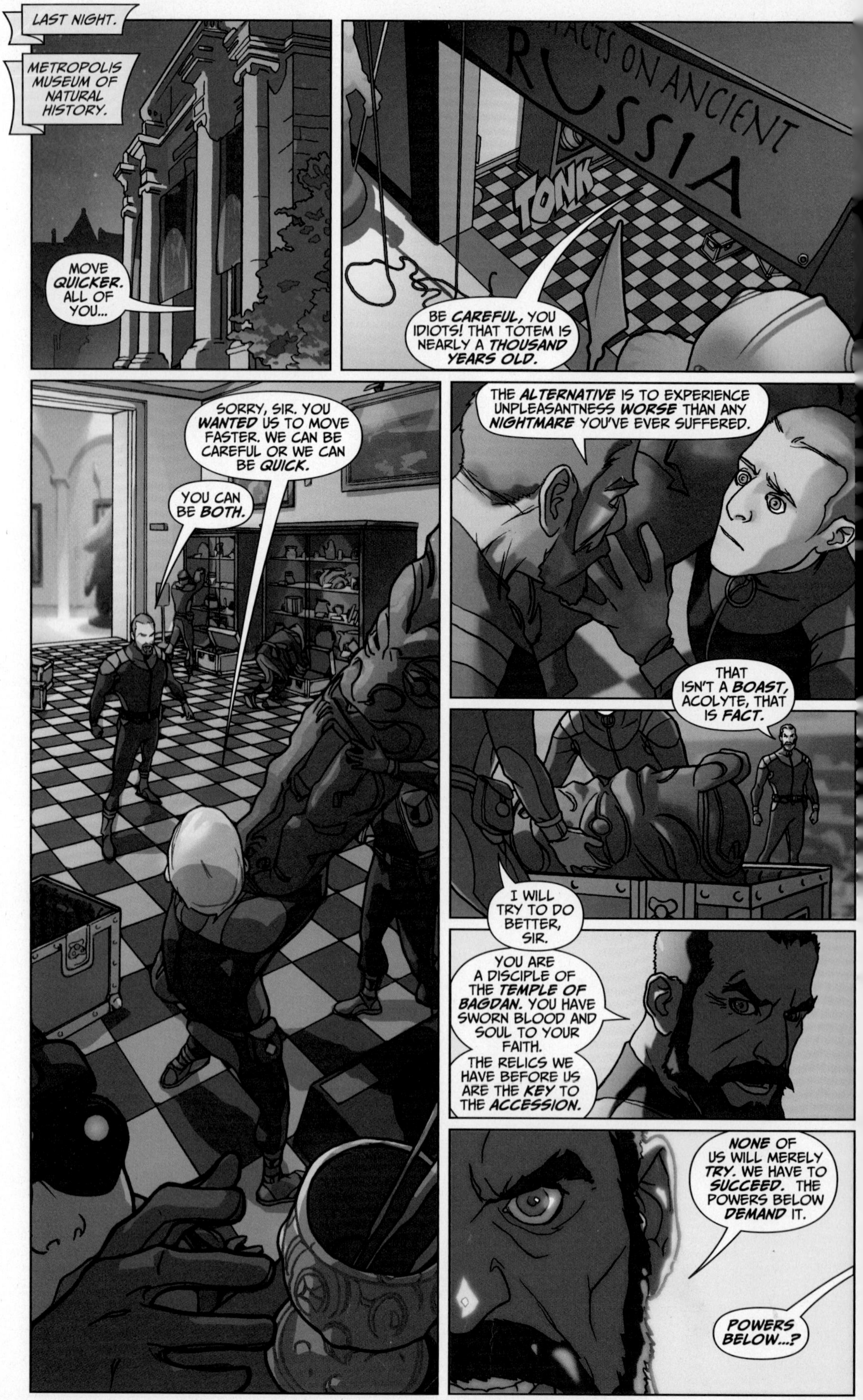
LAST NIGHT.
METROPOLIS MUSEUM OF NATURAL HISTORY.
MOVE QUICKER. ALL OF YOU...
ACTS ON ANCIENT RUSSIA
TONK
BE CAREFUL, YOU IDIOTS! THAT TOTEM IS NEARLY A THOUSAND YEARS OLD.
SORRY, SIR. YOU WANTED US TO MOVE FASTER. WE CAN BE CAREFUL OR WE CAN BE QUICK.
YOU CAN BE BOTH.
THE ALTERNATIVE IS TO EXPERIENCE UNPLEASANTNESS WORSE THAN ANY NIGHTMARE YOU'VE EVER SUFFERED.
THAT ISN'T A BOAST, ACOLYTE, THAT IS FACT.
I WILL TRY TO DO BETTER, SIR.
YOU ARE A DISCIPLE OF THE TEMPLE OF BAGDAN. YOU HAVE SWORN BLOOD AND SOUL TO YOUR FAITH.
THE RELICS WE HAVE BEFORE US ARE THE KEY TO THE ACCESSION.
NONE OF US WILL MERELY TRY. WE HAVE TO SUCCEED. THE POWERS BELOW DEMAND IT.
POWERS BELOW...?

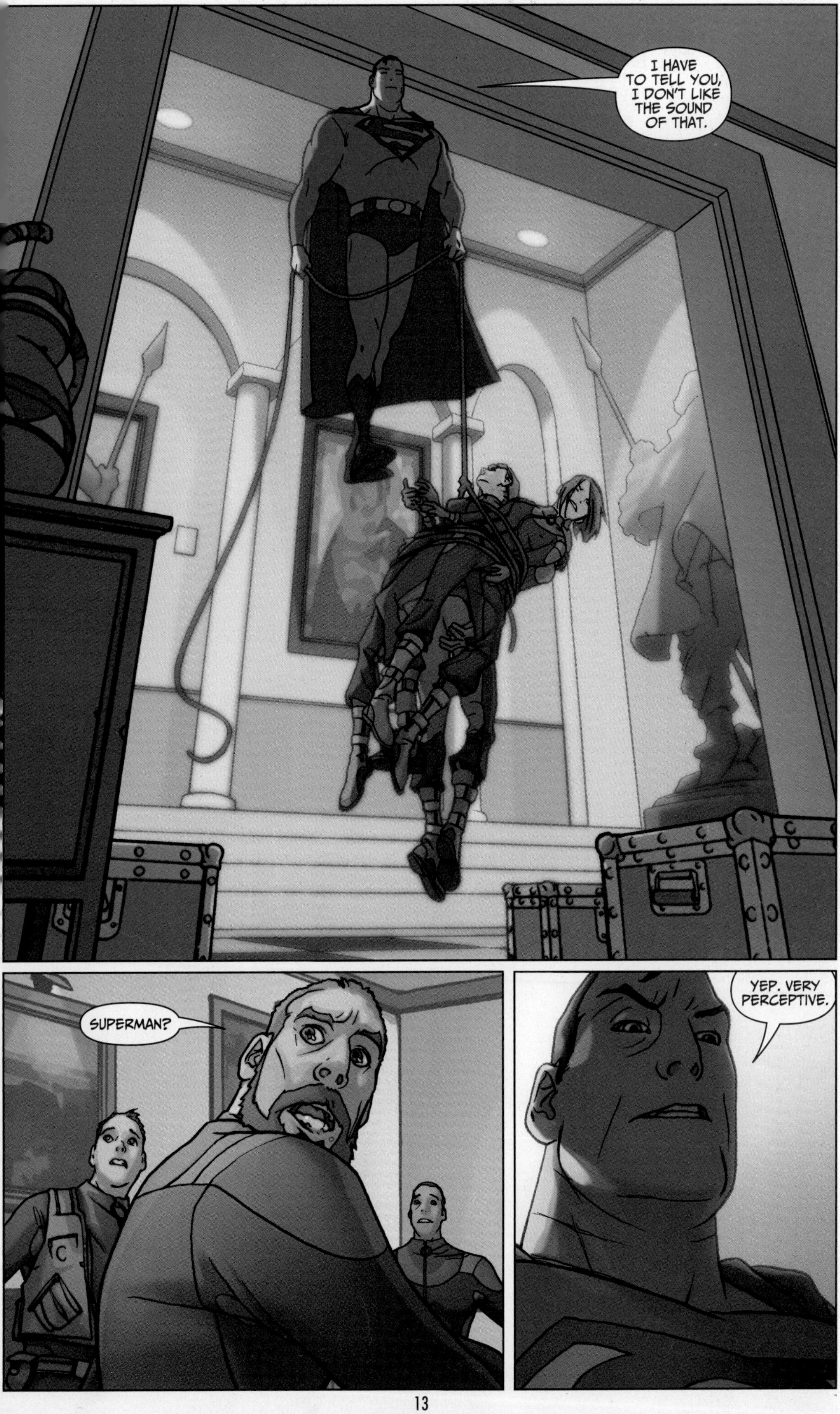
I HAVE TO TELL YOU, I DON'T LIKE THE SOUND OF THAT.
SUPERMAN?
YEP. VERY PERCEPTIVE.

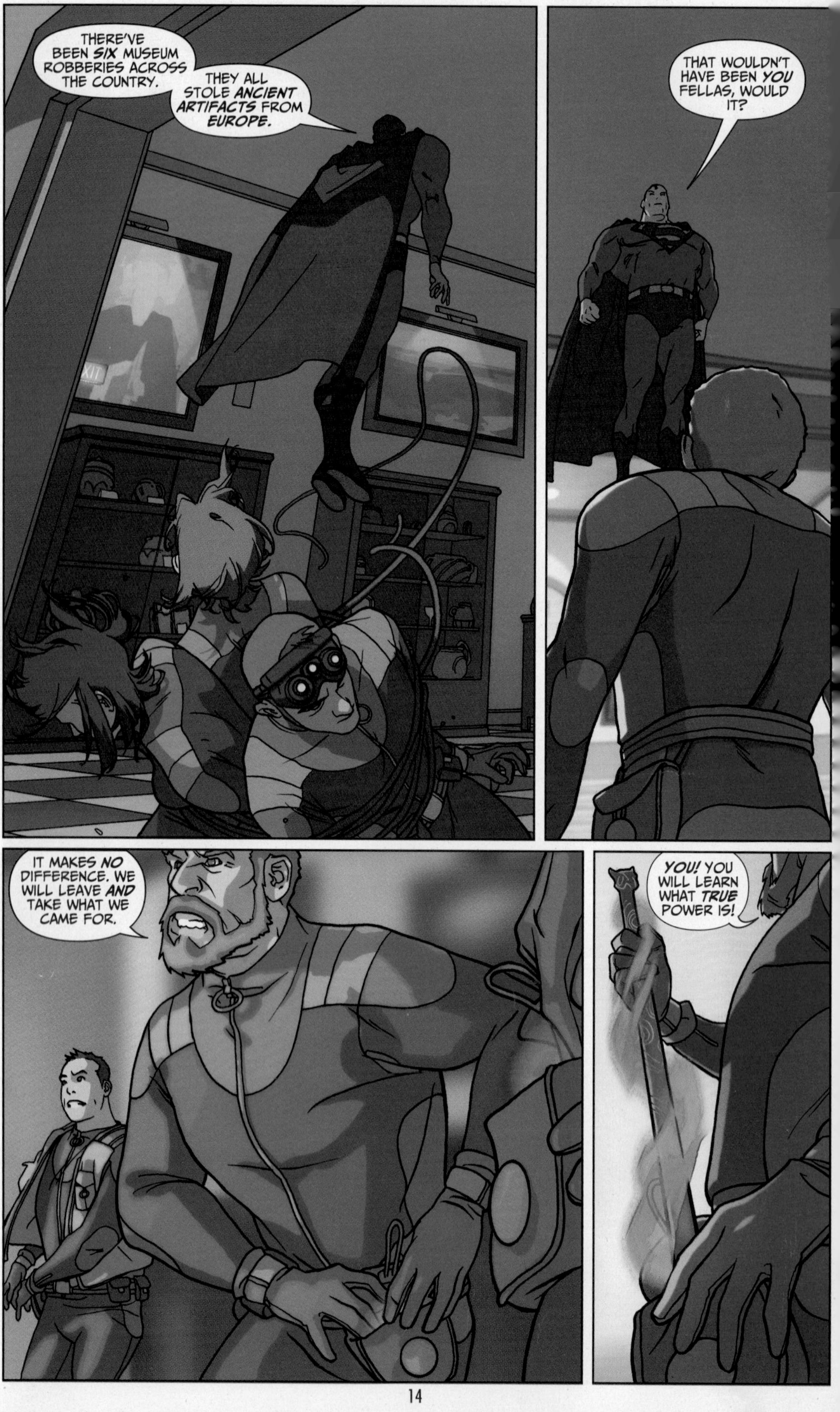

THERE'VE BEEN *SIX* MUSEUM ROBBERIES ACROSS THE COUNTRY.
THEY ALL STOLE *ANCIENT ARTIFACTS* FROM *EUROPE*.
THAT WOULDN'T HAVE BEEN *YOU* FELLAS, WOULD IT?
IT MAKES *NO* DIFFERENCE. WE WILL LEAVE *AND* TAKE WHAT WE CAME FOR.
YOU! YOU WILL LEARN WHAT *TRUE* POWER IS!

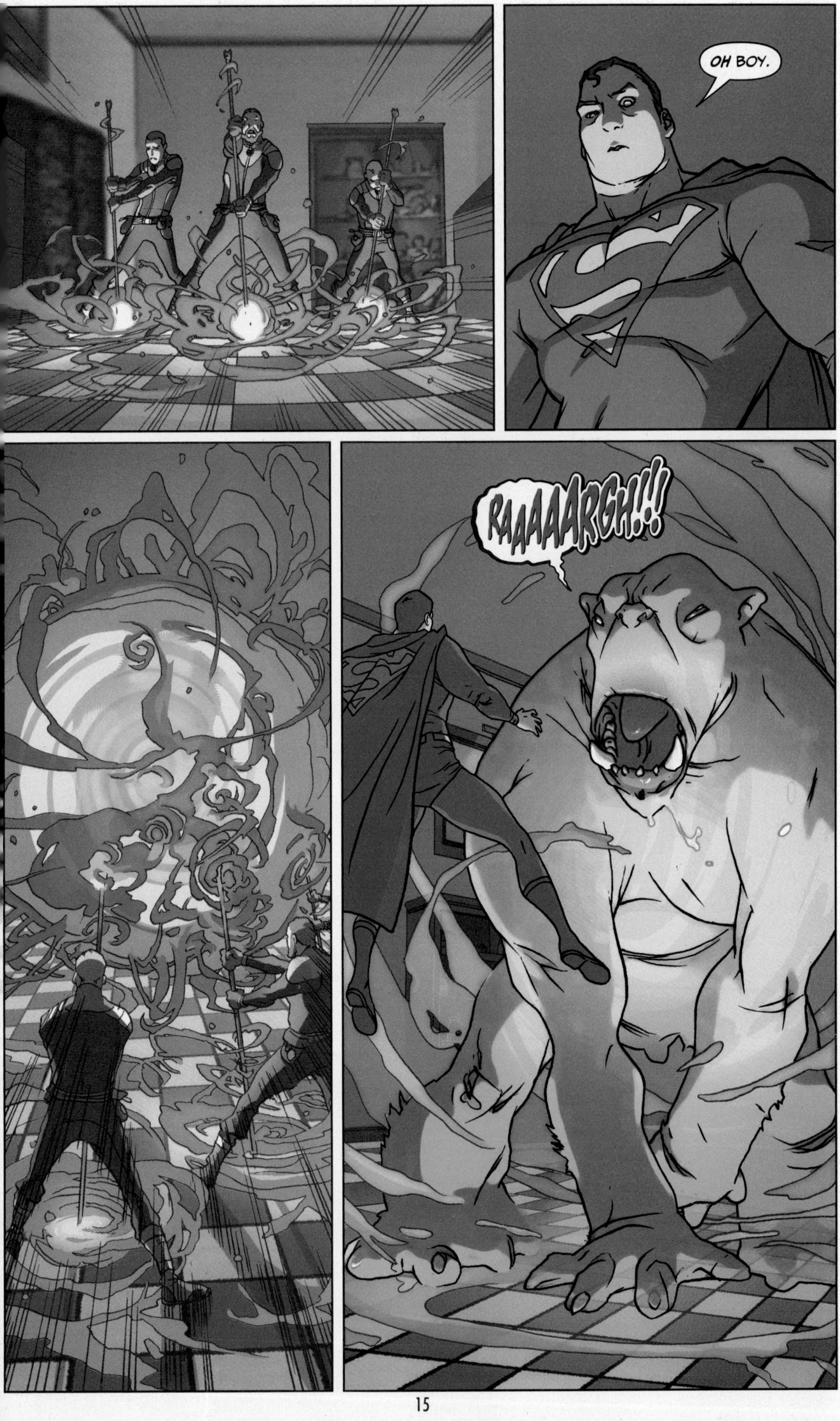
OH BOY.
RAAAAARGH!!!

SO *FAST!* HOW COULD SOMETHING SO *HUGE* MOVE THAT QUI--

HEY!

IT'S *STRONG.* I'VE NEVER FELT *ANYTHING* SO STRONG.

CAN'T-- CAN'T GET HIM *OFF...*

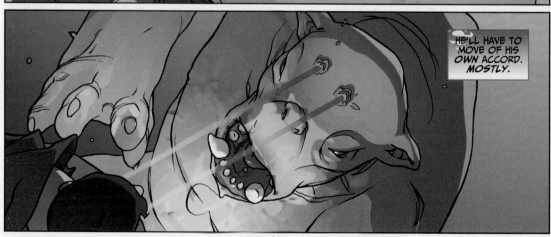

HE'LL HAVE TO MOVE OF HIS OWN ACCORD. *MOSTLY.*

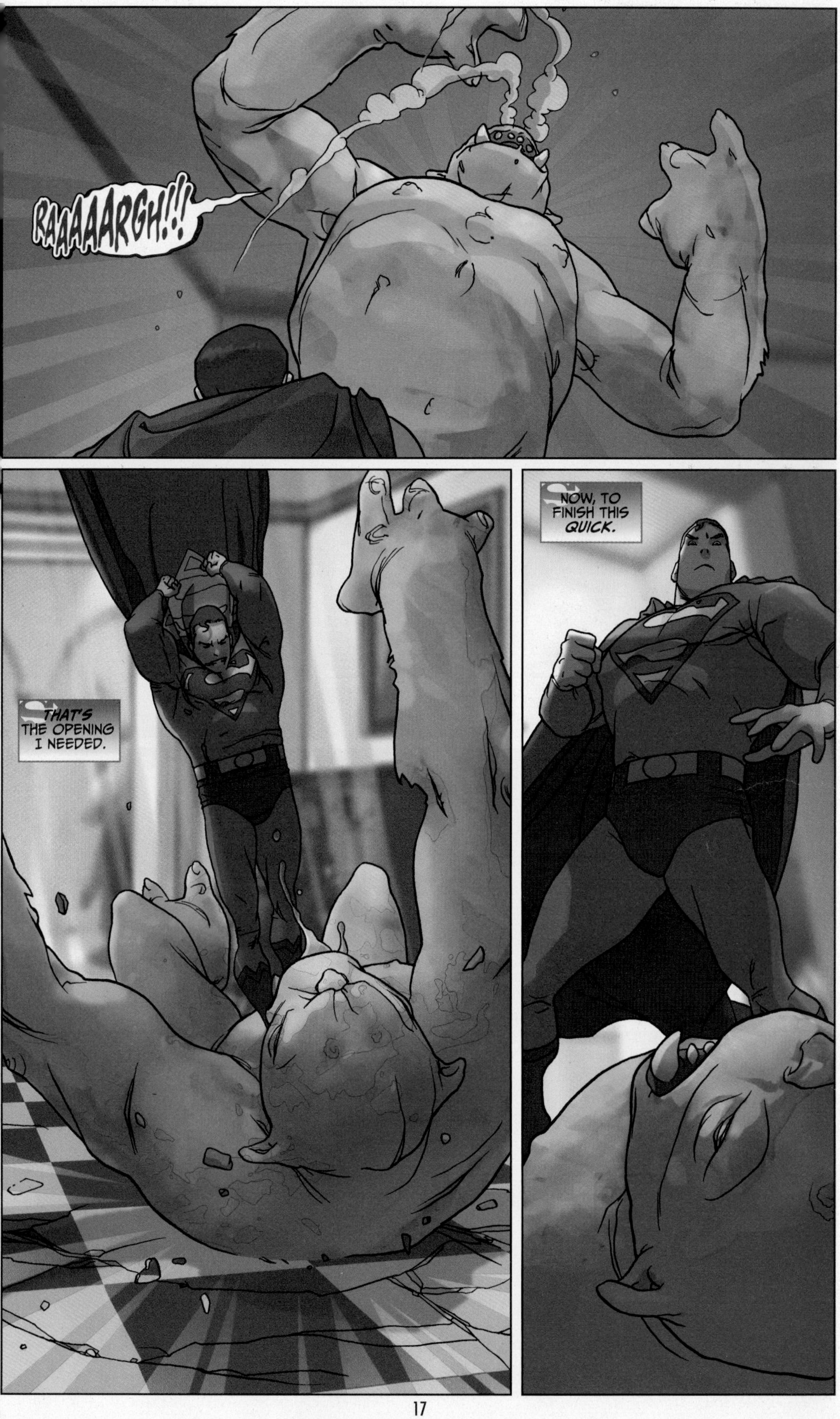
RAAAAARGH!!!
THAT'S THE OPENING I NEEDED.
NOW, TO FINISH THIS QUICK.

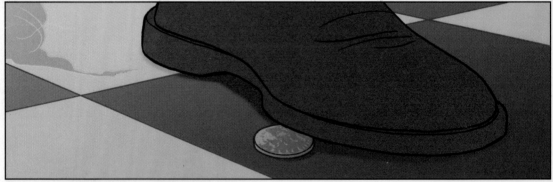

MAGIC.

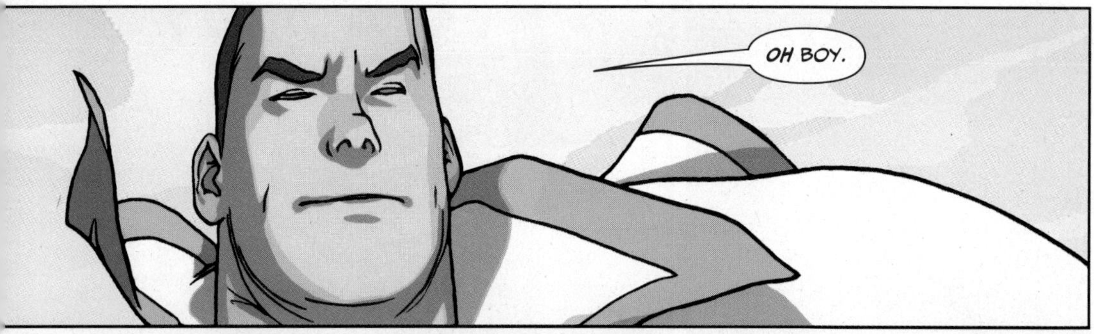
OH BOY.

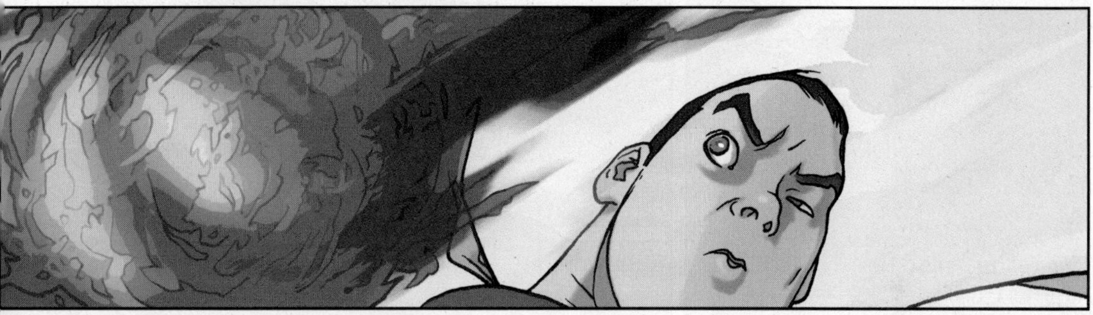

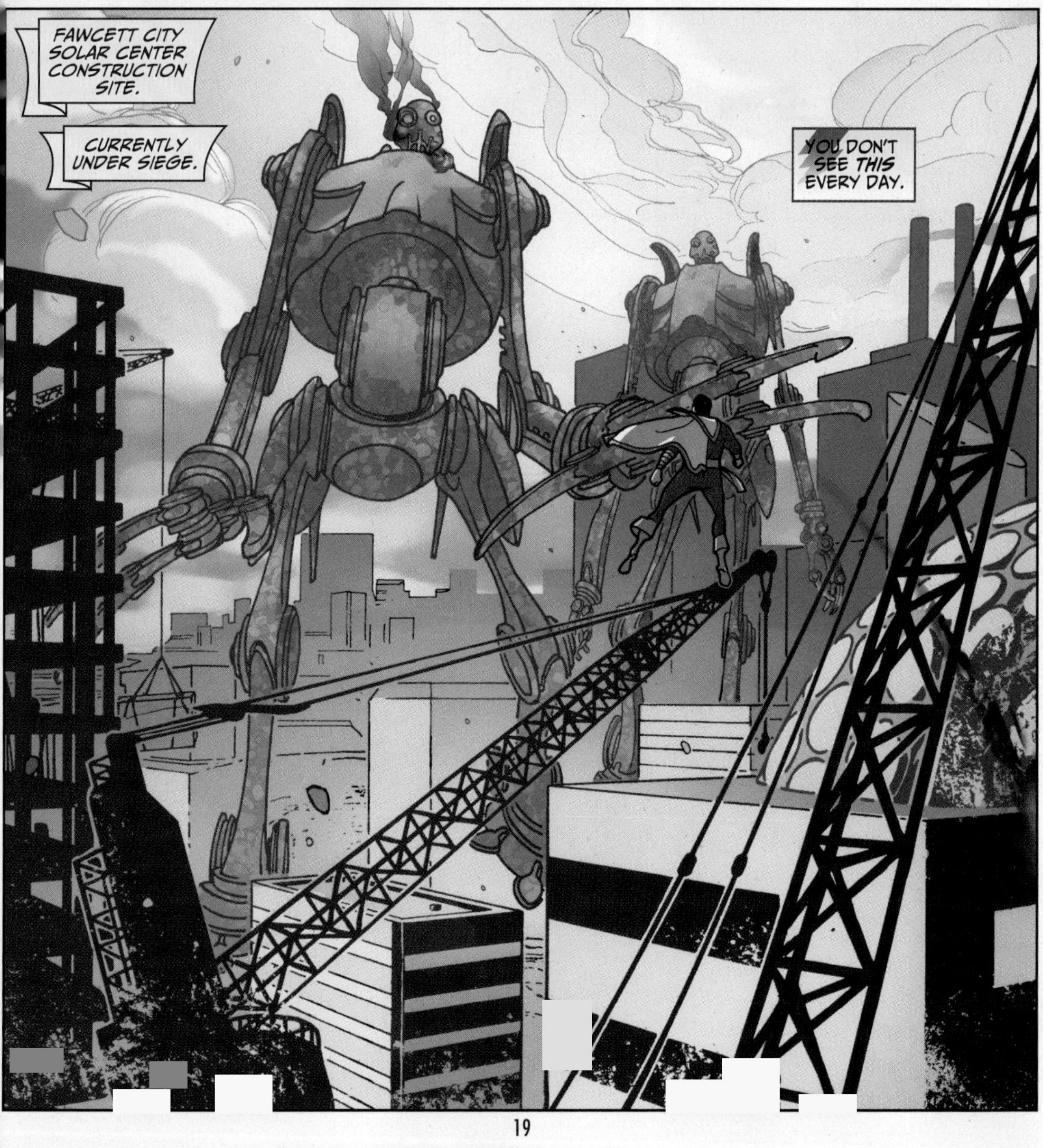
FAWCETT CITY
SOLAR CENTER
CONSTRUCTION
SITE.
CURRENTLY
UNDER SIEGE.
YOU DON'T
SEE THIS
EVERY DAY.

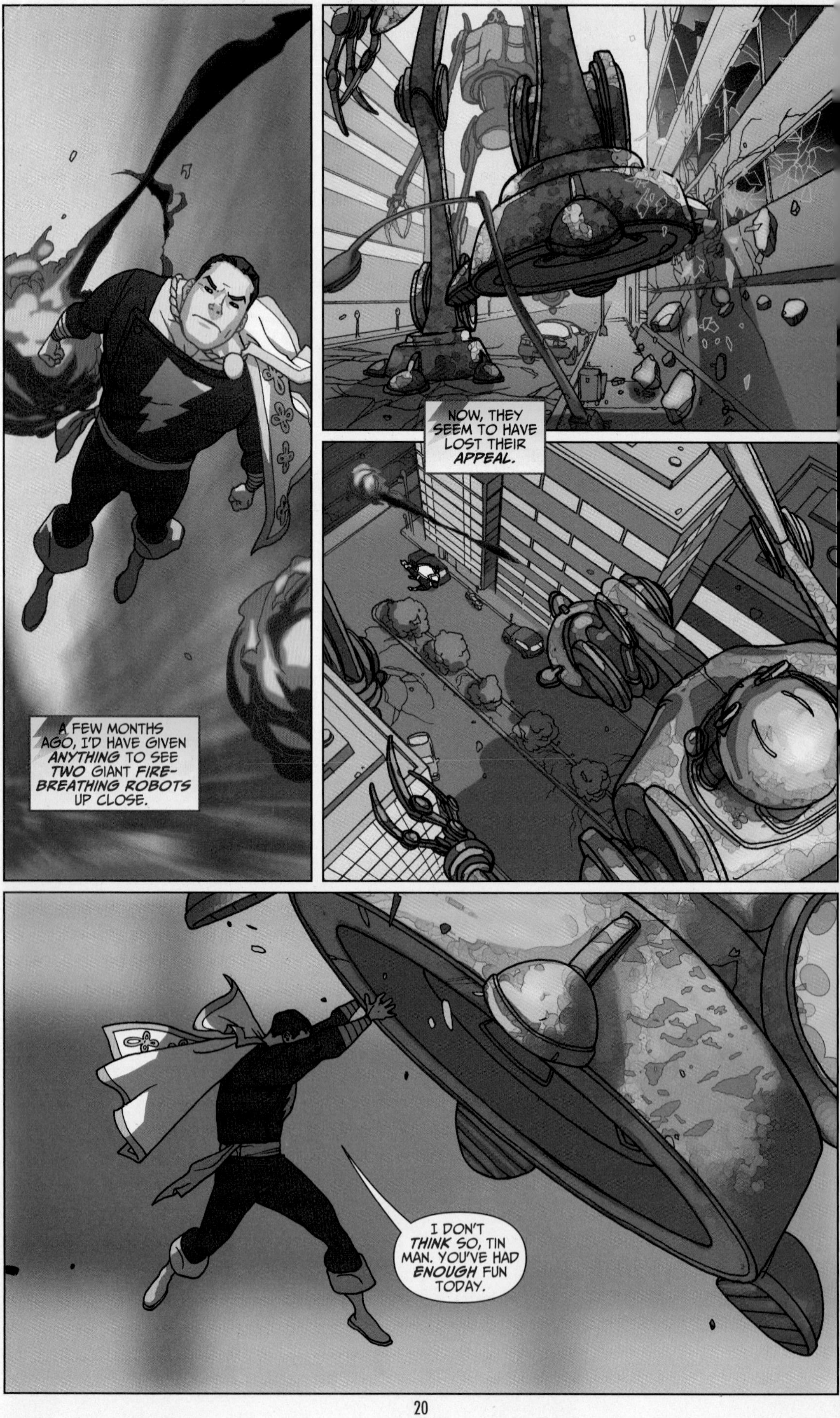

A FEW MONTHS AGO, I'D HAVE GIVEN ANYTHING TO SEE TWO GIANT FIRE-BREATHING ROBOTS UP CLOSE.
NOW, THEY SEEM TO HAVE LOST THEIR APPEAL.
I DON'T THINK SO, TIN MAN. YOU'VE HAD ENOUGH FUN TODAY.

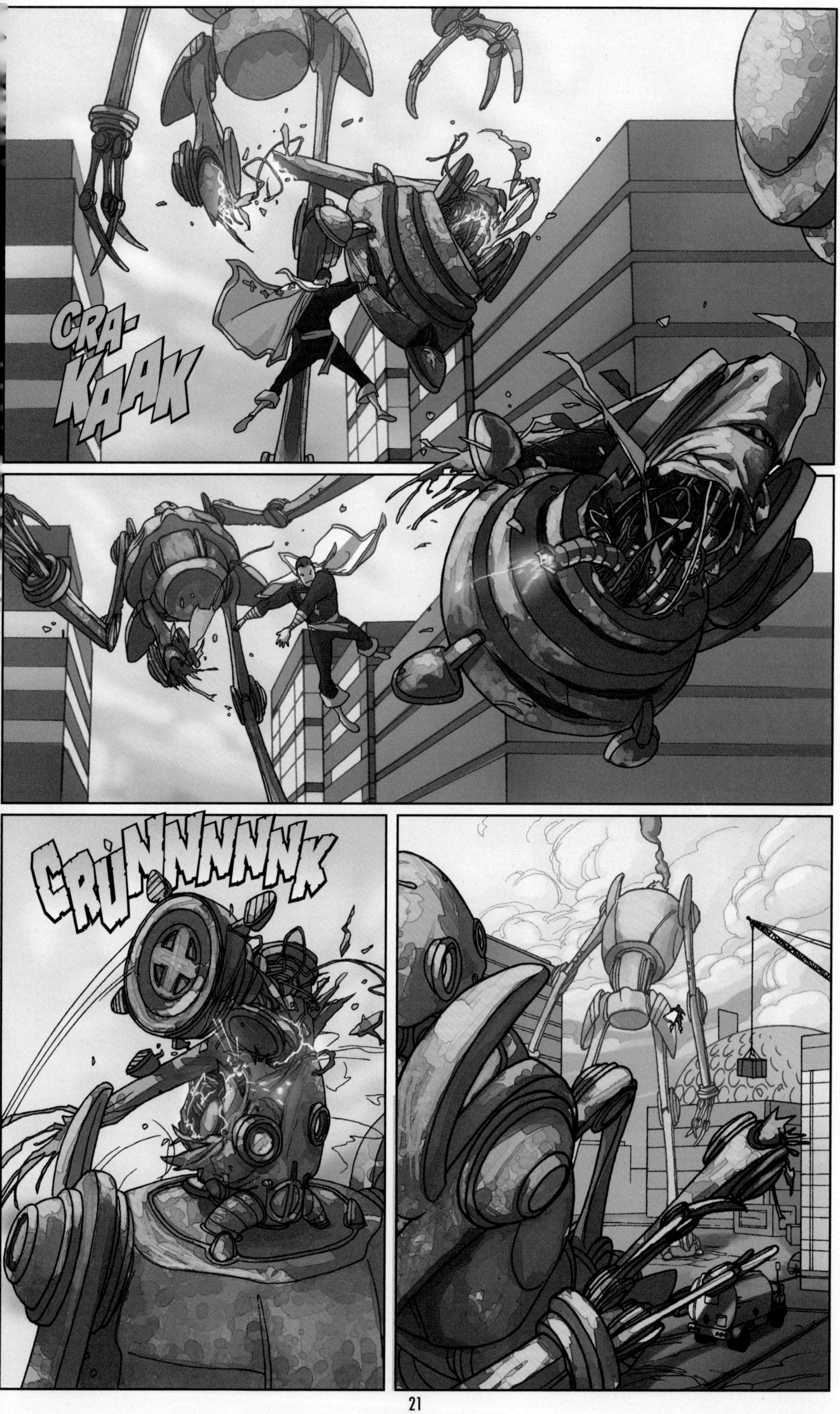
CRA-
KAAK
GRUNNNNNNK

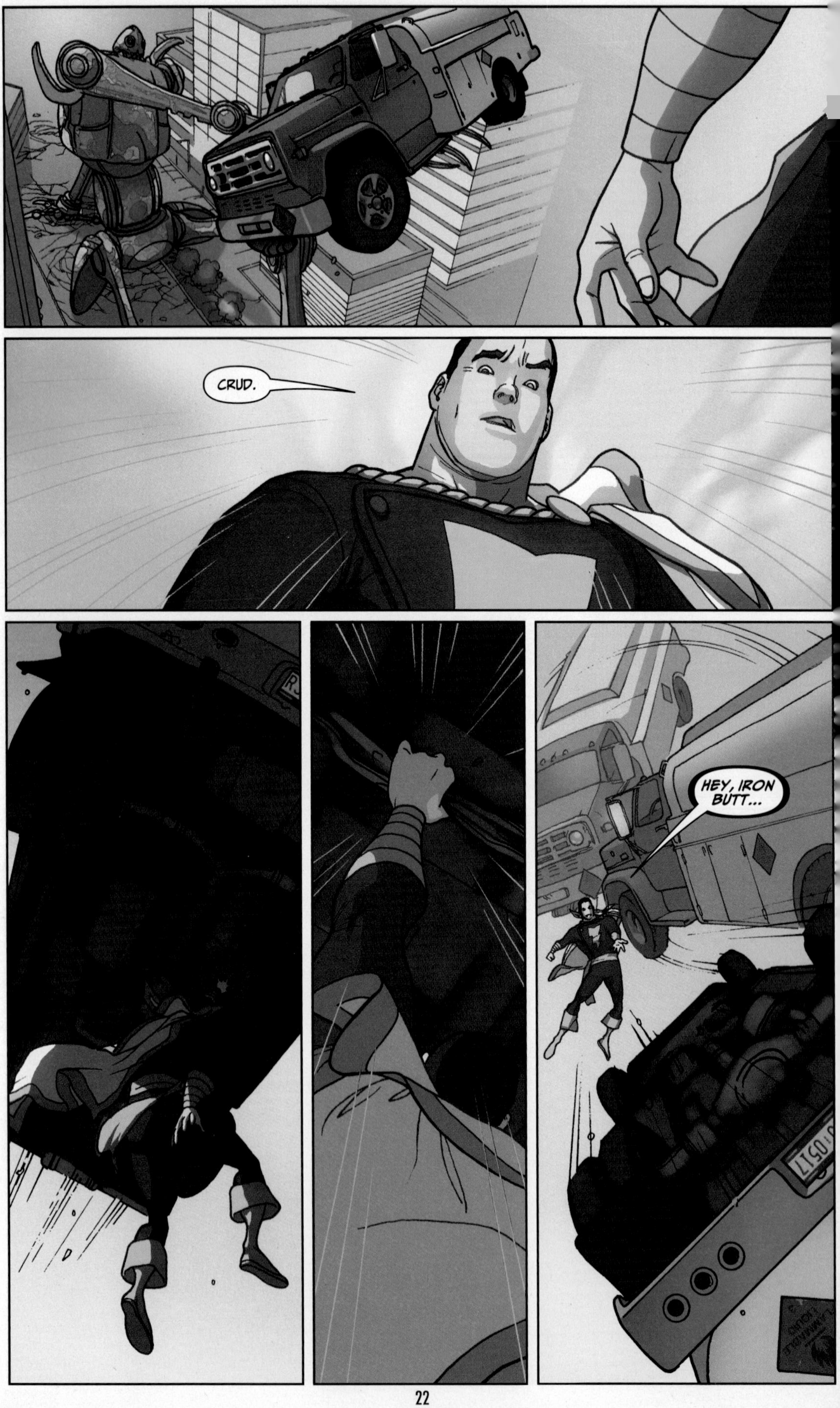
CRUD.
HEY, IRON BUTT...

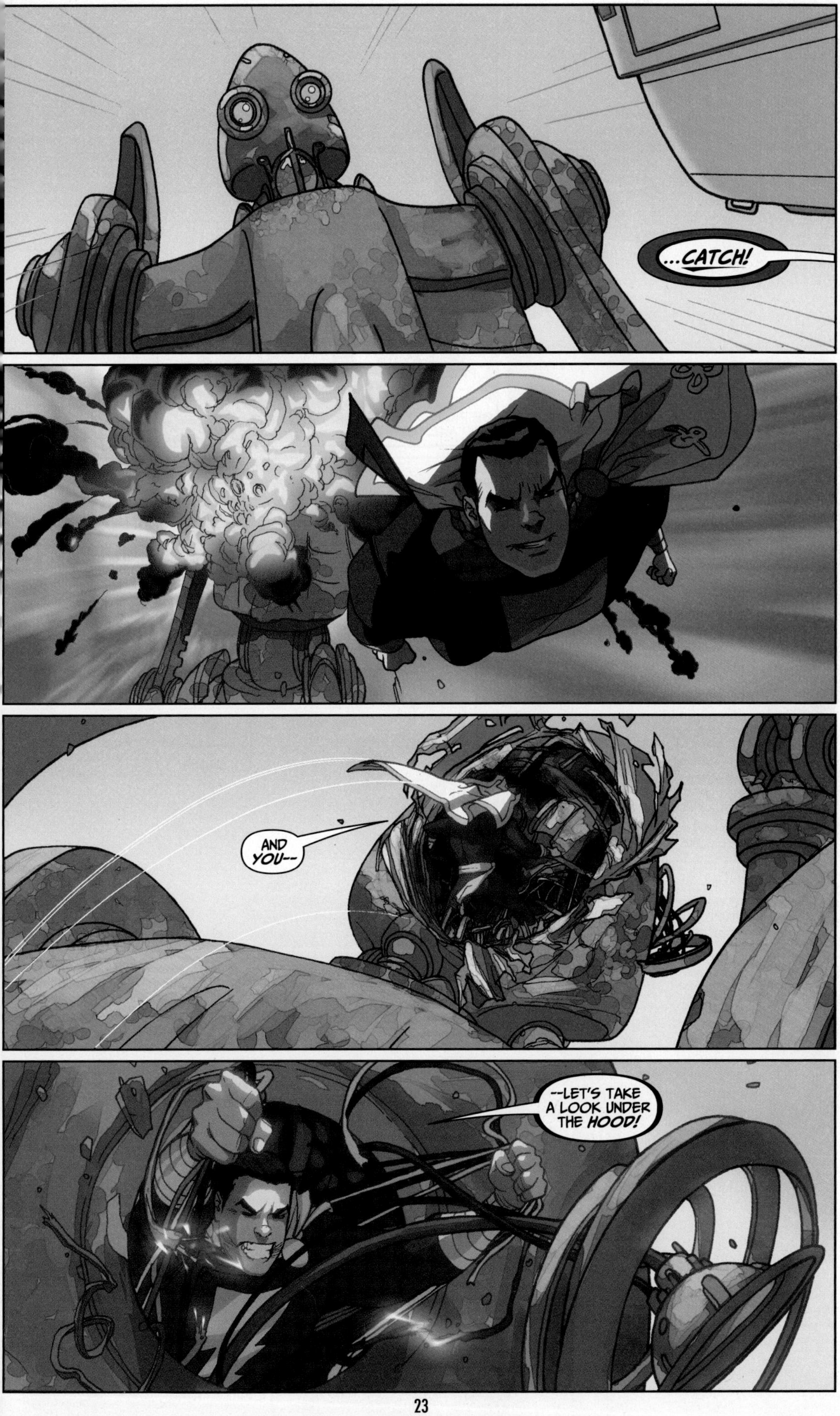
...CATCH!
AND YOU--
--LET'S TAKE A LOOK UNDER THE HOOD!

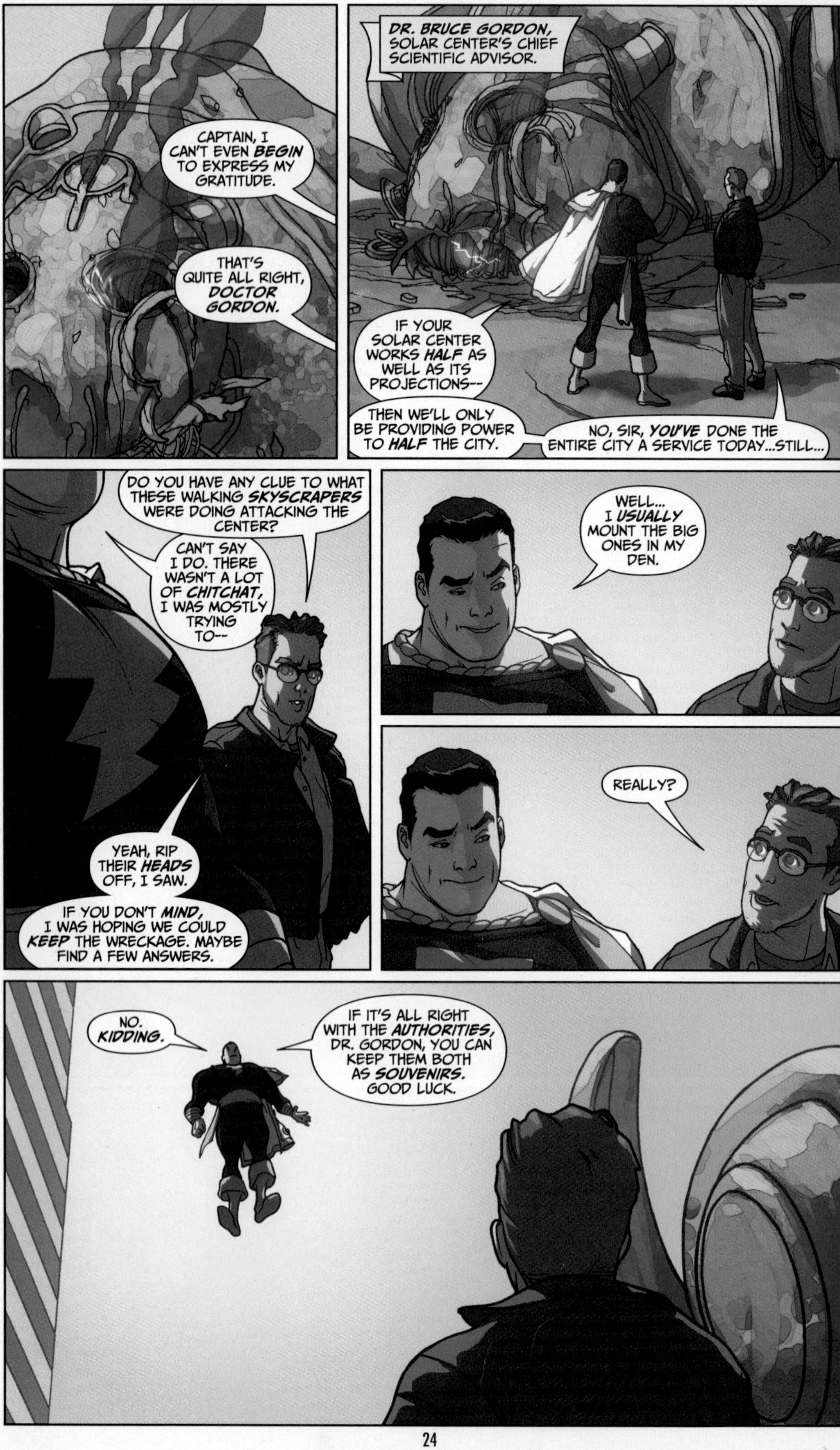
CAPTAIN, I CAN'T EVEN BEGIN TO EXPRESS MY GRATITUDE.
THAT'S QUITE ALL RIGHT, DOCTOR GORDON.
DR. BRUCE GORDON, SOLAR CENTER'S CHIEF SCIENTIFIC ADVISOR.
IF YOUR SOLAR CENTER WORKS HALF AS WELL AS ITS PROJECTIONS--
THEN WE'LL ONLY BE PROVIDING POWER TO HALF THE CITY.
NO, SIR, YOU'VE DONE THE ENTIRE CITY A SERVICE TODAY...STILL...
DO YOU HAVE ANY CLUE TO WHAT THESE WALKING SKYSCRAPERS WERE DOING ATTACKING THE CENTER?
CAN'T SAY I DO. THERE WASN'T A LOT OF CHITCHAT, I WAS MOSTLY TRYING TO--
YEAH, RIP THEIR HEADS OFF, I SAW.
IF YOU DON'T MIND, I WAS HOPING WE COULD KEEP THE WRECKAGE. MAYBE FIND A FEW ANSWERS.
WELL... I USUALLY MOUNT THE BIG ONES IN MY DEN.
REALLY?
NO. KIDDING.
IF IT'S ALL RIGHT WITH THE AUTHORITIES, DR. GORDON, YOU CAN KEEP THEM BOTH AS SOUVENIRS. GOOD LUCK.

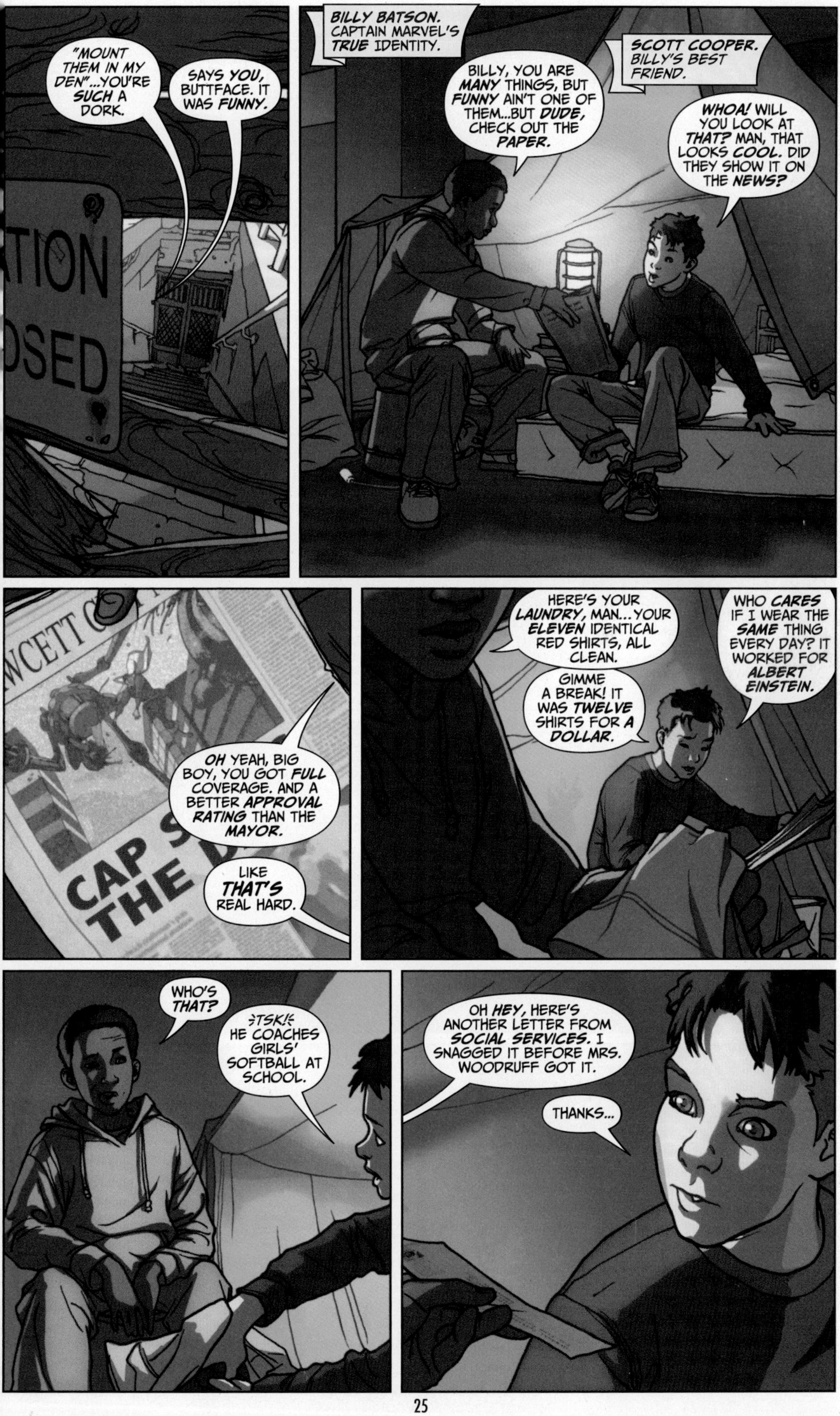
"MOUNT THEM IN MY DEN"...YOU'RE SUCH A DORK.
SAYS YOU, BUTTFACE. IT WAS FUNNY.
ATION
OSED
BILLY BATSON. CAPTAIN MARVEL'S TRUE IDENTITY.
SCOTT COOPER. BILLY'S BEST FRIEND.
BILLY, YOU ARE MANY THINGS, BUT FUNNY AIN'T ONE OF THEM...BUT DUDE, CHECK OUT THE PAPER.
WHOA! WILL YOU LOOK AT THAT? MAN, THAT LOOKS COOL. DID THEY SHOW IT ON THE NEWS?
WCETT
CAP
THE
OH YEAH, BIG BOY, YOU GOT FULL COVERAGE. AND A BETTER APPROVAL RATING THAN THE MAYOR.
LIKE THAT'S REAL HARD.
HERE'S YOUR LAUNDRY, MAN... YOUR ELEVEN IDENTICAL RED SHIRTS, ALL CLEAN.
WHO CARES IF I WEAR THE SAME THING EVERY DAY? IT WORKED FOR ALBERT EINSTEIN.
GIMME A BREAK! IT WAS TWELVE SHIRTS FOR A DOLLAR.
WHO'S THAT?
TSK! HE COACHES GIRLS' SOFTBALL AT SCHOOL.
OH HEY, HERE'S ANOTHER LETTER FROM SOCIAL SERVICES. I SNAGGED IT BEFORE MRS. WOODRUFF GOT IT.
THANKS...

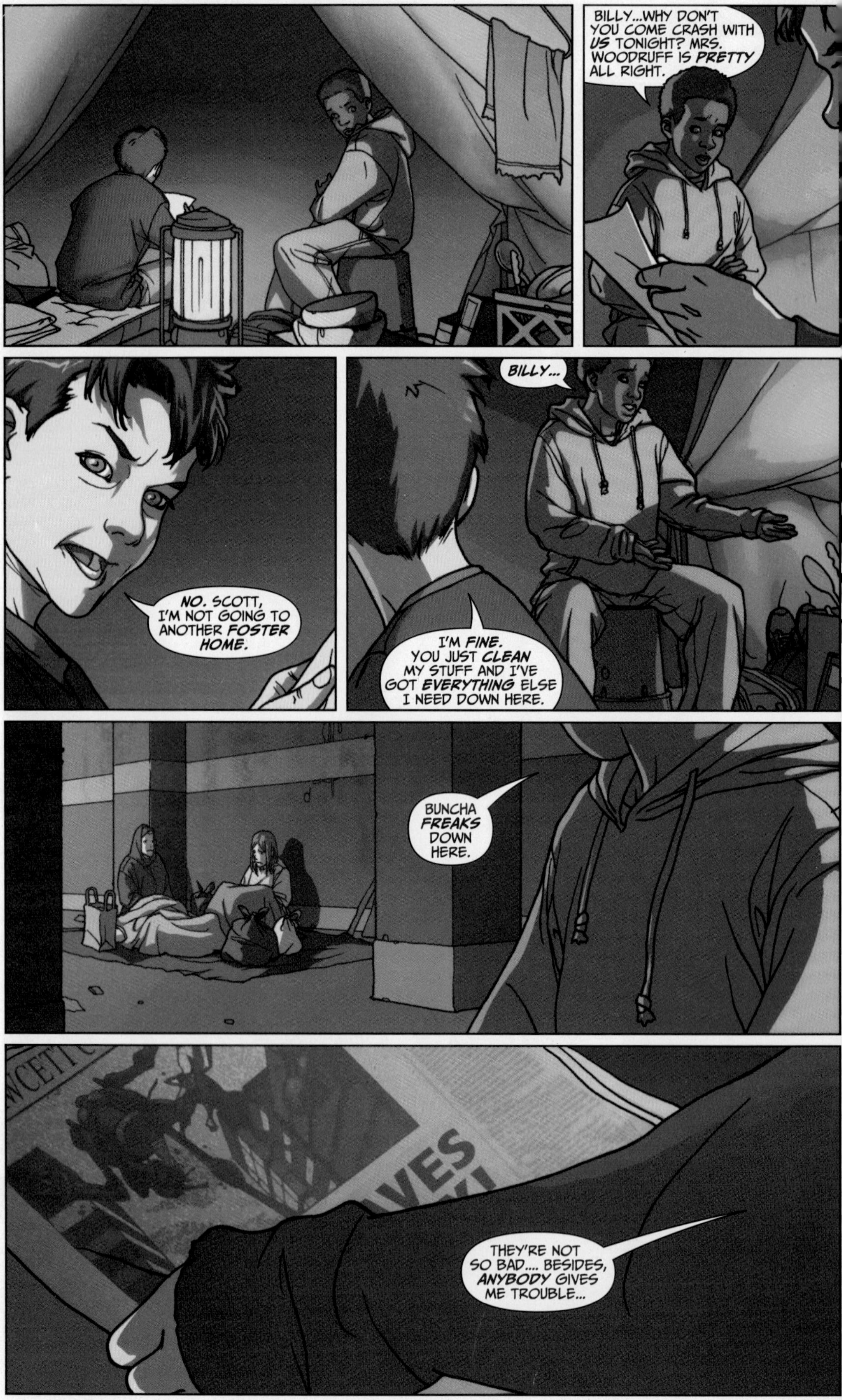

BILLY...WHY DON'T YOU COME CRASH WITH *US* TONIGHT? MRS. WOODRUFF IS *PRETTY* ALL RIGHT.
NO. SCOTT, I'M NOT GOING TO ANOTHER *FOSTER HOME.*
BILLY...
I'M *FINE.* YOU JUST *CLEAN* MY STUFF AND I'VE GOT *EVERYTHING* ELSE I NEED DOWN HERE.
BUNCHA *FREAKS* DOWN HERE.
THEY'RE NOT SO BAD.... BESIDES, *ANYBODY* GIVES ME TROUBLE...

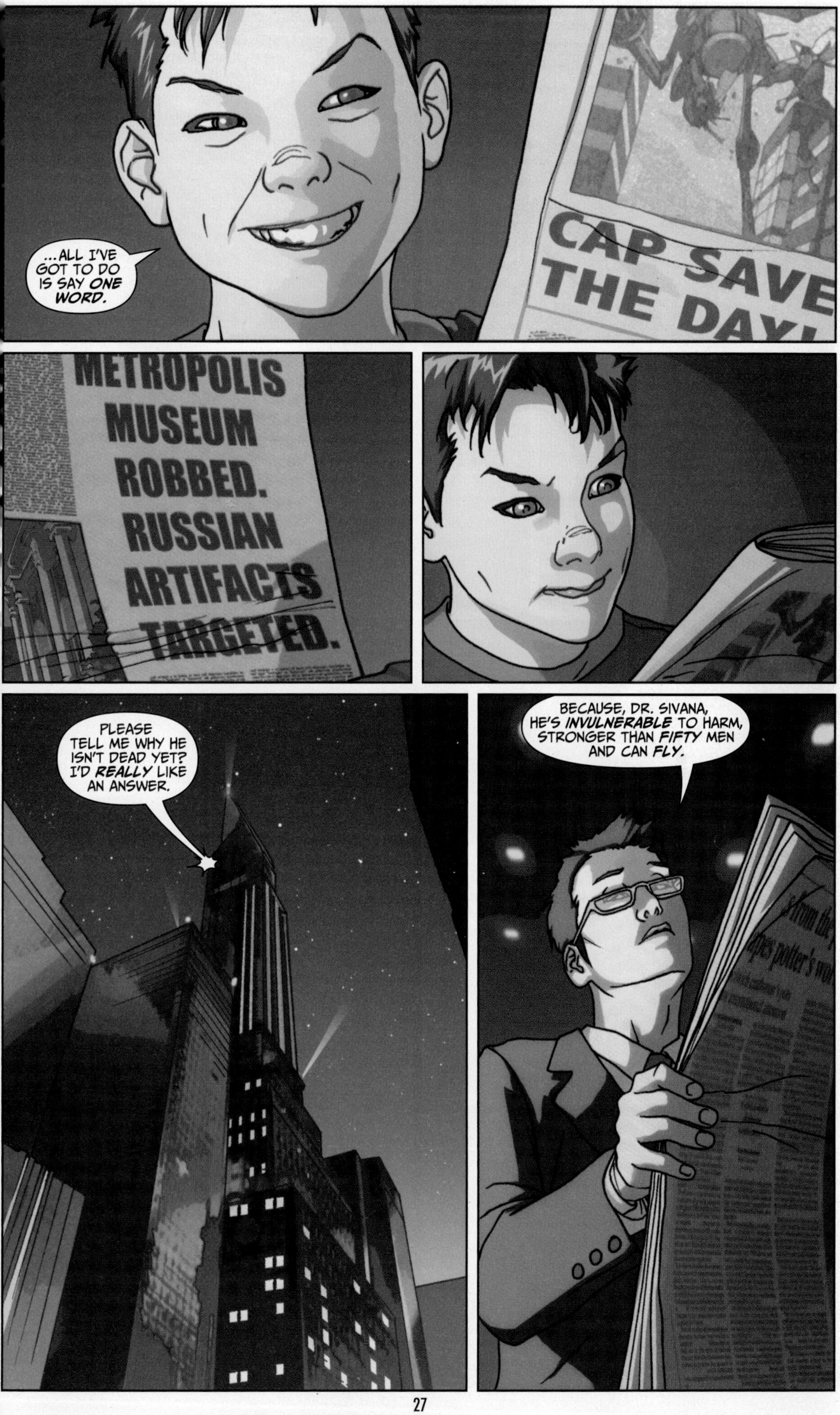
...ALL I'VE GOT TO DO IS SAY ONE WORD.
CAP SAVES THE DAY!
METROPOLIS MUSEUM ROBBED. RUSSIAN ARTIFACTS TARGETED.
PLEASE TELL ME WHY HE ISN'T DEAD YET? I'D REALLY LIKE AN ANSWER.
BECAUSE, DR. SIVANA, HE'S INVULNERABLE TO HARM, STRONGER THAN FIFTY MEN AND CAN FLY.

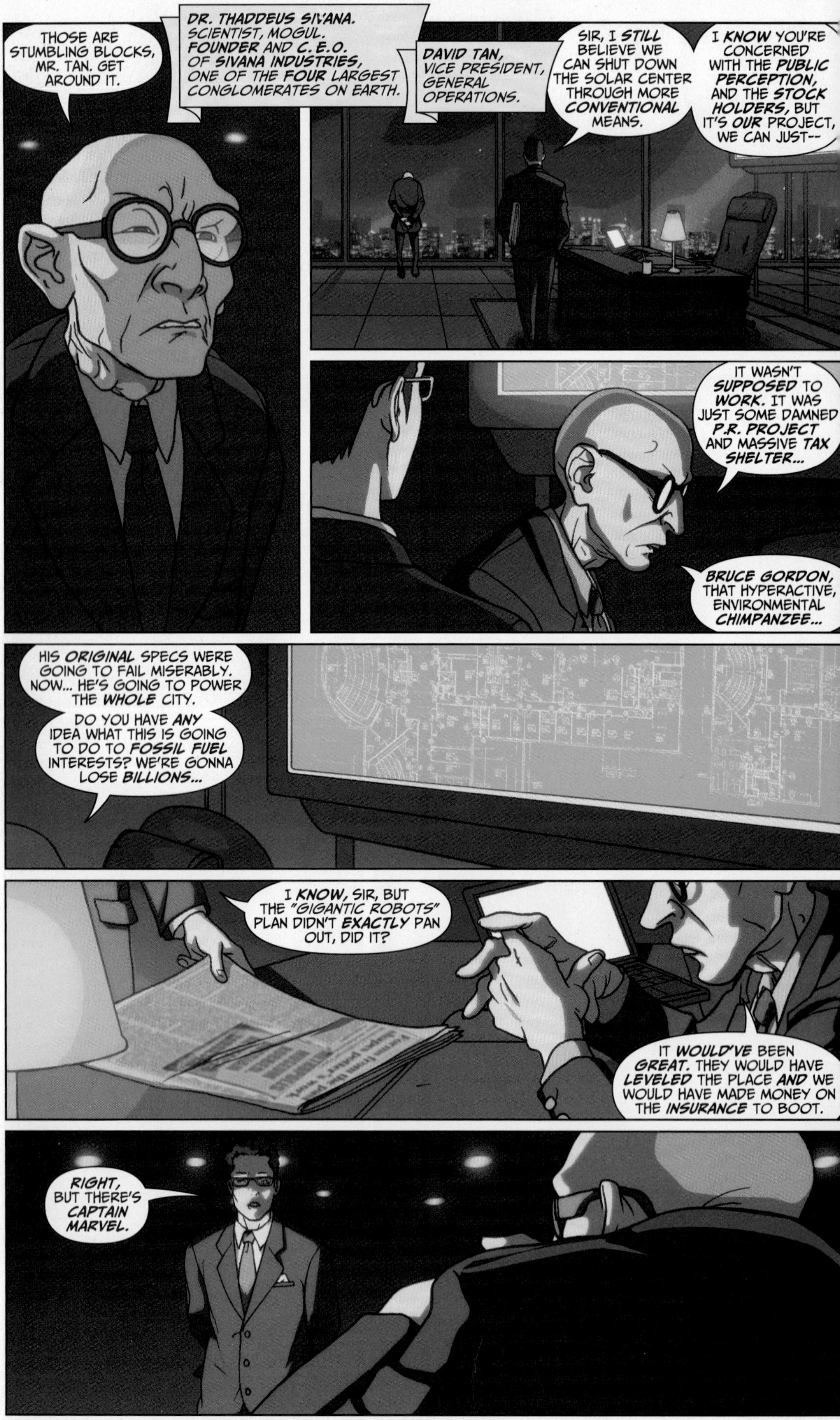

THOSE ARE STUMBLING BLOCKS, MR. TAN. GET AROUND IT.
DR. THADDEUS SIVANA. SCIENTIST, MOGUL. FOUNDER AND C.E.O. OF SIVANA INDUSTRIES, ONE OF THE FOUR LARGEST CONGLOMERATES ON EARTH.
DAVID TAN, VICE PRESIDENT, GENERAL OPERATIONS.
SIR, I STILL BELIEVE WE CAN SHUT DOWN THE SOLAR CENTER THROUGH MORE CONVENTIONAL MEANS.
I KNOW YOU'RE CONCERNED WITH THE PUBLIC PERCEPTION, AND THE STOCK HOLDERS, BUT IT'S OUR PROJECT, WE CAN JUST--
IT WASN'T SUPPOSED TO WORK. IT WAS JUST SOME DAMNED P.R. PROJECT AND MASSIVE TAX SHELTER...
BRUCE GORDON, THAT HYPERACTIVE, ENVIRONMENTAL CHIMPANZEE...
HIS ORIGINAL SPECS WERE GOING TO FAIL MISERABLY. NOW... HE'S GOING TO POWER THE WHOLE CITY.
DO YOU HAVE ANY IDEA WHAT THIS IS GOING TO DO TO FOSSIL FUEL INTERESTS? WE'RE GONNA LOSE BILLIONS...
I KNOW, SIR, BUT THE "GIGANTIC ROBOTS" PLAN DIDN'T EXACTLY PAN OUT, DID IT?
IT WOULD'VE BEEN GREAT. THEY WOULD HAVE LEVELED THE PLACE AND WE WOULD HAVE MADE MONEY ON THE INSURANCE TO BOOT.
RIGHT, BUT THERE'S CAPTAIN MARVEL.

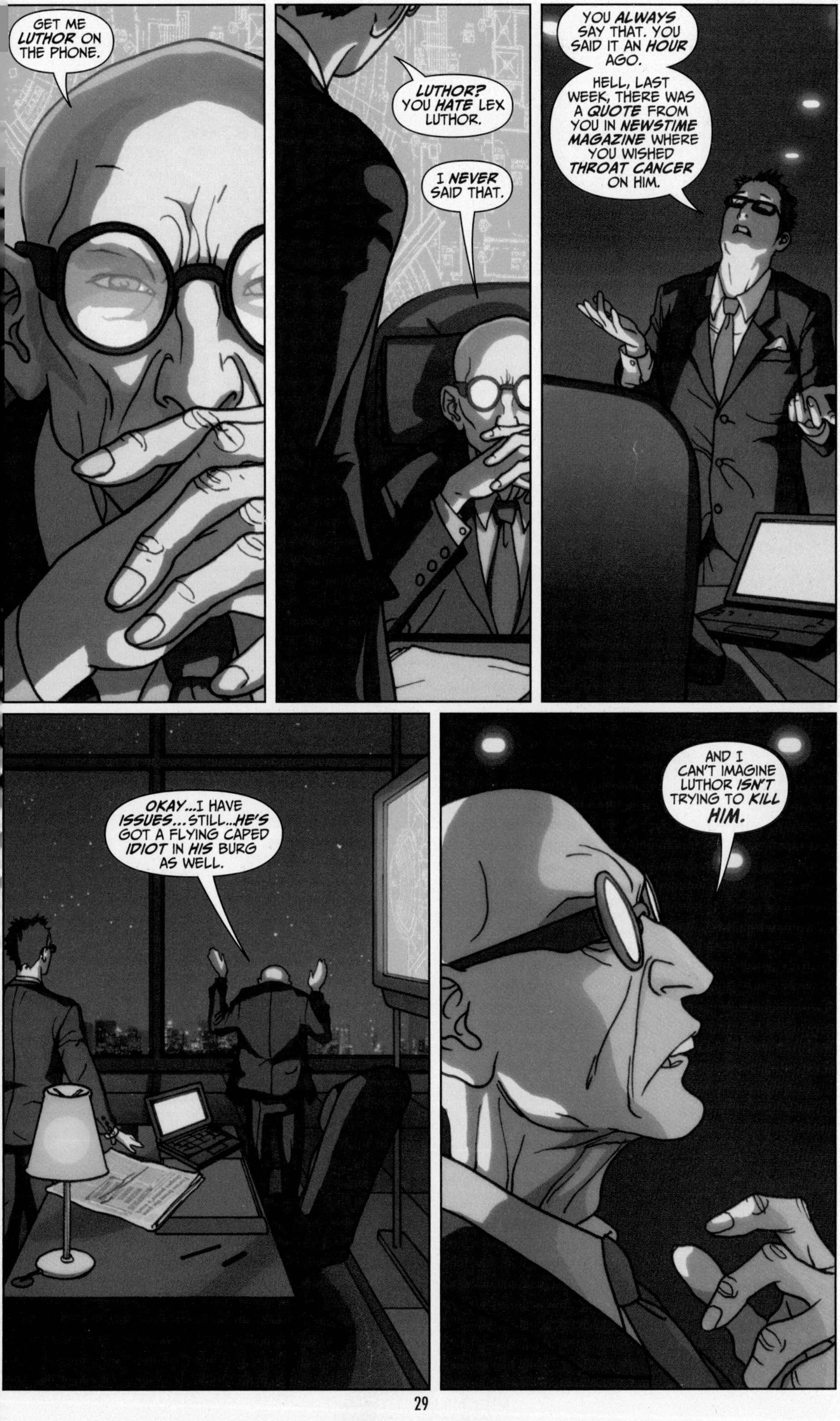
GET ME LUTHOR ON THE PHONE.
LUTHOR? YOU HATE LEX LUTHOR.
I NEVER SAID THAT.
YOU ALWAYS SAY THAT. YOU SAID IT AN HOUR AGO.
HELL, LAST WEEK, THERE WAS A QUOTE FROM YOU IN NEWSTIME MAGAZINE WHERE YOU WISHED THROAT CANCER ON HIM.
OKAY...I HAVE ISSUES...STILL...HE'S GOT A FLYING CAPED IDIOT IN HIS BURG AS WELL.
AND I CAN'T IMAGINE LUTHOR ISN'T TRYING TO KILL HIM.

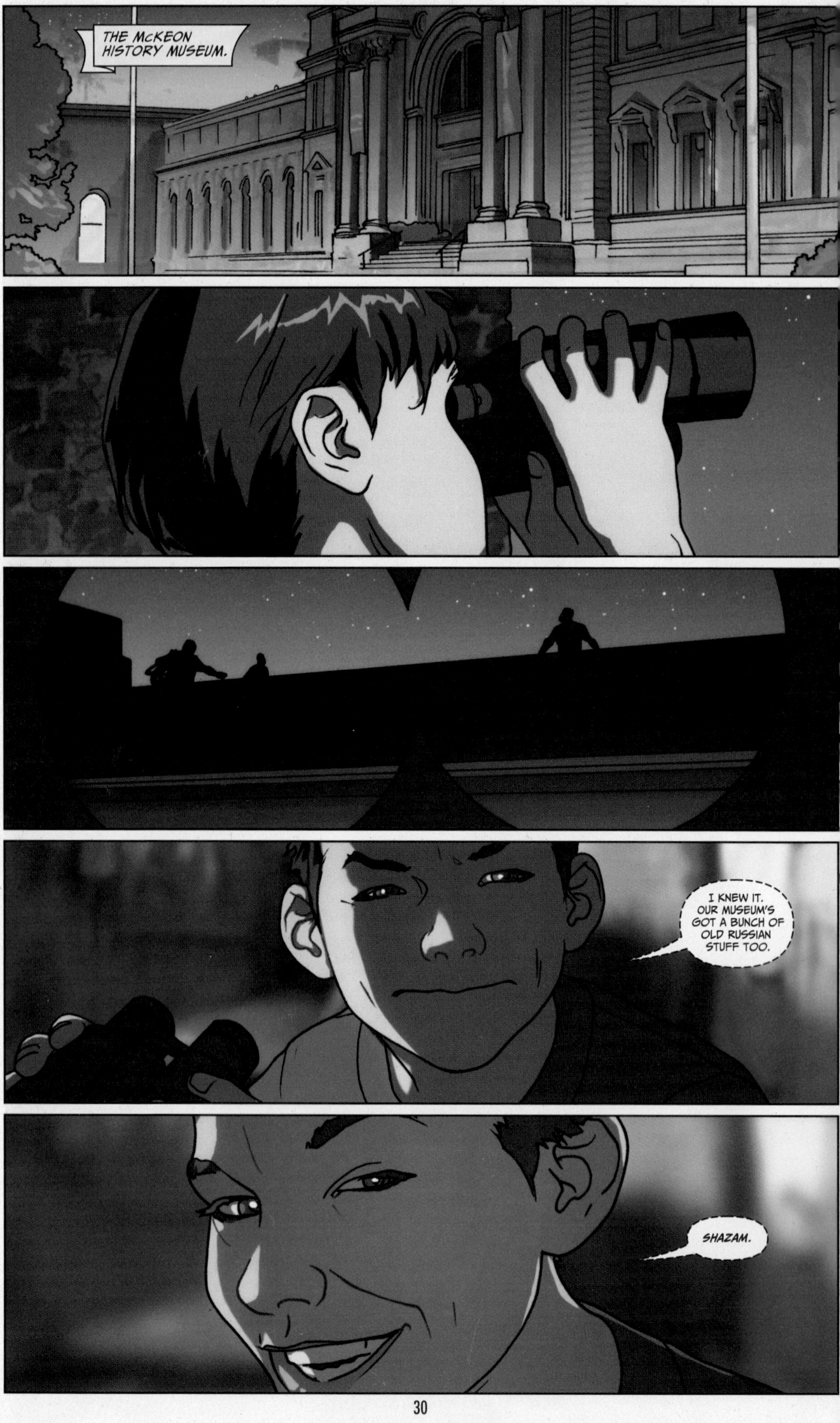
THE McKEON HISTORY MUSEUM.
I KNEW IT. OUR MUSEUM'S GOT A BUNCH OF OLD RUSSIAN STUFF TOO.
SHAZAM.

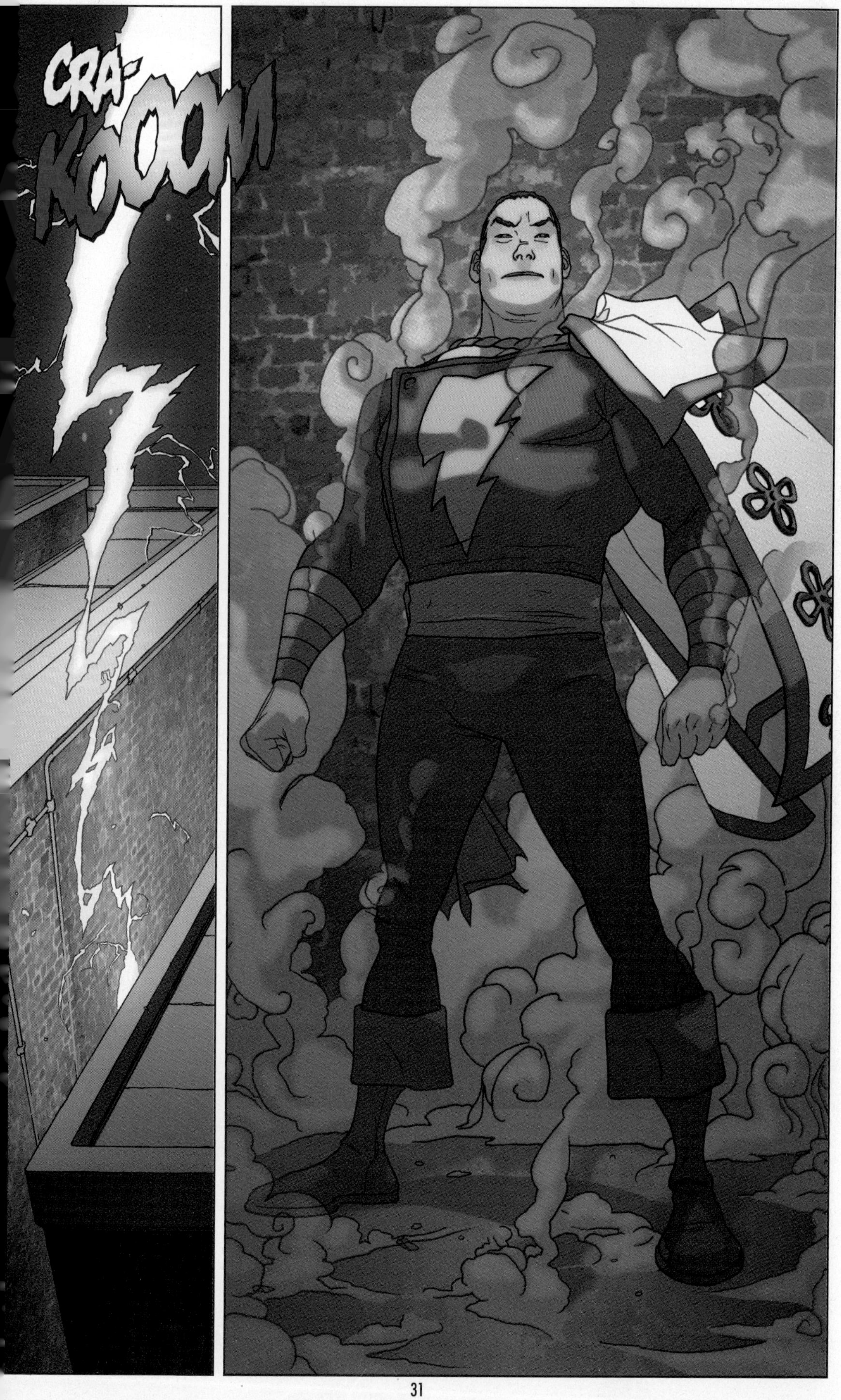
CRA-
KOOOM

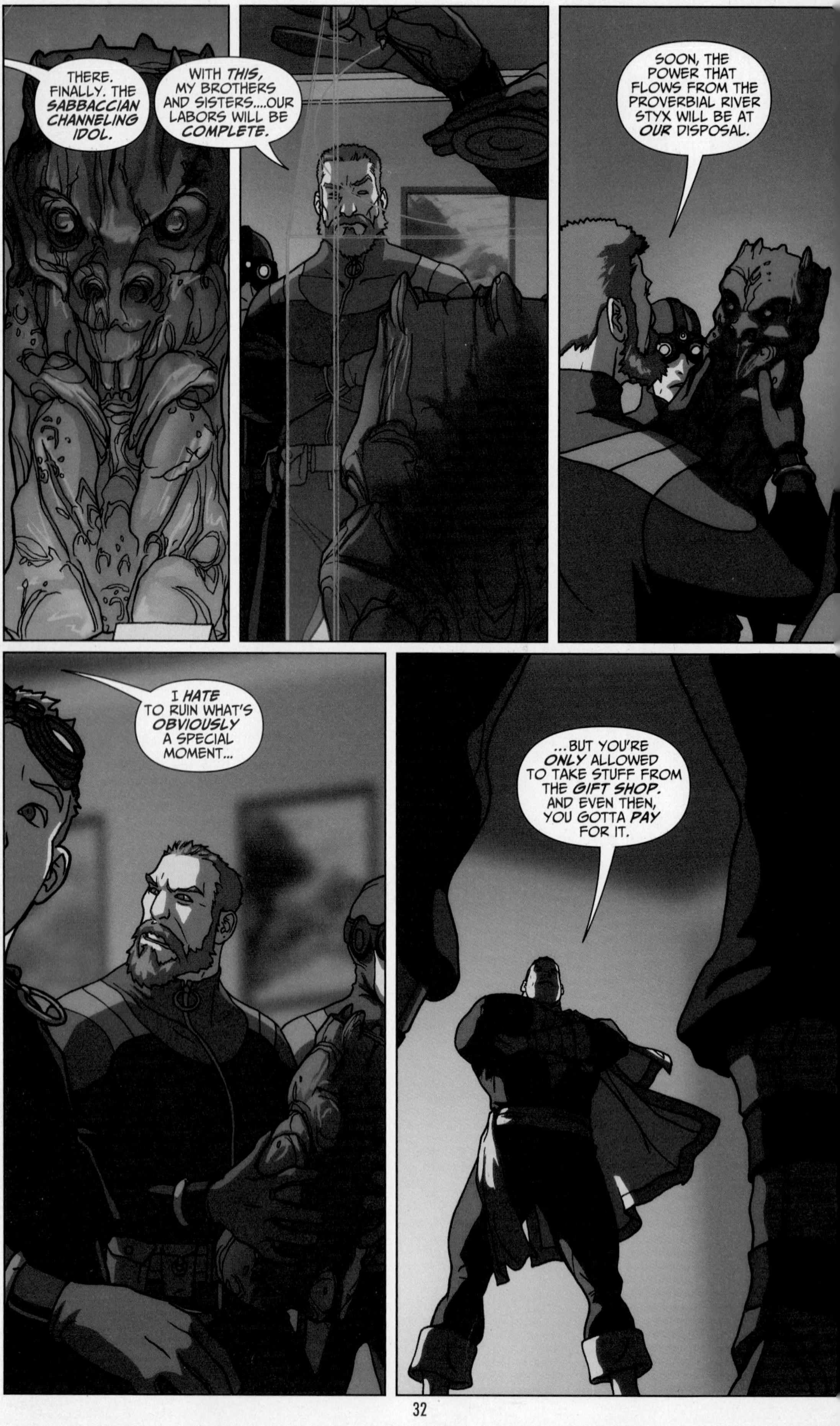
THERE. FINALLY. THE SABBACCIAN CHANNELING IDOL.
WITH THIS, MY BROTHERS AND SISTERS....OUR LABORS WILL BE COMPLETE.
SOON, THE POWER THAT FLOWS FROM THE PROVERBIAL RIVER STYX WILL BE AT OUR DISPOSAL.
I HATE TO RUIN WHAT'S OBVIOUSLY A SPECIAL MOMENT...
...BUT YOU'RE ONLY ALLOWED TO TAKE STUFF FROM THE GIFT SHOP. AND EVEN THEN, YOU GOTTA PAY FOR IT.

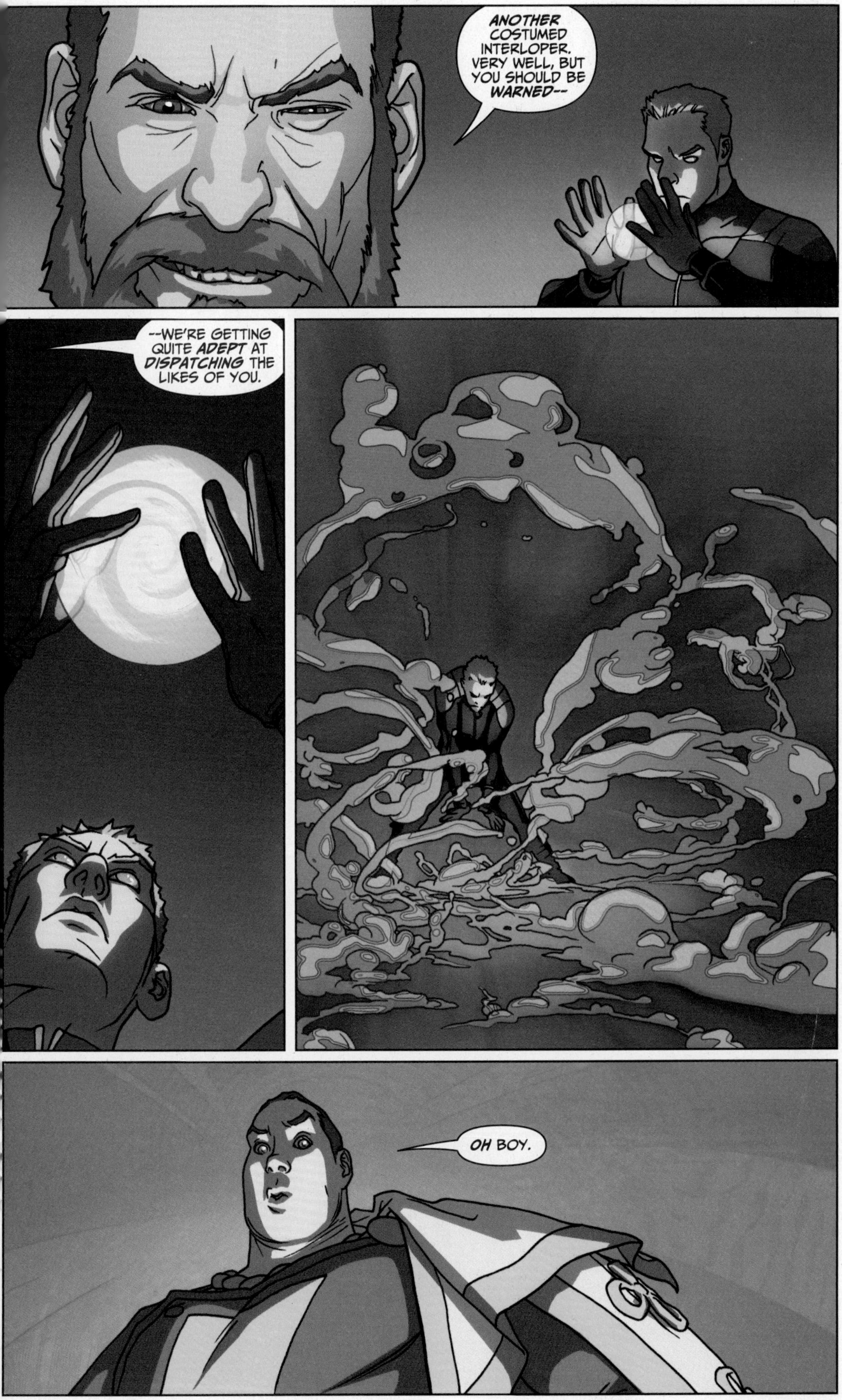
ANOTHER COSTUMED INTERLOPER. VERY WELL, BUT YOU SHOULD BE WARNED--
--WE'RE GETTING QUITE ADEPT AT DISPATCHING THE LIKES OF YOU.
OH BOY.

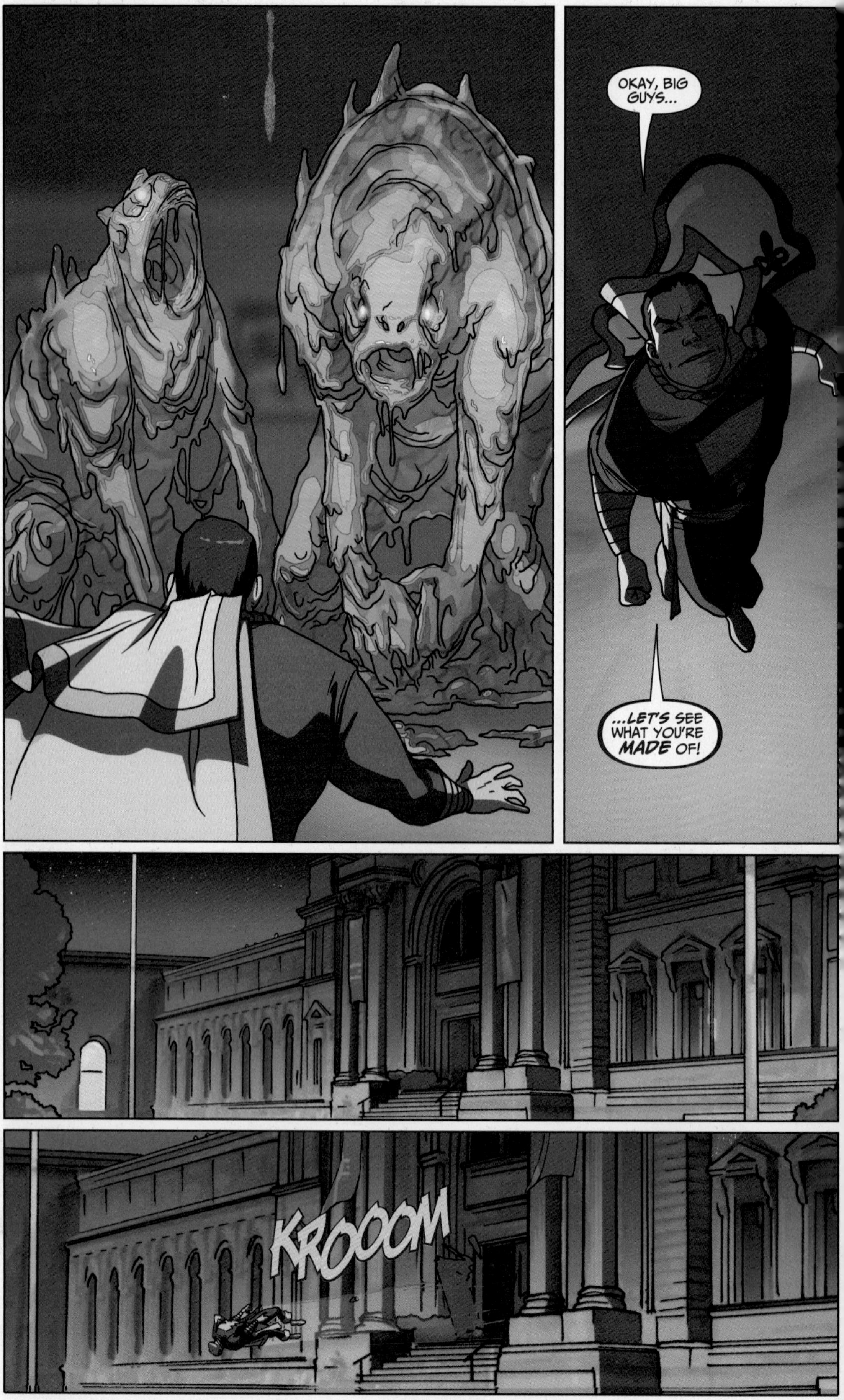
OKAY, BIG GUYS...
...LET'S SEE WHAT YOU'RE MADE OF!
KROOOM

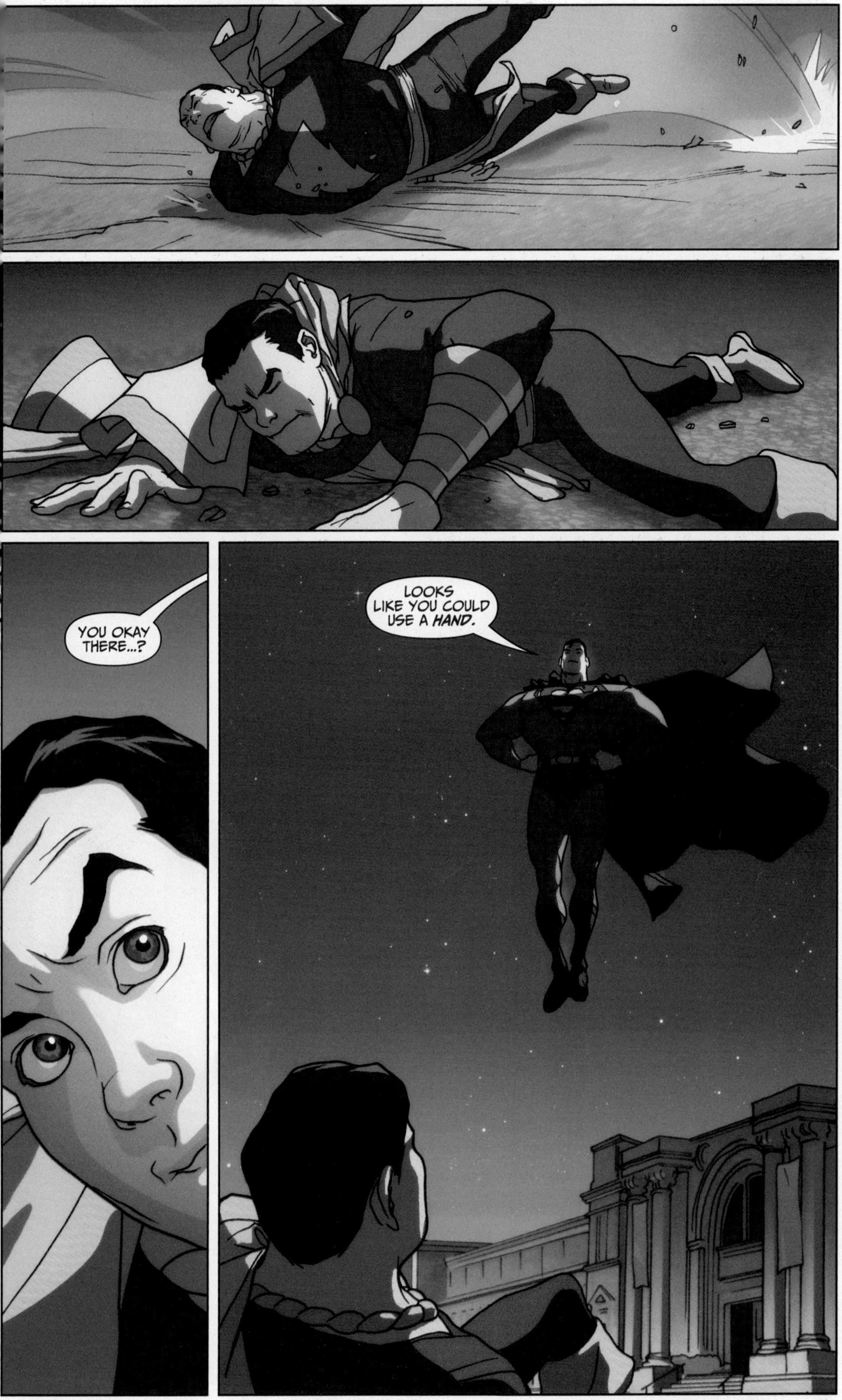
YOU OKAY THERE...?
LOOKS LIKE YOU COULD USE A HAND.

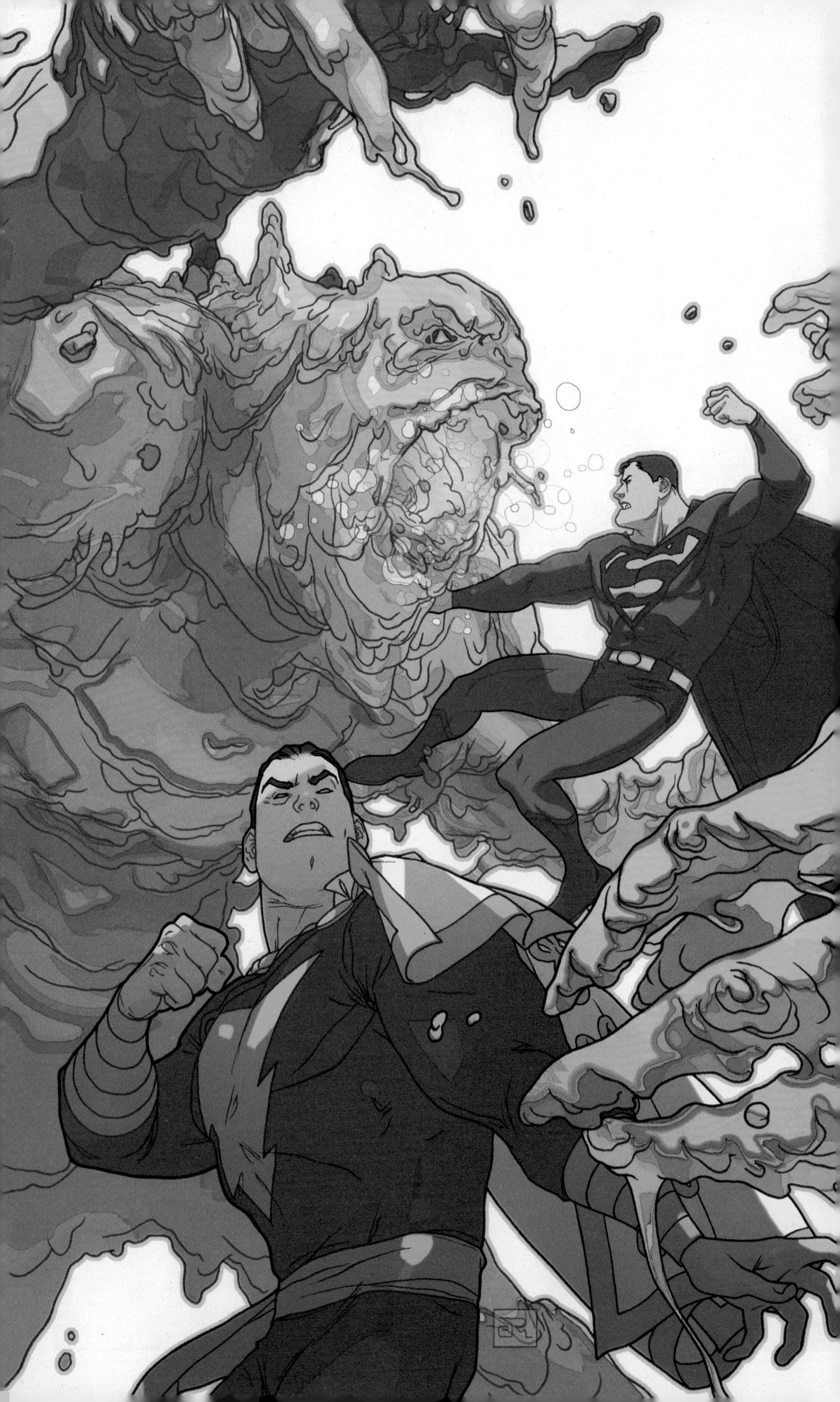

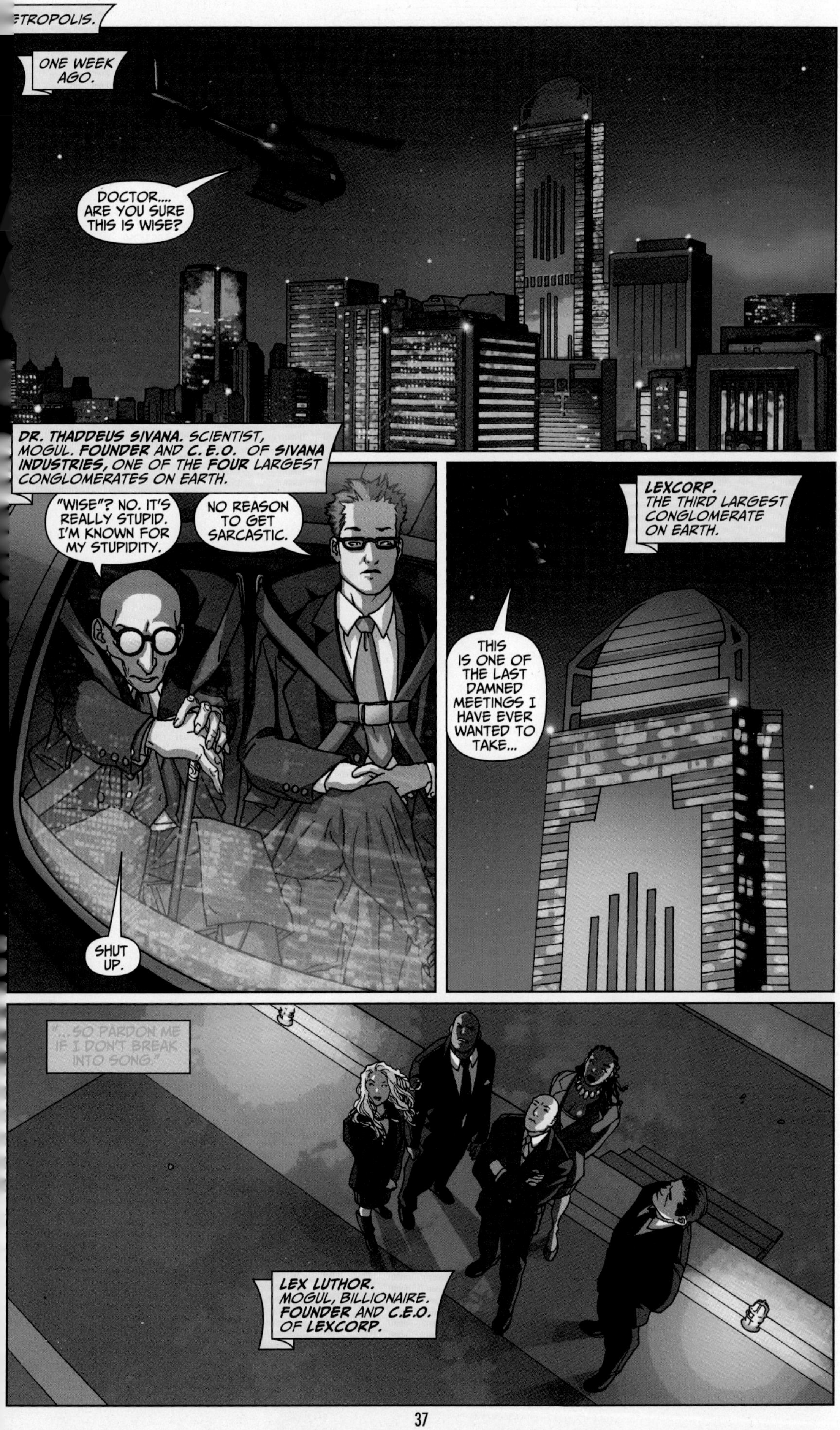
ETROPOLIS.
ONE WEEK AGO.
DOCTOR.... ARE YOU SURE THIS IS WISE?
DR. THADDEUS SIVANA. SCIENTIST, MOGUL. FOUNDER AND C.E.O. OF SIVANA INDUSTRIES, ONE OF THE FOUR LARGEST CONGLOMERATES ON EARTH.
"WISE"? NO. IT'S REALLY STUPID. I'M KNOWN FOR MY STUPIDITY.
NO REASON TO GET SARCASTIC.
SHUT UP.
LEXCORP. THE THIRD LARGEST CONGLOMERATE ON EARTH.
THIS IS ONE OF THE LAST DAMNED MEETINGS I HAVE EVER WANTED TO TAKE...
"...SO PARDON ME IF I DON'T BREAK INTO SONG."
LEX LUTHOR. MOGUL, BILLIONAIRE. FOUNDER AND C.E.O. OF LEXCORP.

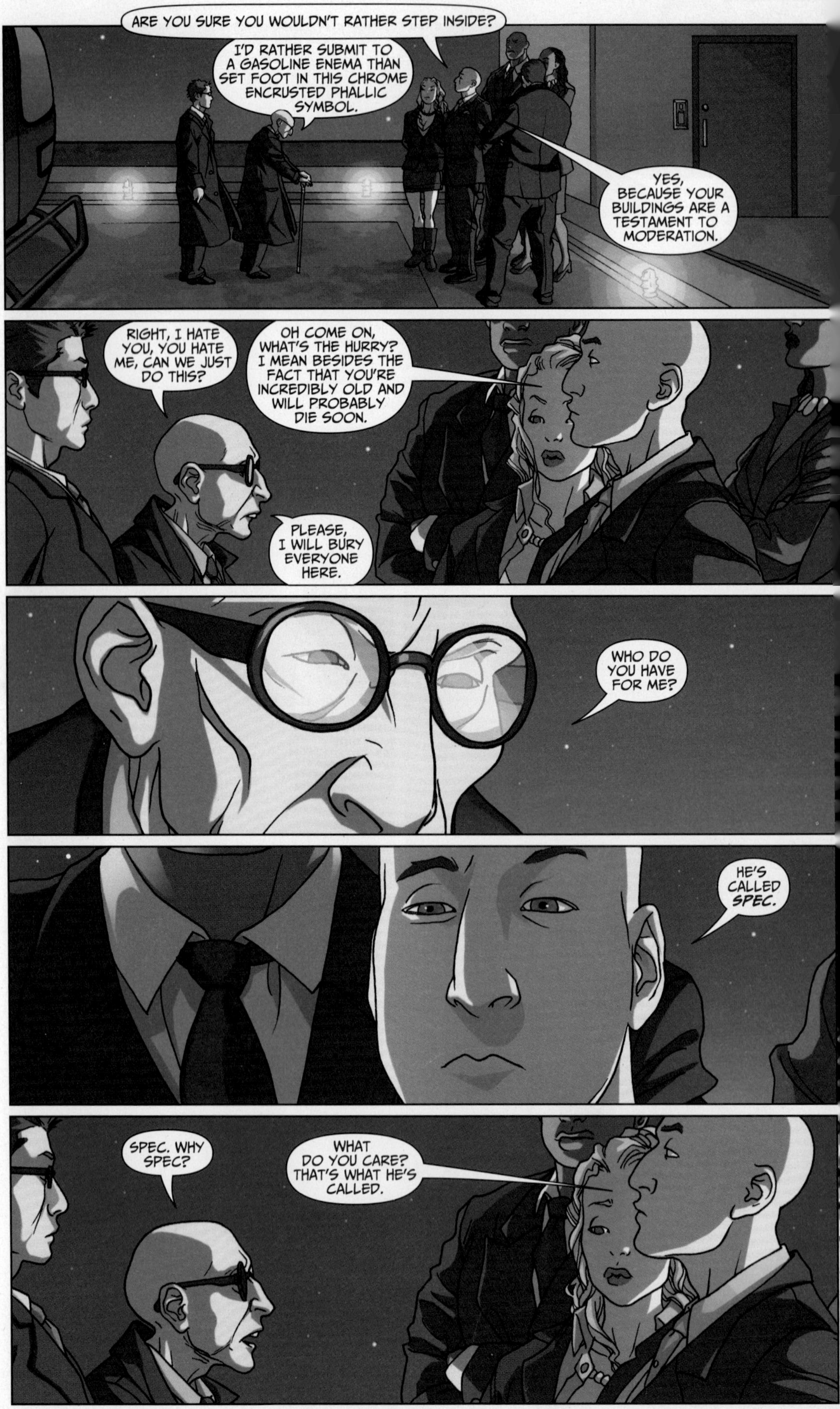
ARE YOU SURE YOU WOULDN'T RATHER STEP INSIDE?
I'D RATHER SUBMIT TO A GASOLINE ENEMA THAN SET FOOT IN THIS CHROME ENCRUSTED PHALLIC SYMBOL.
YES, BECAUSE YOUR BUILDINGS ARE A TESTAMENT TO MODERATION.
RIGHT, I HATE YOU, YOU HATE ME, CAN WE JUST DO THIS?
OH COME ON, WHAT'S THE HURRY? I MEAN BESIDES THE FACT THAT YOU'RE INCREDIBLY OLD AND WILL PROBABLY DIE SOON.
PLEASE, I WILL BURY EVERYONE HERE.
WHO DO YOU HAVE FOR ME?
HE'S CALLED *SPEC.*
SPEC. WHY SPEC?
WHAT DO YOU CARE? THAT'S WHAT HE'S CALLED.

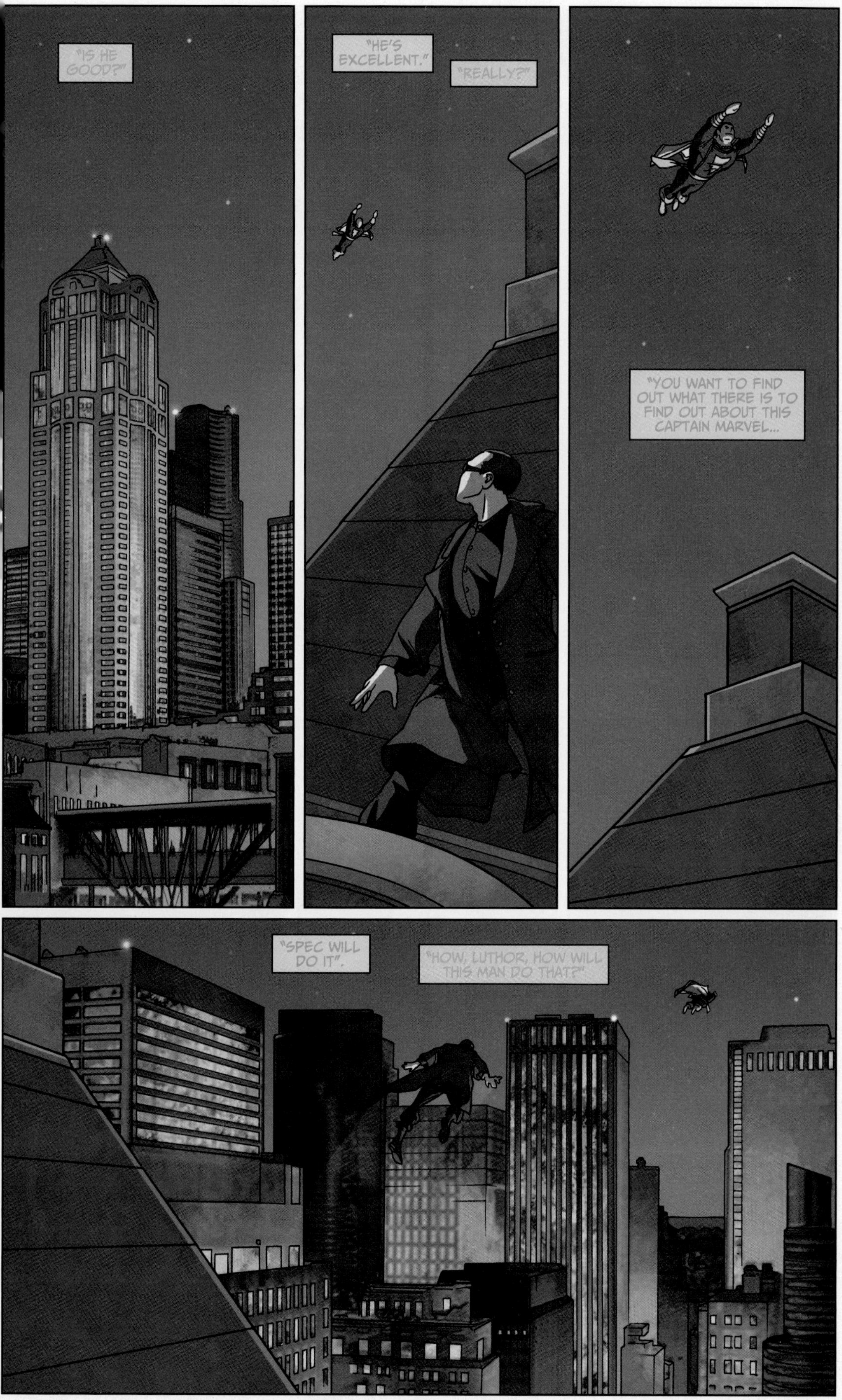
"IS HE GOOD?"
"HE'S EXCELLENT."
"REALLY?"
"YOU WANT TO FIND OUT WHAT THERE IS TO FIND OUT ABOUT THIS CAPTAIN MARVEL...
"SPEC WILL DO IT".
"HOW, LUTHOR, HOW WILL THIS MAN DO THAT?"

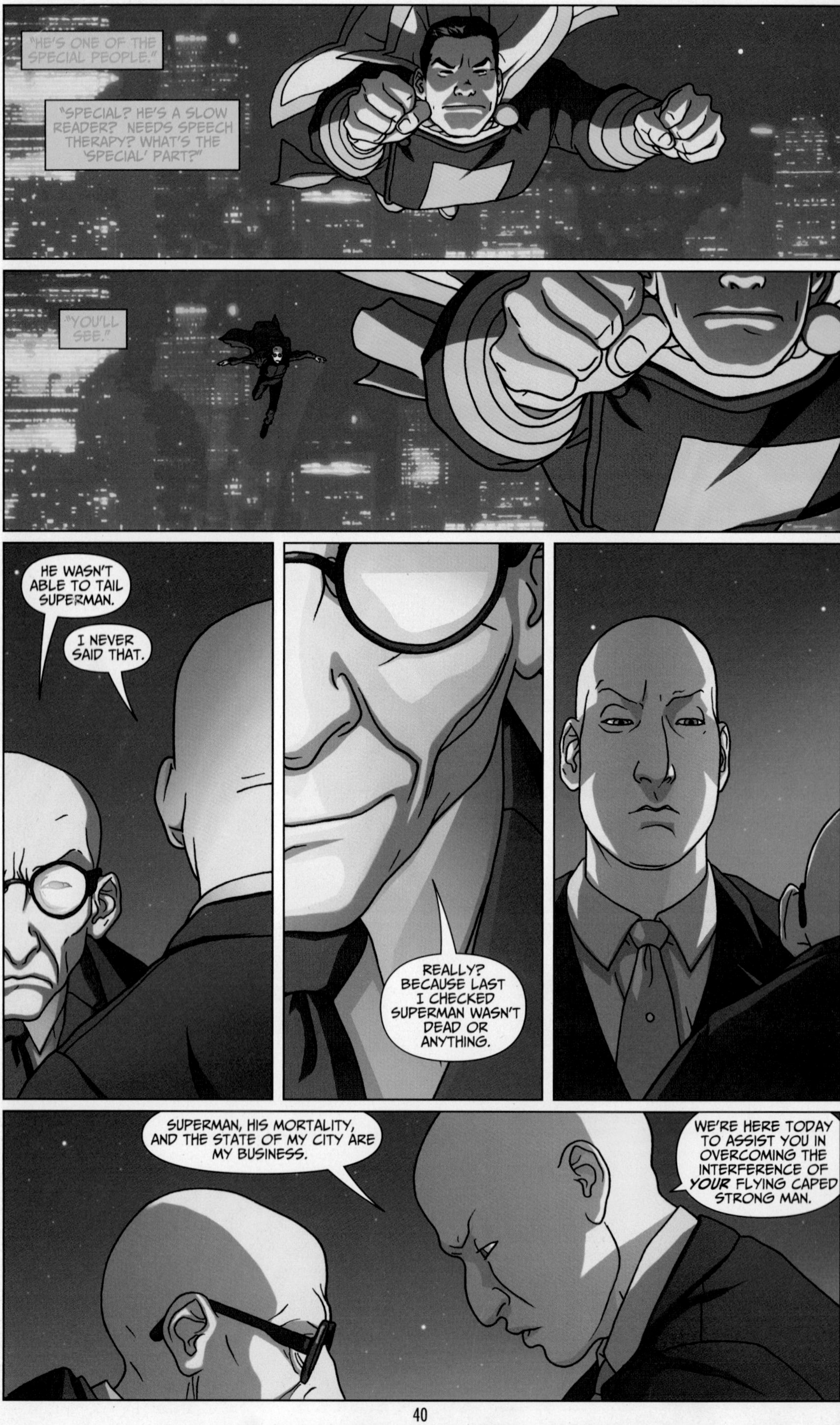
"HE'S ONE OF THE SPECIAL PEOPLE."
"SPECIAL? HE'S A SLOW READER? NEEDS SPEECH THERAPY? WHAT'S THE 'SPECIAL' PART?"
"YOU'LL SEE."
HE WASN'T ABLE TO TAIL SUPERMAN.
I NEVER SAID THAT.
REALLY? BECAUSE LAST I CHECKED SUPERMAN WASN'T DEAD OR ANYTHING.
SUPERMAN, HIS MORTALITY, AND THE STATE OF MY CITY ARE MY BUSINESS.
WE'RE HERE TODAY TO ASSIST YOU IN OVERCOMING THE INTERFERENCE OF *YOUR* FLYING CAPED STRONG MAN.

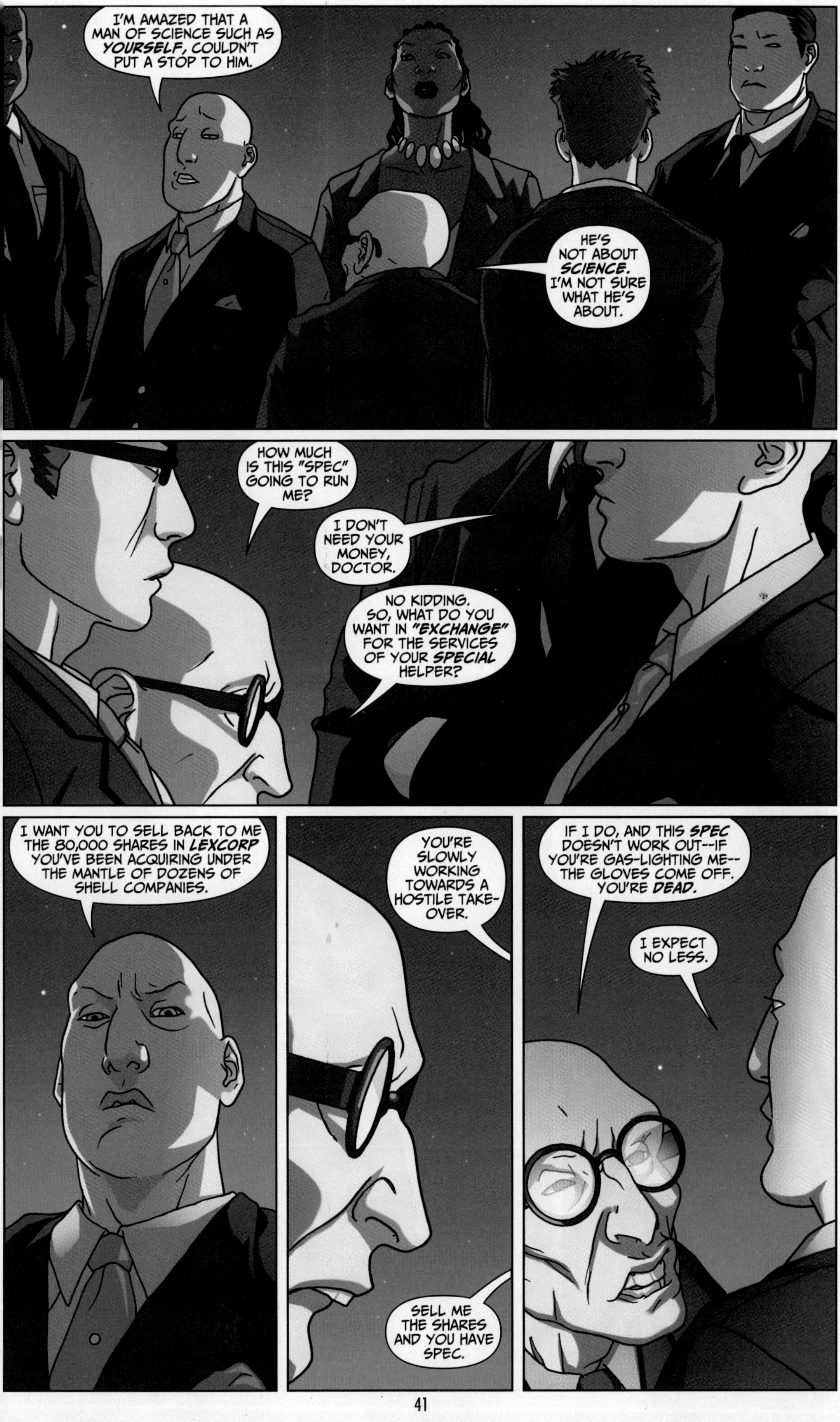

I'M AMAZED THAT A MAN OF SCIENCE SUCH AS YOURSELF, COULDN'T PUT A STOP TO HIM.
HE'S NOT ABOUT SCIENCE. I'M NOT SURE WHAT HE'S ABOUT.
HOW MUCH IS THIS "SPEC" GOING TO RUN ME?
I DON'T NEED YOUR MONEY, DOCTOR.
NO KIDDING. SO, WHAT DO YOU WANT IN "EXCHANGE" FOR THE SERVICES OF YOUR SPECIAL HELPER?
I WANT YOU TO SELL BACK TO ME THE 80,000 SHARES IN LEXCORP YOU'VE BEEN ACQUIRING UNDER THE MANTLE OF DOZENS OF SHELL COMPANIES.
YOU'RE SLOWLY WORKING TOWARDS A HOSTILE TAKE-OVER.
SELL ME THE SHARES AND YOU HAVE SPEC.
IF I DO, AND THIS SPEC DOESN'T WORK OUT--IF YOU'RE GAS-LIGHTING ME--THE GLOVES COME OFF. YOU'RE DEAD.
I EXPECT NO LESS.

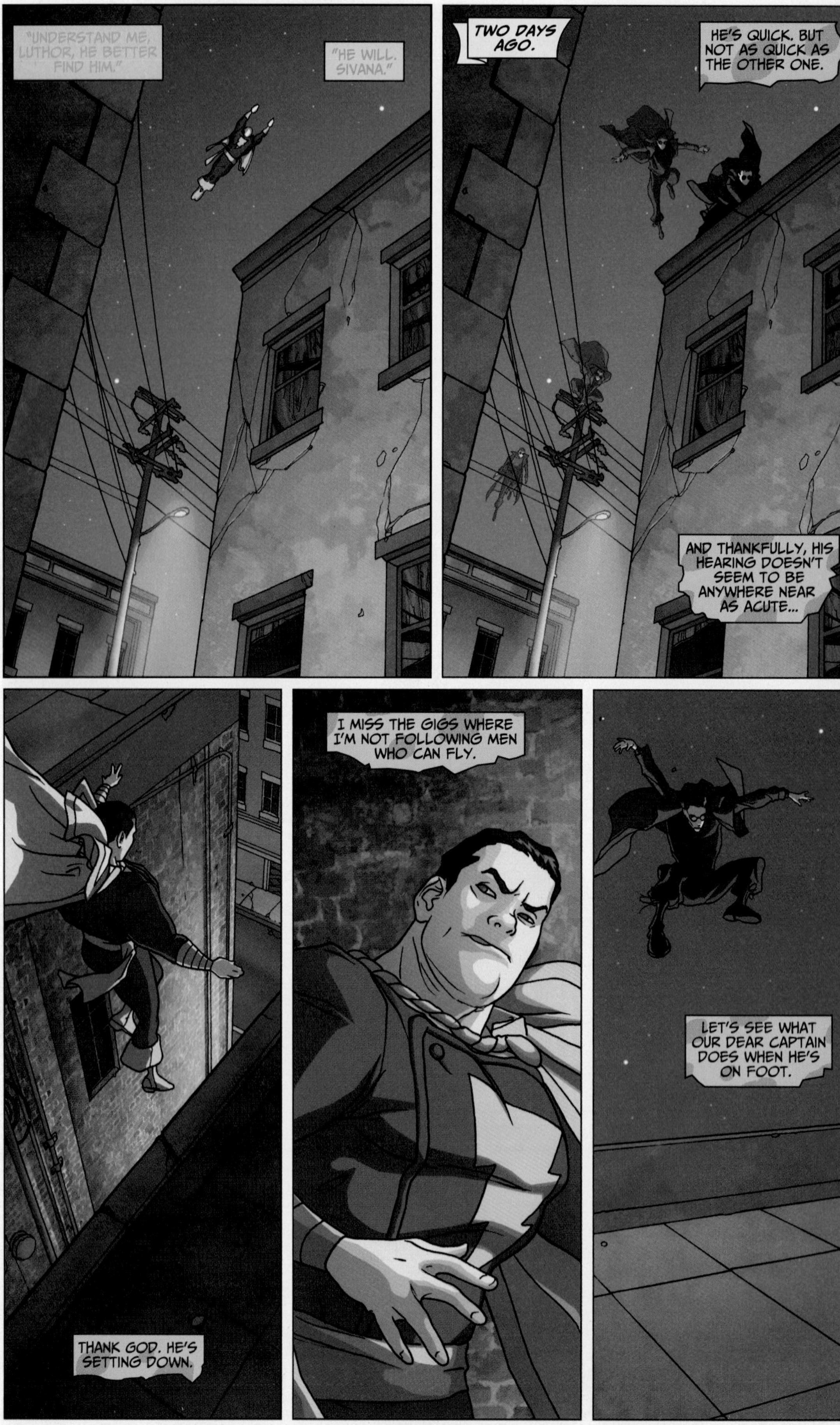
"UNDERSTAND ME, LUTHOR, HE BETTER FIND HIM."
"HE WILL. SIVANA."
TWO DAYS AGO.
HE'S QUICK. BUT NOT AS QUICK AS THE OTHER ONE.
AND THANKFULLY, HIS HEARING DOESN'T SEEM TO BE ANYWHERE NEAR AS ACUTE...
THANK GOD. HE'S SETTING DOWN.
I MISS THE GIGS WHERE I'M NOT FOLLOWING MEN WHO CAN FLY.
LET'S SEE WHAT OUR DEAR CAPTAIN DOES WHEN HE'S ON FOOT.

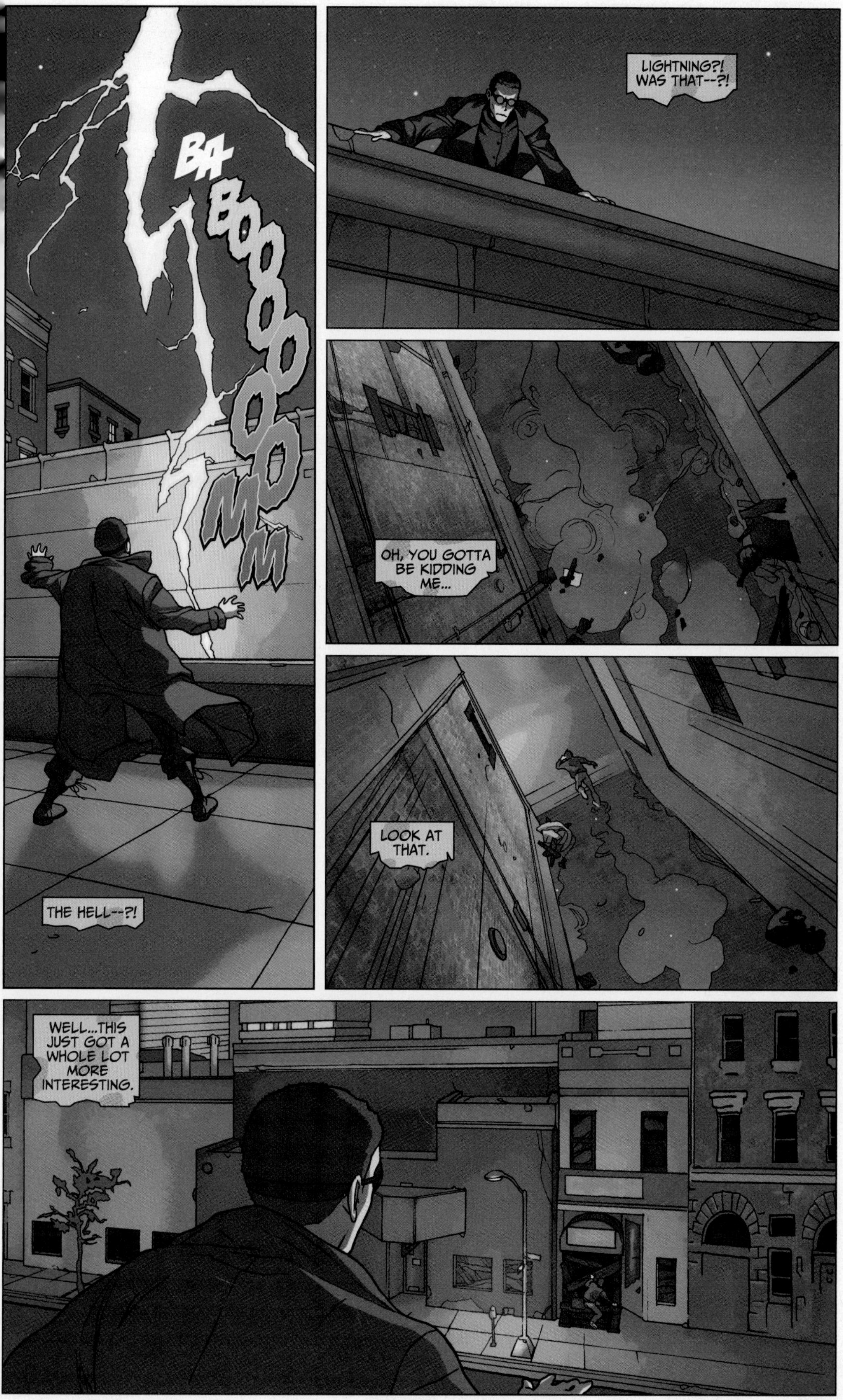
BA
BOOOOOOOOOMM
THE HELL--?!
LIGHTNING?! WAS THAT--?!
OH, YOU GOTTA BE KIDDING ME...
LOOK AT THAT.
WELL...THIS JUST GOT A WHOLE LOT MORE INTERESTING.

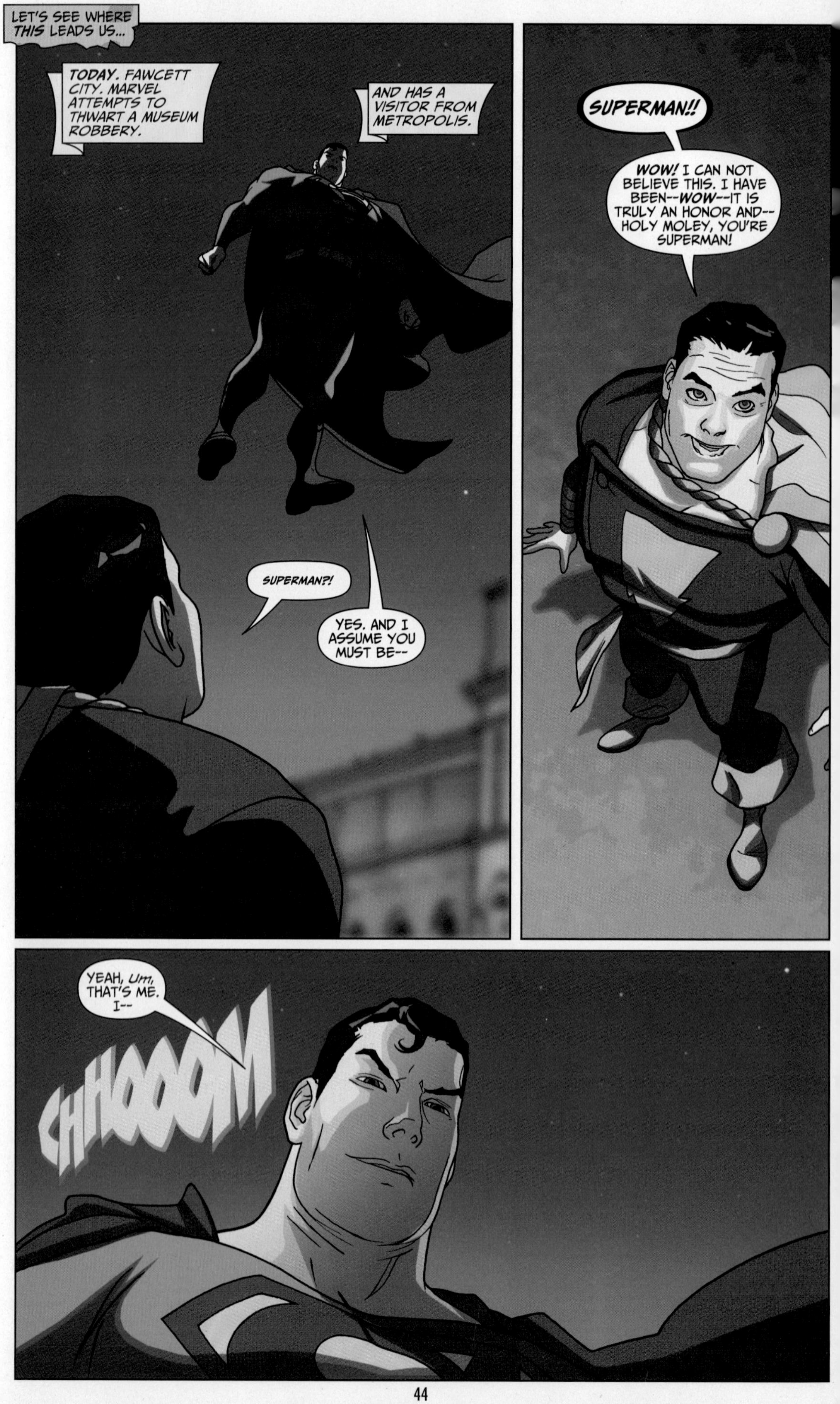
LET'S SEE WHERE THIS LEADS US...
TODAY. FAWCETT CITY. MARVEL ATTEMPTS TO THWART A MUSEUM ROBBERY.
AND HAS A VISITOR FROM METROPOLIS.
SUPERMAN?!
YES. AND I ASSUME YOU MUST BE--
SUPERMAN!!
WOW! I CAN NOT BELIEVE THIS. I HAVE BEEN--WOW--IT IS TRULY AN HONOR AND--HOLY MOLEY, YOU'RE SUPERMAN!
YEAH, UM, THAT'S ME. I--
CHHOOOM

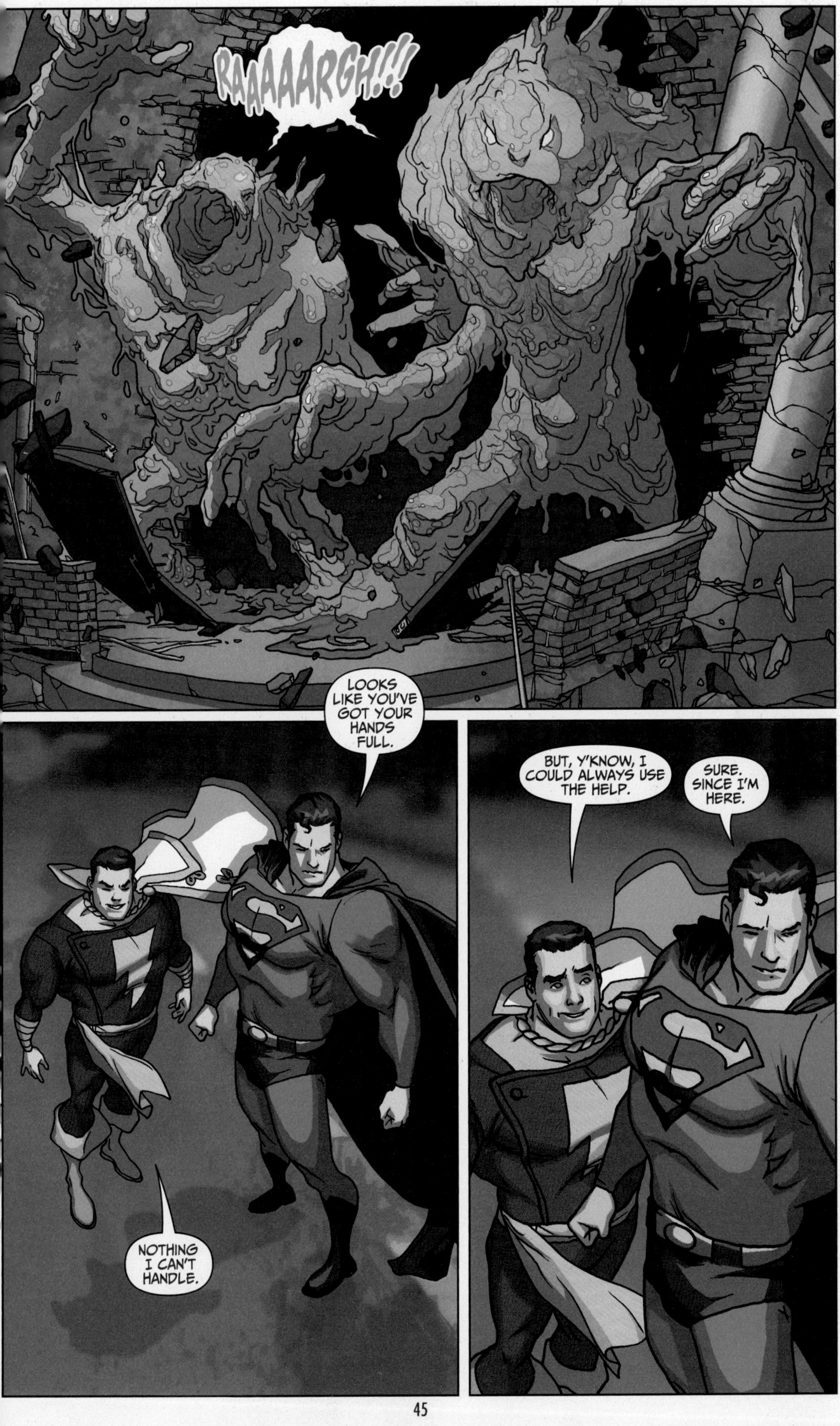
RAAAAARGH!!!
LOOKS LIKE YOU'VE GOT YOUR HANDS FULL.
NOTHING I CAN'T HANDLE.
BUT, Y'KNOW, I COULD ALWAYS USE THE HELP.
SURE. SINCE I'M HERE.

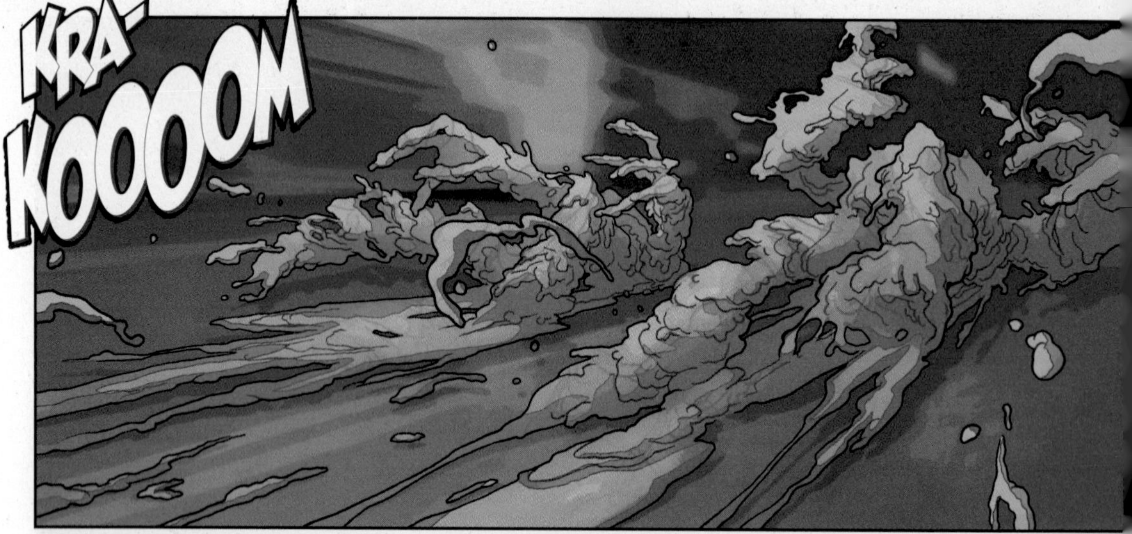
KRA-KOOOOM

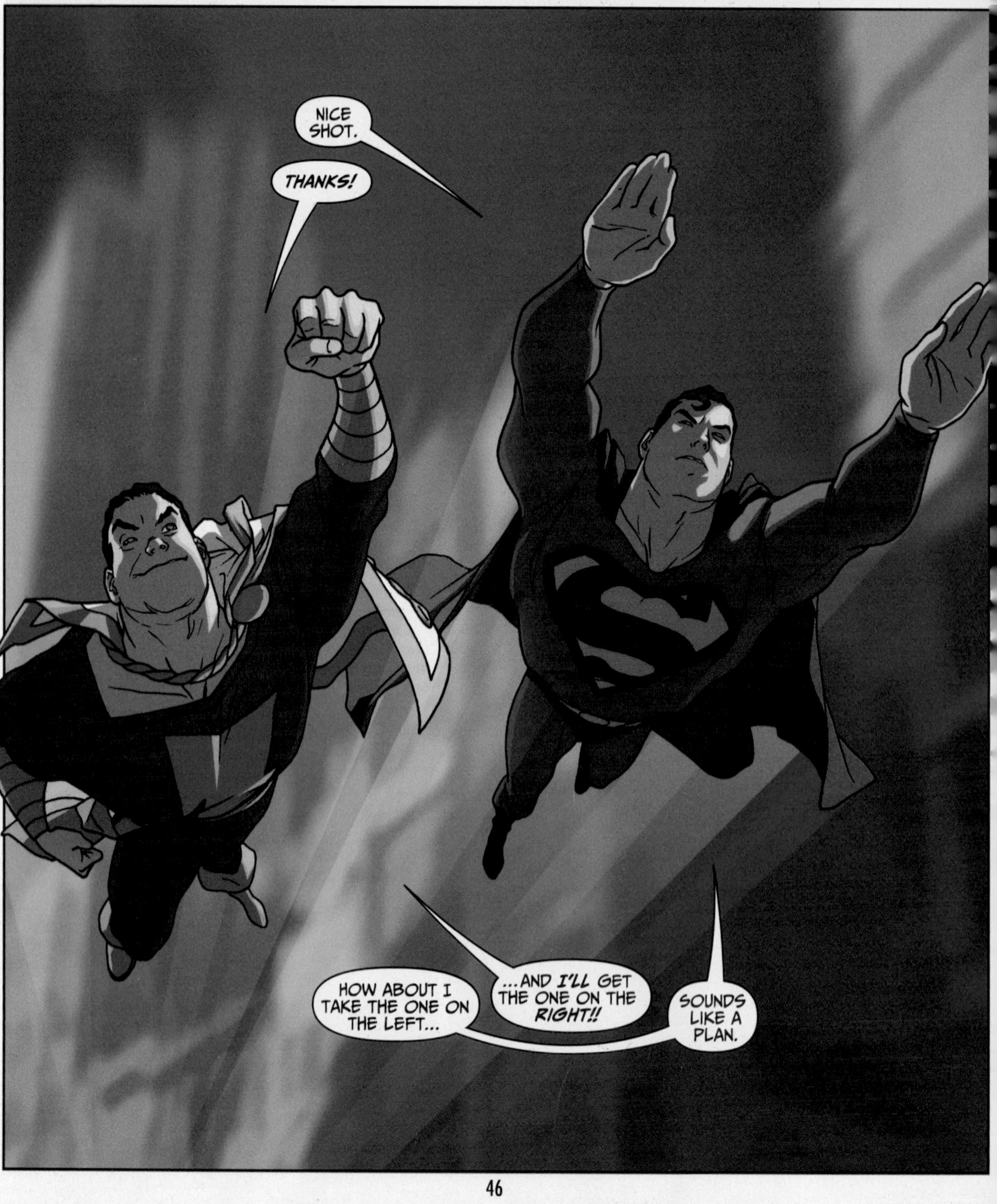
NICE SHOT.
THANKS!
HOW ABOUT I TAKE THE ONE ON THE LEFT...
...AND I'LL GET THE ONE ON THE RIGHT!!
SOUNDS LIKE A PLAN.

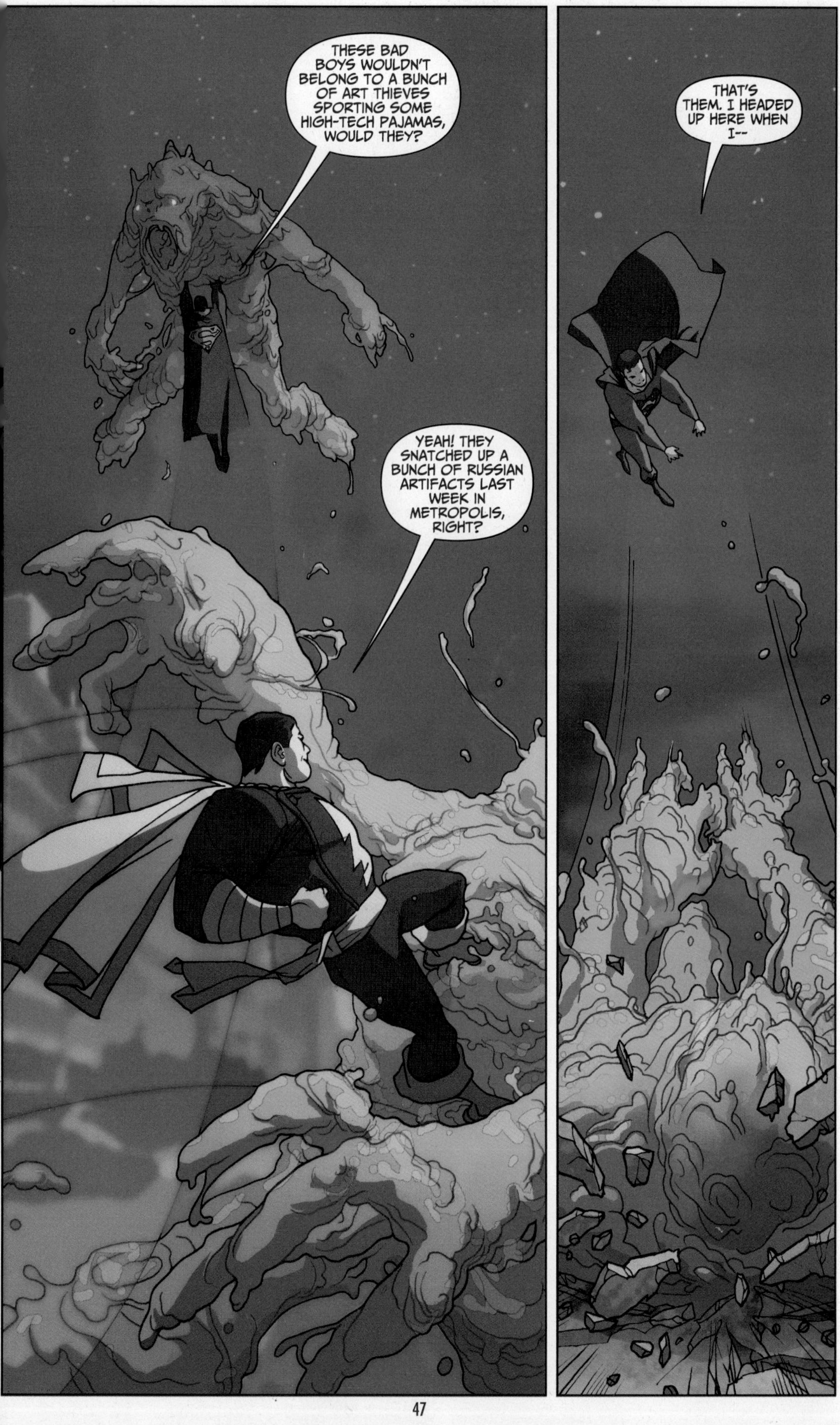

THESE BAD BOYS WOULDN'T BELONG TO A BUNCH OF ART THIEVES SPORTING SOME HIGH-TECH PAJAMAS, WOULD THEY?
YEAH! THEY SNATCHED UP A BUNCH OF RUSSIAN ARTIFACTS LAST WEEK IN METROPOLIS, RIGHT?
THAT'S THEM. I HEADED UP HERE WHEN I--

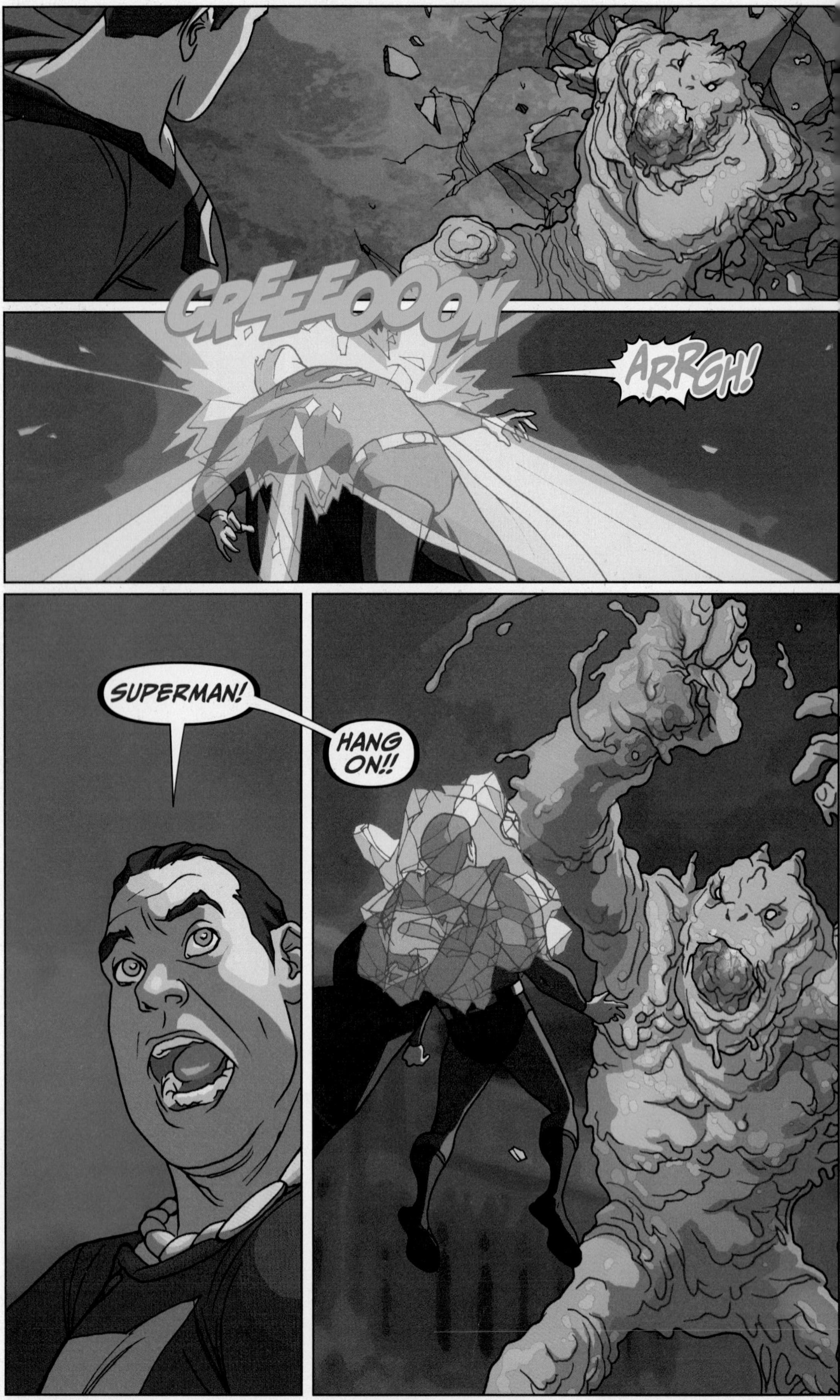

CREEEOOOK
ARRGH!
SUPERMAN!
HANG ON!!

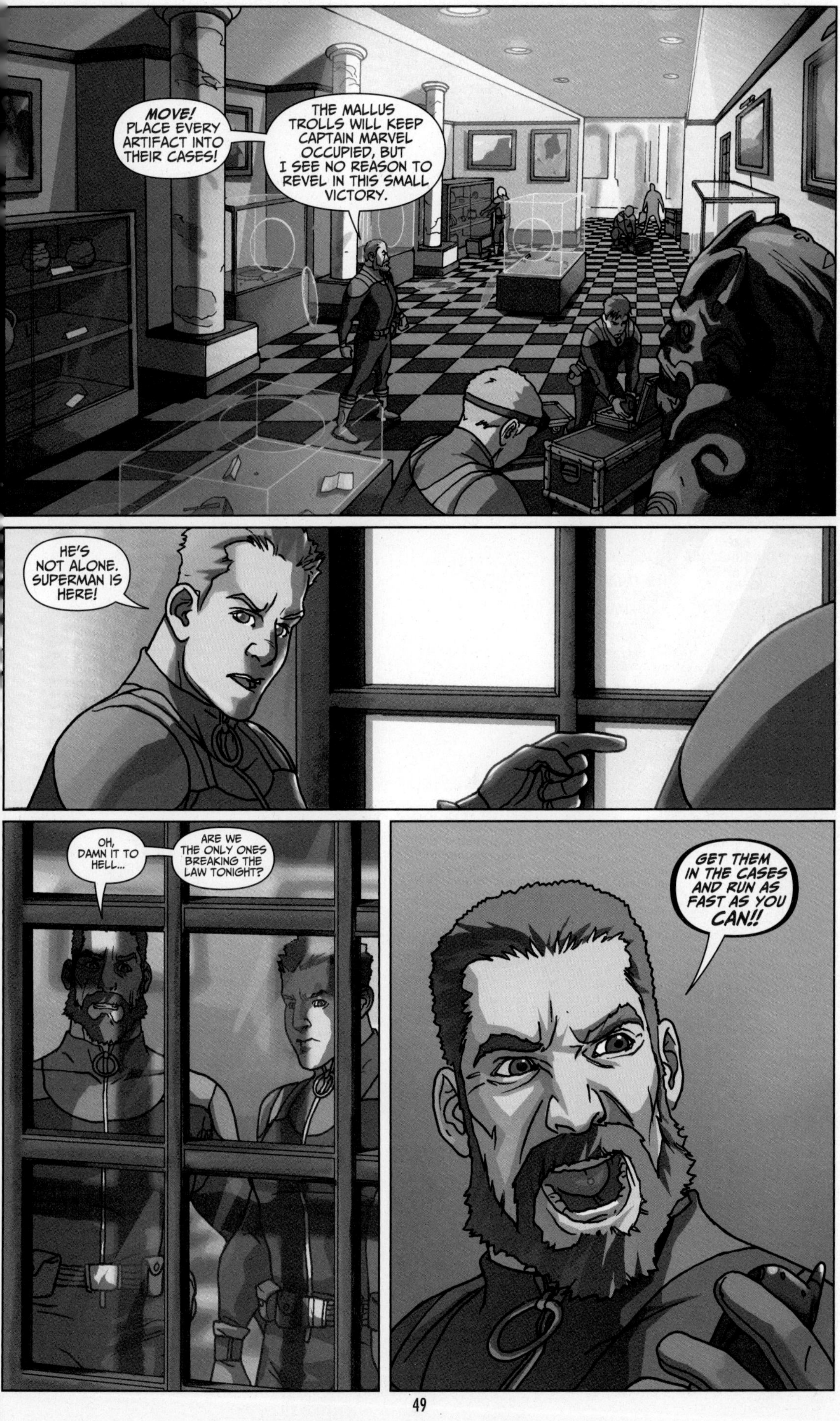
MOVE! PLACE EVERY ARTIFACT INTO THEIR CASES!
THE MALLUS TROLLS WILL KEEP CAPTAIN MARVEL OCCUPIED, BUT I SEE NO REASON TO REVEL IN THIS SMALL VICTORY.
HE'S NOT ALONE. SUPERMAN IS HERE!
OH, DAMN IT TO HELL...
ARE WE THE ONLY ONES BREAKING THE LAW TONIGHT?
GET THEM IN THE CASES AND RUN AS FAST AS YOU CAN!!

IT'S ME. TELL ME YOU HAVE HIM.

WE DO, BUT SIR, I, UM, I DON'T MEAN TO IN ANY WAY QUESTION OUR DIRECTION--

WHAT THE HELL IS WRONG?!!

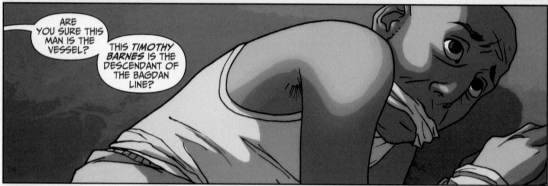

ARE YOU SURE THIS MAN IS THE VESSEL?

THIS *TIMOTHY BARNES* IS THE DESCENDANT OF THE BAGDAN LINE?

THAT'S HIM. I DO NOT WANT HIM INJURED.

HE WILL SOON UNDERSTAND THE GIFT WE ARE BESTOWING UPON HIM.

BUT NOW, WE SEEM TO HAVE ATTRACTED FAR TOO MUCH ATTENTION. WE ARE SHORT ON TIME.

CALL DR. SIVANA, INFORM HIM THAT WE HAVE EVERYTHING WE NEED.

WE WILL BEGIN IN ONE HOUR.

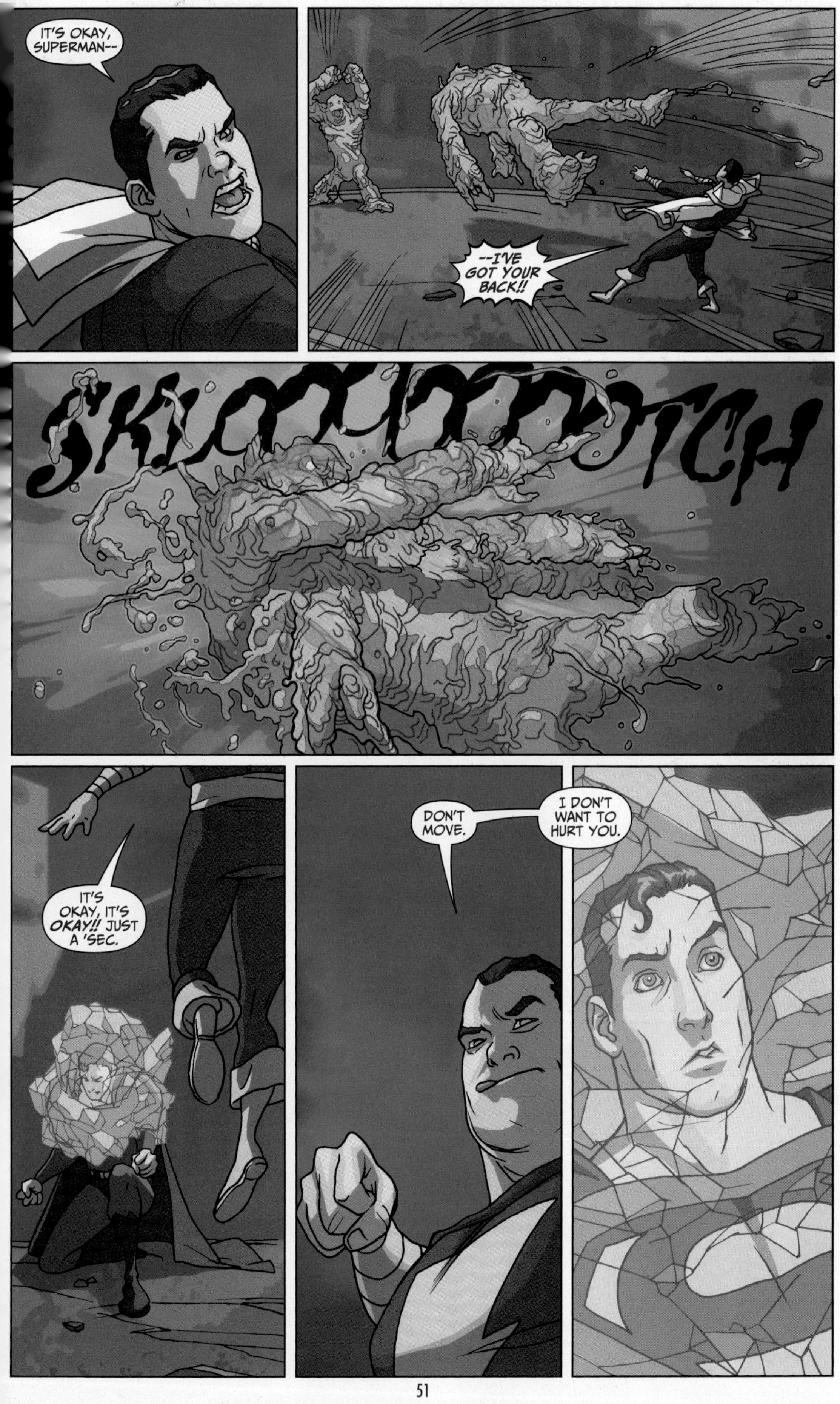
IT'S OKAY, SUPERMAN--
--I'VE GOT YOUR BACK!!
IT'S OKAY, IT'S OKAY!! JUST A 'SEC.
DON'T MOVE.
I DON'T WANT TO HURT YOU.

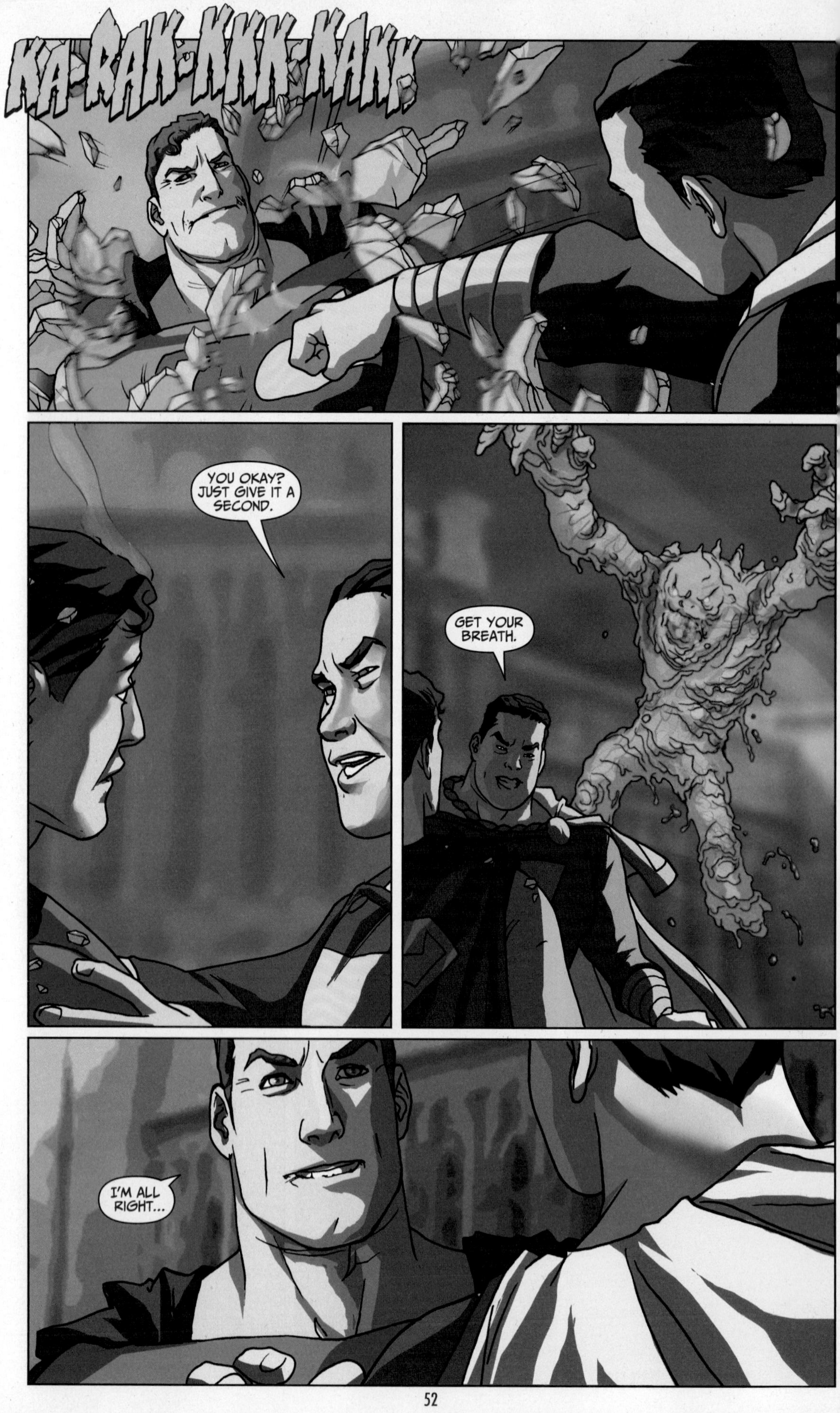
KA-RAK-KKK-KAKK
YOU OKAY? JUST GIVE IT A SECOND.
GET YOUR BREATH.
I'M ALL RIGHT...

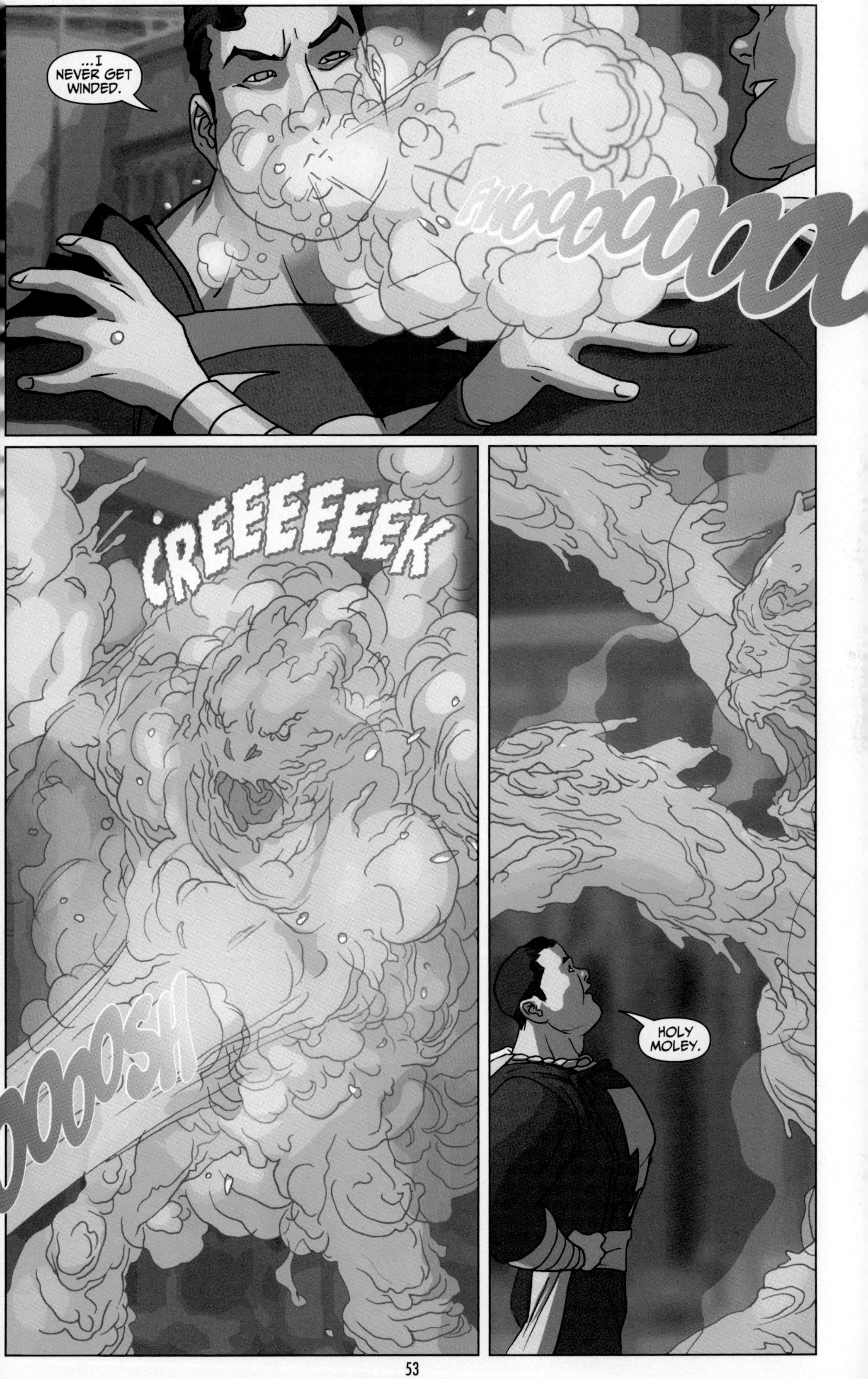
...I NEVER GET WINDED.
FWOOOOOOOO
CREEEEEEK
OOOOSH
HOLY MOLEY.

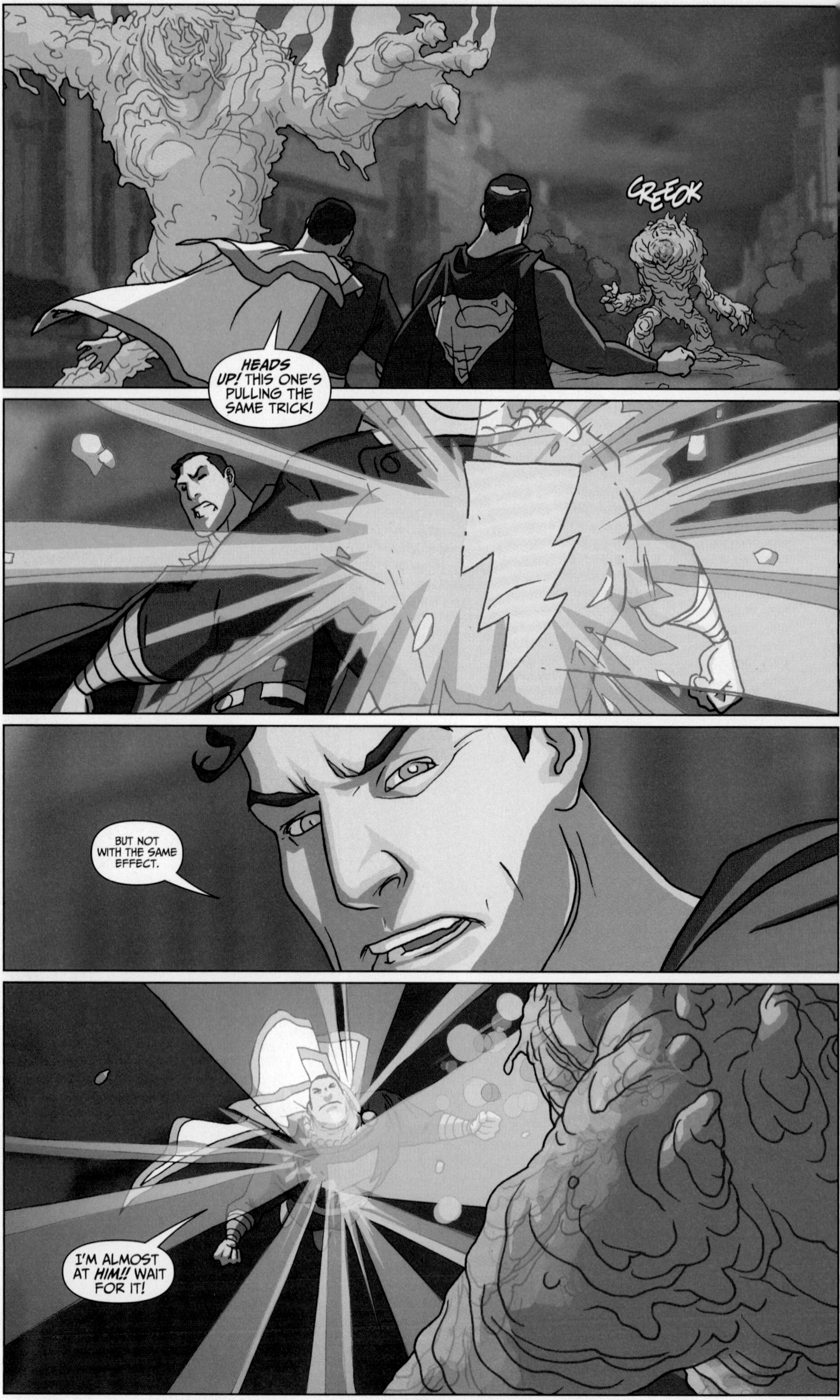
CREEOK
HEADS UP! THIS ONE'S PULLING THE SAME TRICK!
BUT NOT WITH THE SAME EFFECT.
I'M ALMOST AT HIM!! WAIT FOR IT!

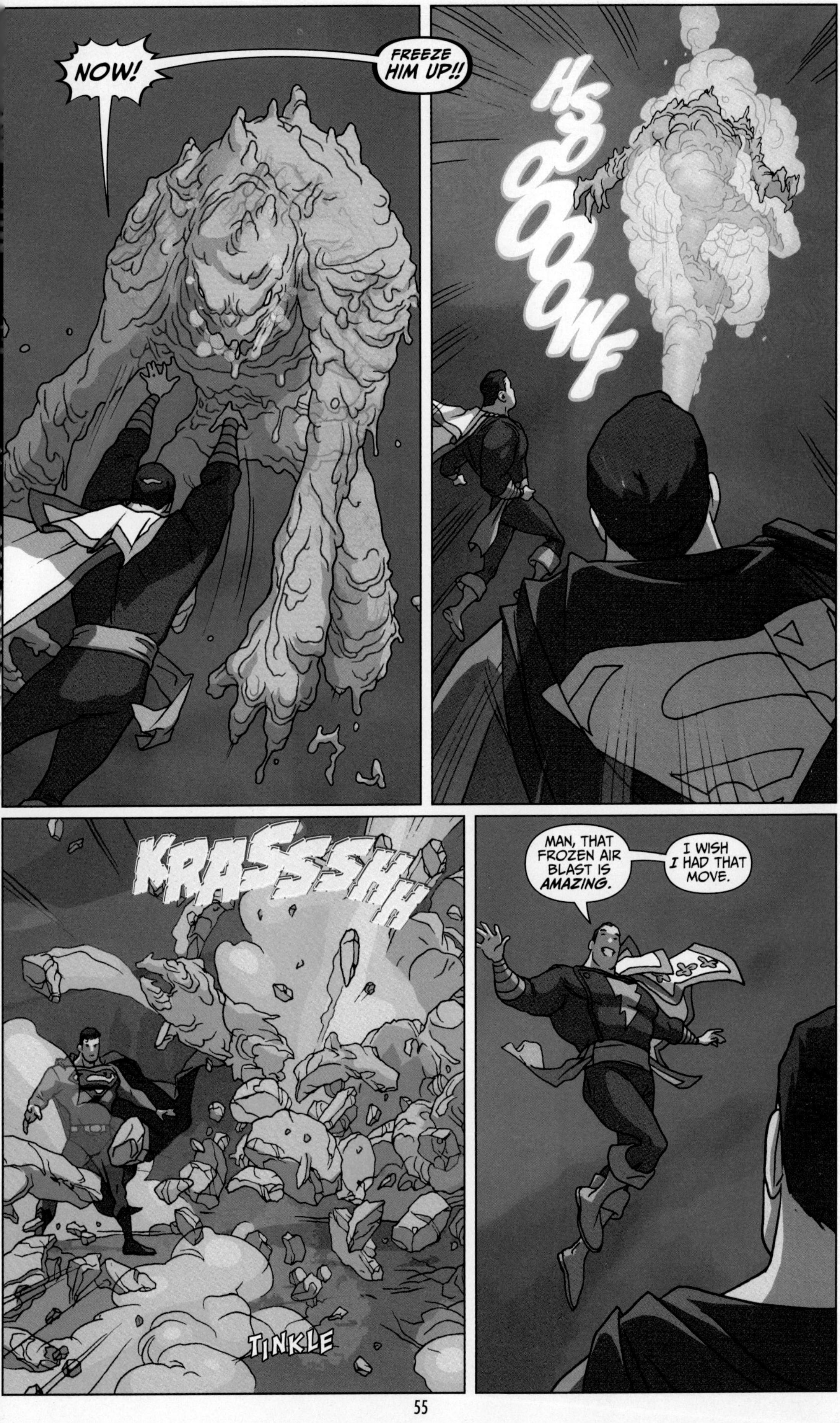
NOW!
FREEZE HIM UP!!
HSOOOOOWF
KRASSSHH
TINKLE
MAN, THAT FROZEN AIR BLAST IS AMAZING.
I WISH I HAD THAT MOVE.

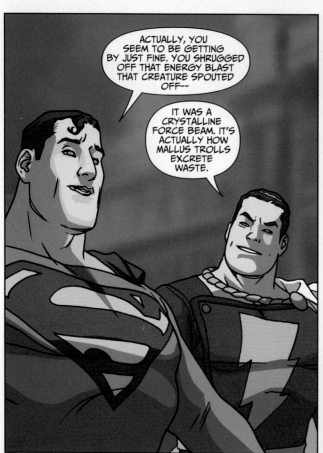

ACTUALLY, YOU SEEM TO BE GETTING BY JUST FINE. YOU SHRUGGED OFF THAT ENERGY BLAST THAT CREATURE SPOUTED OFF--

IT WAS A CRYSTALLINE FORCE BEAM. IT'S ACTUALLY HOW MALLUS TROLLS EXCRETE WASTE.

YOU FOUGHT THOSE MONSTERS BEFORE?

NO. I JUST KNOW THINGS.

WISDOM OF SOLOMON.

OH, SO YOU'RE A "SCHOLAR" AS WELL.

NO, I, UM... SORT OF. YES. I JUST KNOW THINGS.

LISTEN... I DON'T MEAN TO IMPOSE, BUT...

DO YOU HAVE SOME TIME TO TALK?

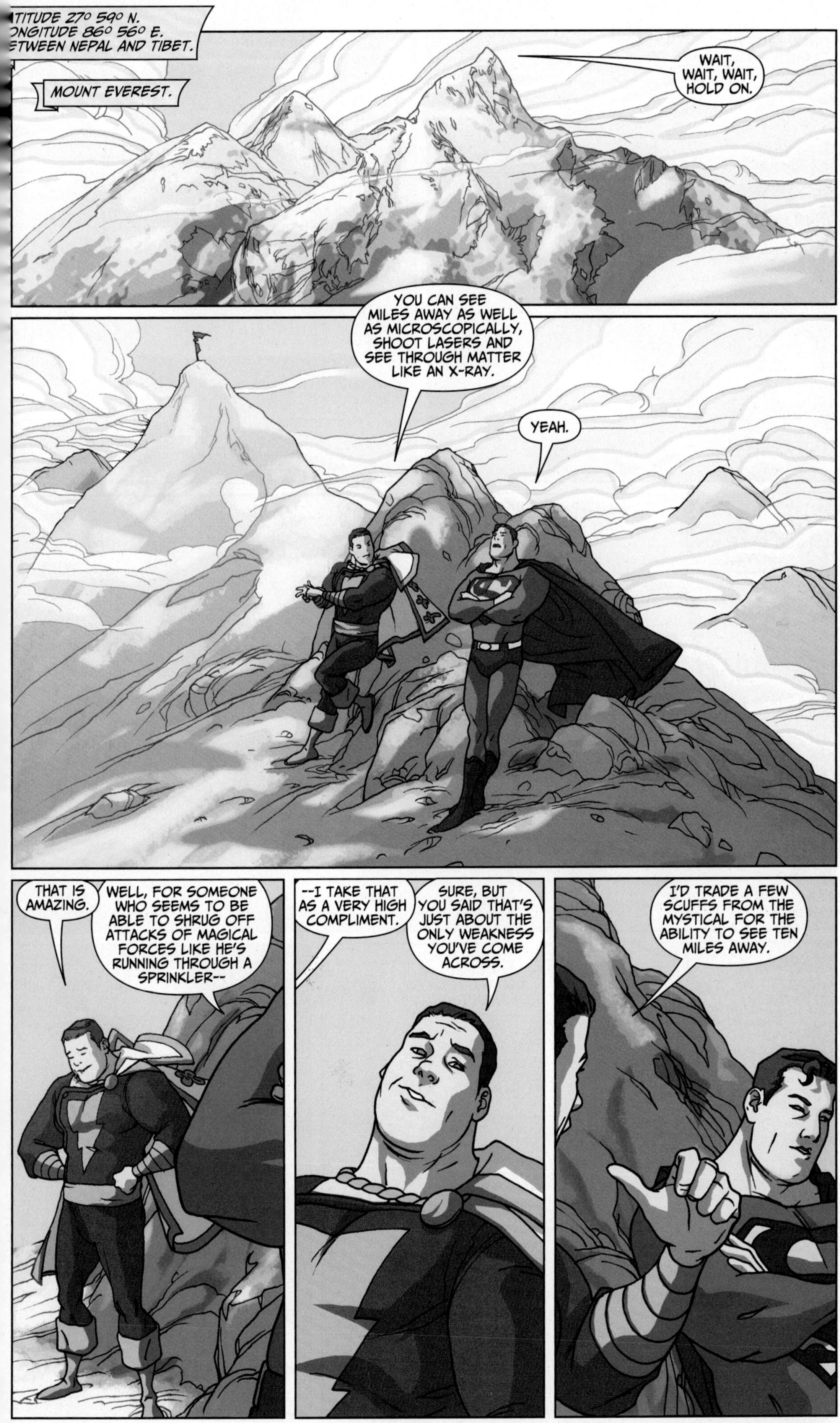
ATITUDE 27° 59° N.
ONGITUDE 86° 56° E.
ETWEEN NEPAL AND TIBET.
MOUNT EVEREST.
WAIT, WAIT, WAIT, HOLD ON.
YOU CAN SEE MILES AWAY AS WELL AS MICROSCOPICALLY, SHOOT LASERS AND SEE THROUGH MATTER LIKE AN X-RAY.
YEAH.
THAT IS AMAZING.
WELL, FOR SOMEONE WHO SEEMS TO BE ABLE TO SHRUG OFF ATTACKS OF MAGICAL FORCES LIKE HE'S RUNNING THROUGH A SPRINKLER--
--I TAKE THAT AS A VERY HIGH COMPLIMENT.
SURE, BUT YOU SAID THAT'S JUST ABOUT THE ONLY WEAKNESS YOU'VE COME ACROSS.
I'D TRADE A FEW SCUFFS FROM THE MYSTICAL FOR THE ABILITY TO SEE TEN MILES AWAY.

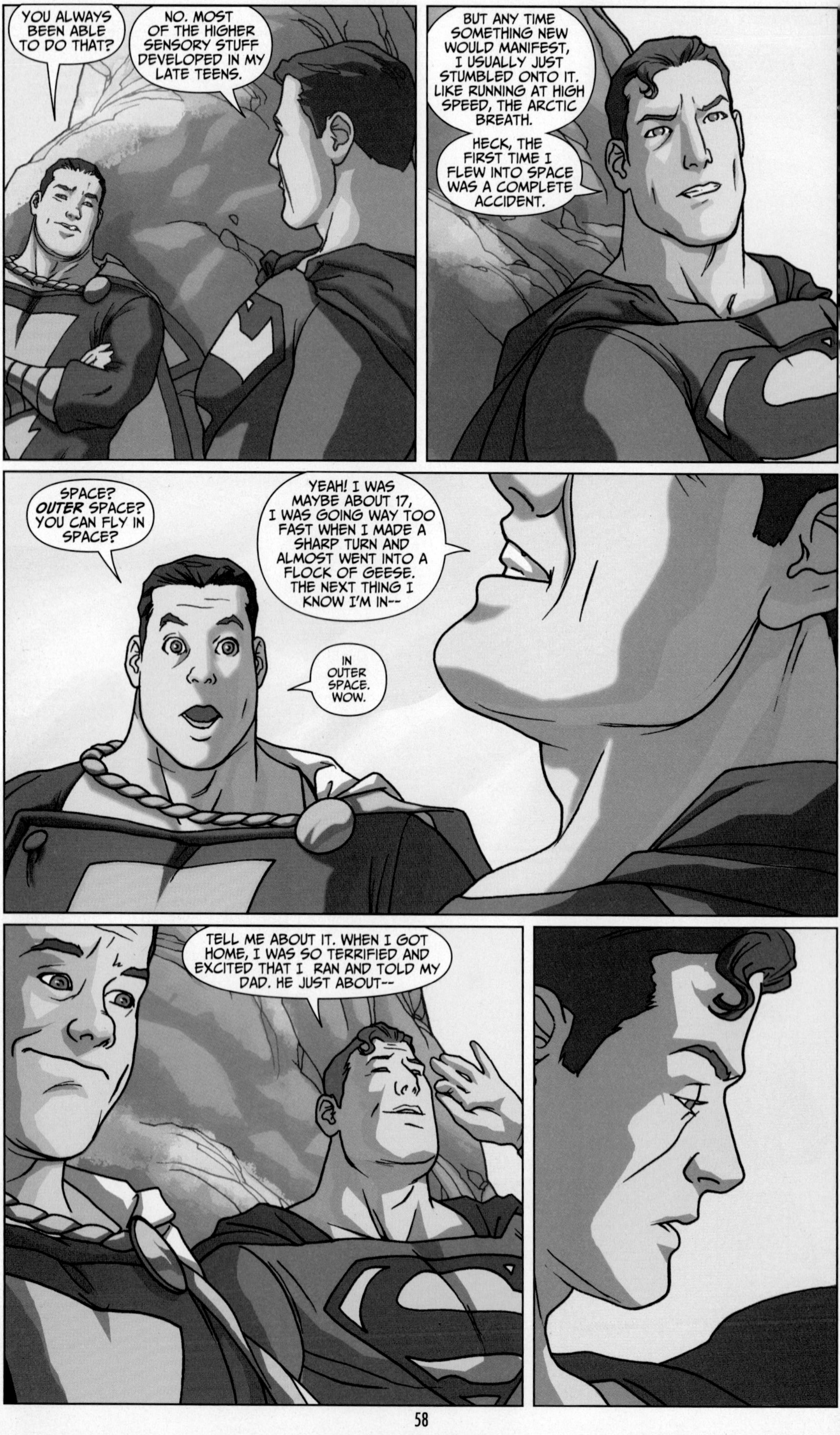

YOU ALWAYS BEEN ABLE TO DO THAT?
NO. MOST OF THE HIGHER SENSORY STUFF DEVELOPED IN MY LATE TEENS.
BUT ANY TIME SOMETHING NEW WOULD MANIFEST, I USUALLY JUST STUMBLED ONTO IT. LIKE RUNNING AT HIGH SPEED, THE ARCTIC BREATH.
HECK, THE FIRST TIME I FLEW INTO SPACE WAS A COMPLETE ACCIDENT.
SPACE? *OUTER* SPACE? YOU CAN FLY IN SPACE?
YEAH! I WAS MAYBE ABOUT 17, I WAS GOING WAY TOO FAST WHEN I MADE A SHARP TURN AND ALMOST WENT INTO A FLOCK OF GEESE. THE NEXT THING I KNOW I'M IN--
IN OUTER SPACE. WOW.
TELL ME ABOUT IT. WHEN I GOT HOME, I WAS SO TERRIFIED AND EXCITED THAT I RAN AND TOLD MY DAD. HE JUST ABOUT--

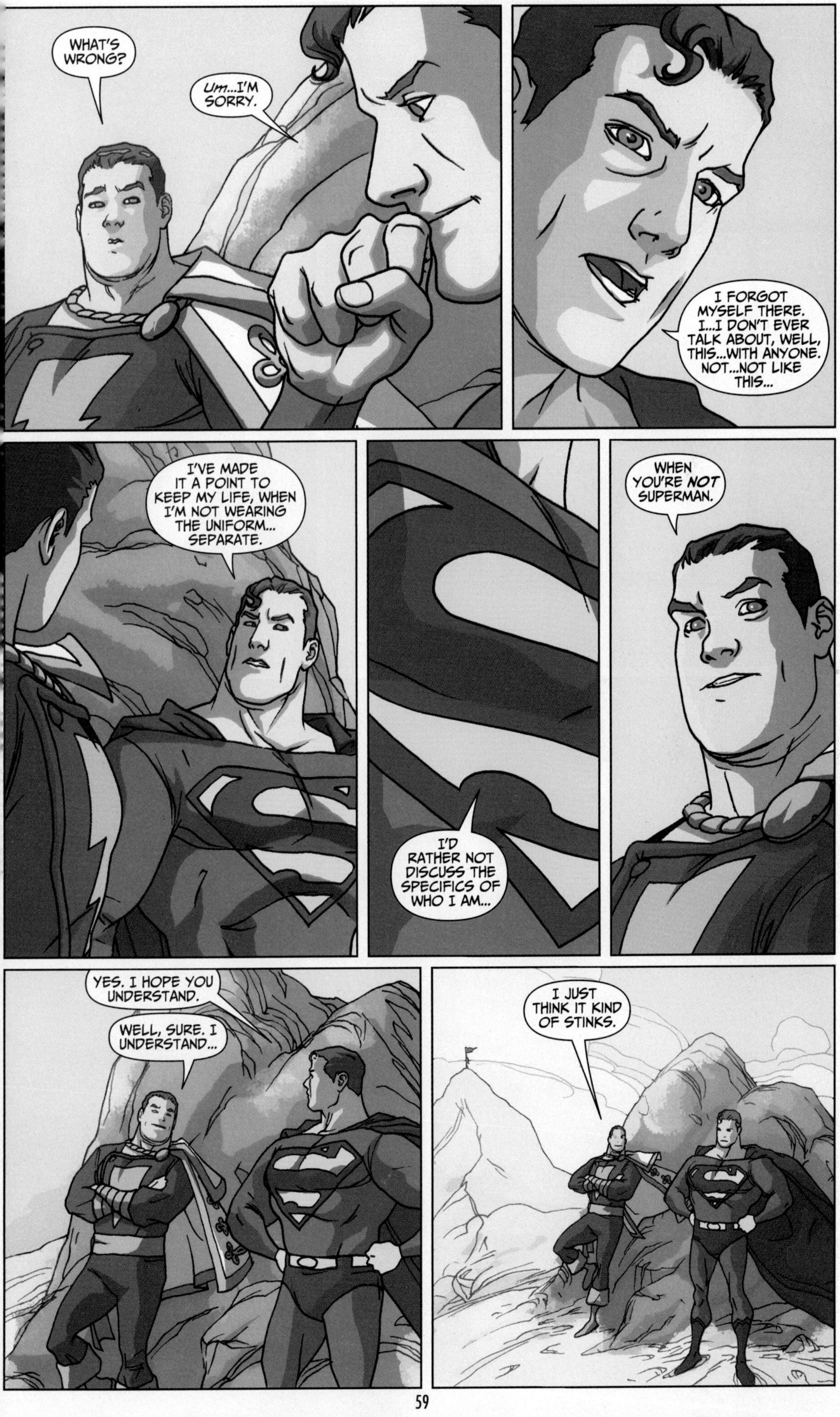
WHAT'S WRONG?
Um...I'M SORRY.
I FORGOT MYSELF THERE. I...I DON'T EVER TALK ABOUT, WELL, THIS...WITH ANYONE. NOT...NOT LIKE THIS...
I'VE MADE IT A POINT TO KEEP MY LIFE, WHEN I'M NOT WEARING THE UNIFORM... SEPARATE.
I'D RATHER NOT DISCUSS THE SPECIFICS OF WHO I AM...
WHEN YOU'RE NOT SUPERMAN.
YES. I HOPE YOU UNDERSTAND.
WELL, SURE. I UNDERSTAND...
I JUST THINK IT KIND OF STINKS.

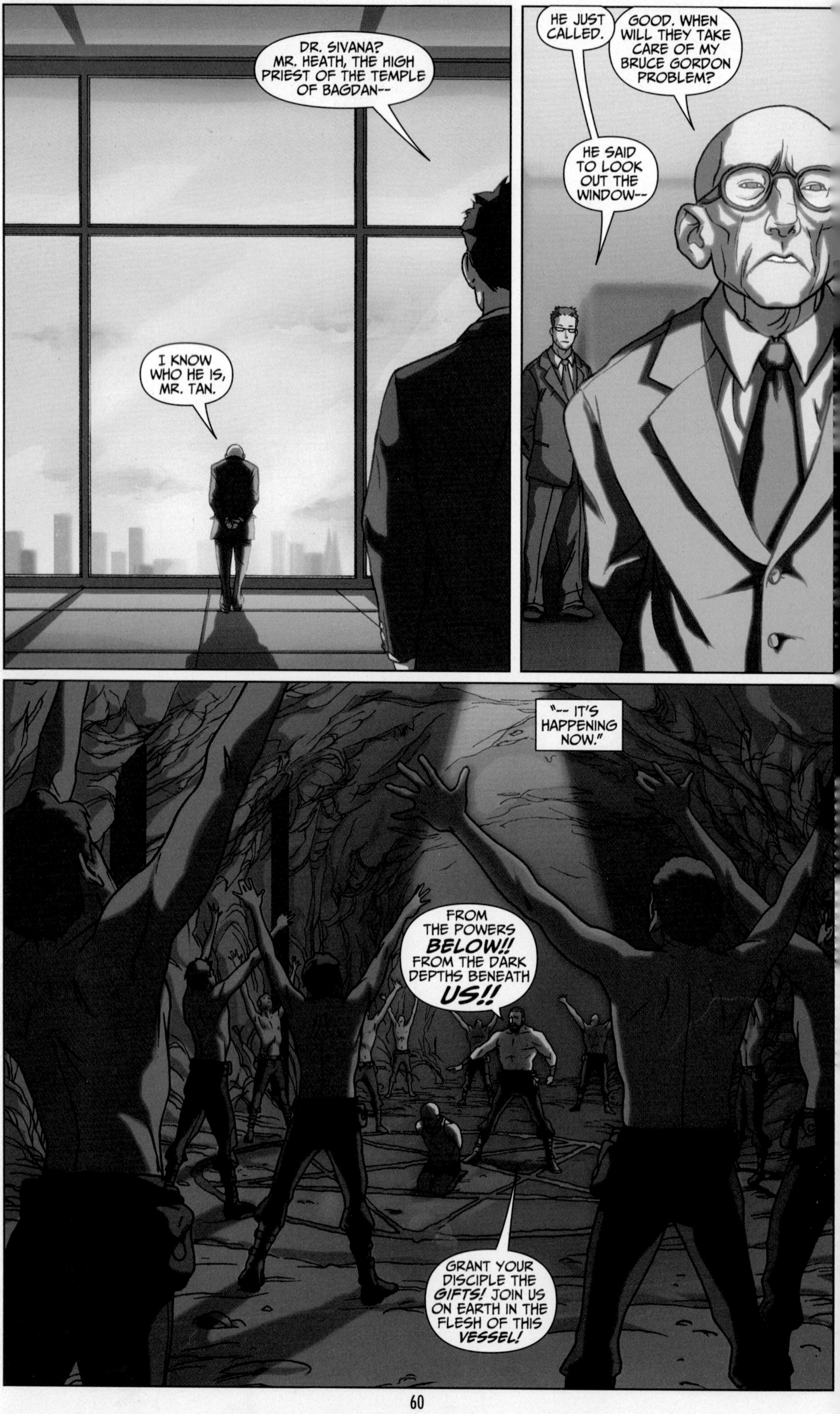
DR. SIVANA? MR. HEATH, THE HIGH PRIEST OF THE TEMPLE OF BAGDAN--
I KNOW WHO HE IS, MR. TAN.
HE JUST CALLED.
GOOD. WHEN WILL THEY TAKE CARE OF MY BRUCE GORDON PROBLEM?
HE SAID TO LOOK OUT THE WINDOW--
"-- IT'S HAPPENING NOW."
FROM THE POWERS BELOW!! FROM THE DARK DEPTHS BENEATH US!!
GRANT YOUR DISCIPLE THE GIFTS! JOIN US ON EARTH IN THE FLESH OF THIS VESSEL!

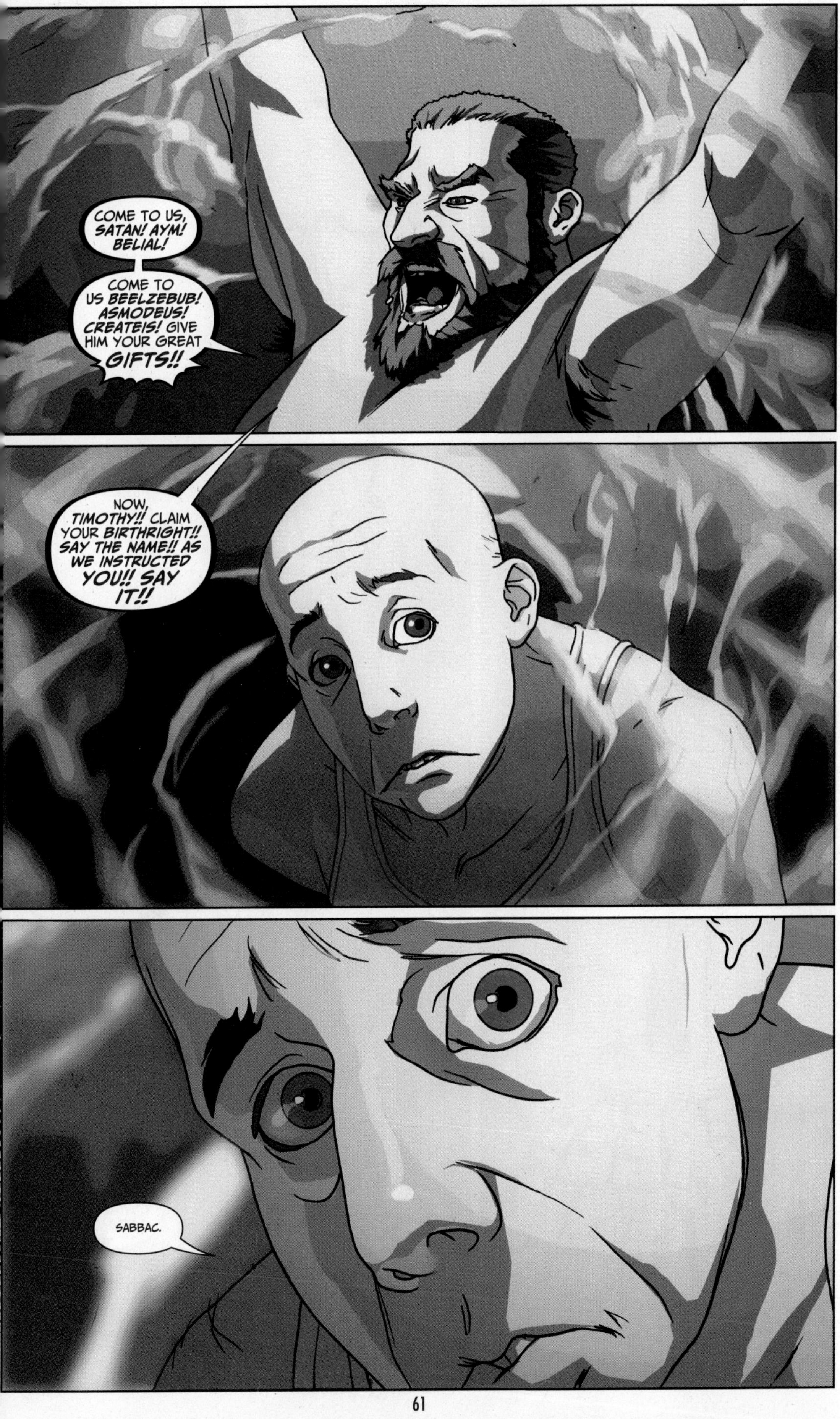
COME TO US, SATAN! AYM! BELIAL!
COME TO US BEELZEBUB! ASMODEUS! CREATEIS! GIVE HIM YOUR GREAT GIFTS!!
NOW, TIMOTHY!! CLAIM YOUR BIRTHRIGHT!! SAY THE NAME!! AS WE INSTRUCTED YOU!! SAY IT!!
SABBAC.

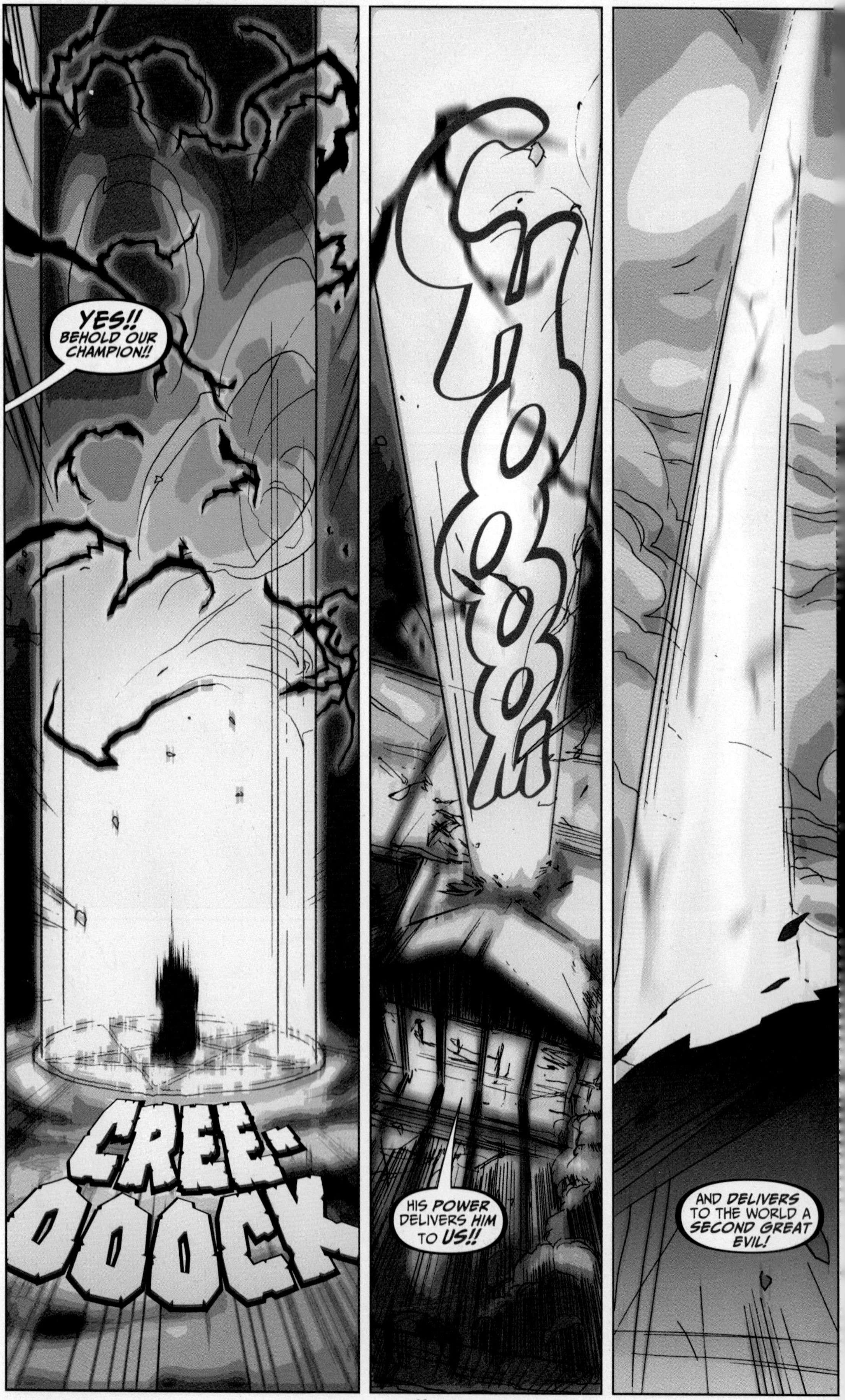
YES!! BEHOLD OUR CHAMPION!!
CREE-OOOCK
HIS POWER DELIVERS HIM TO US!!
AND DELIVERS TO THE WORLD A SECOND GREAT EVIL!

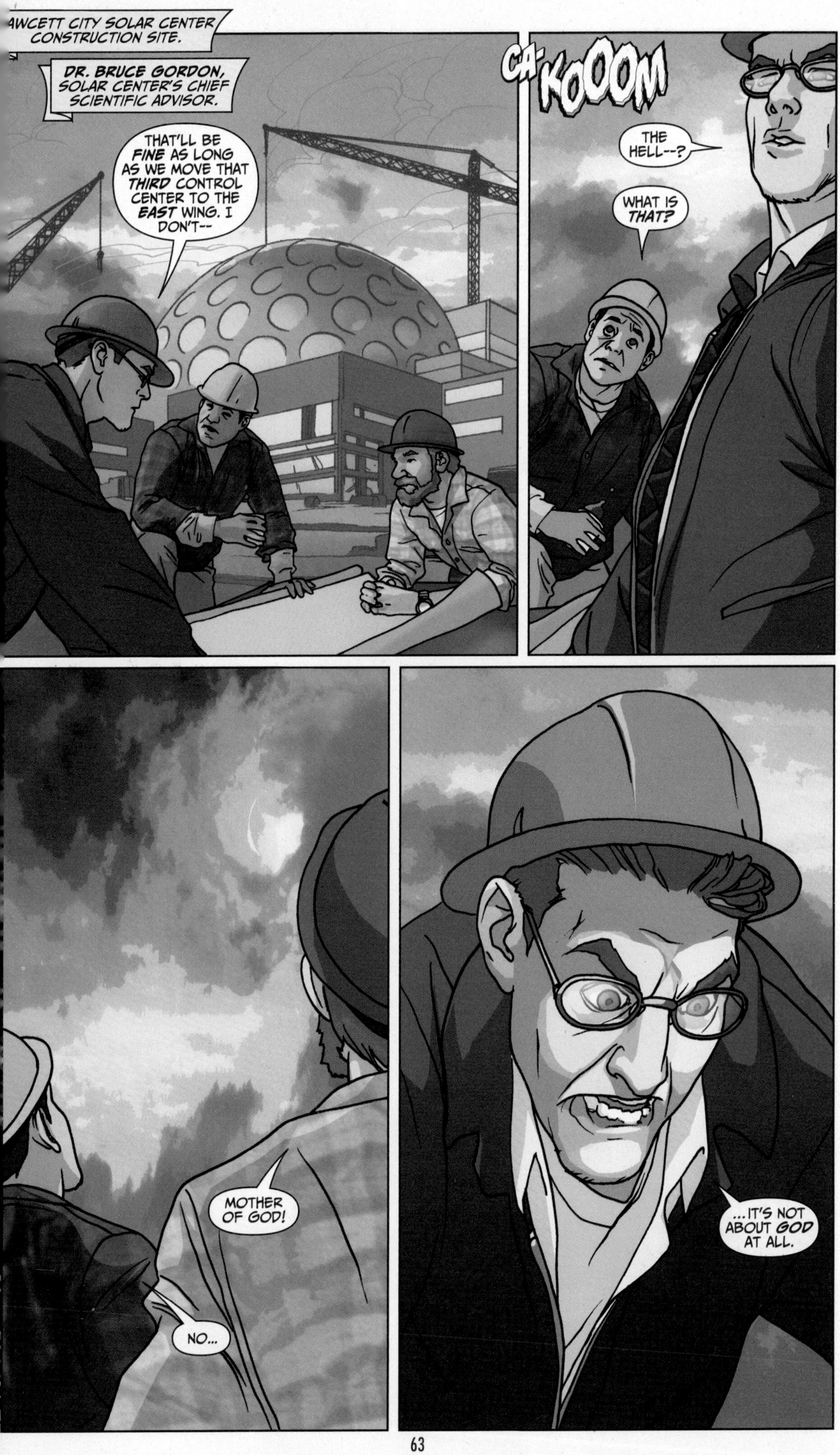
AWCETT CITY SOLAR CENTER CONSTRUCTION SITE.
DR. BRUCE GORDON, SOLAR CENTER'S CHIEF SCIENTIFIC ADVISOR.
THAT'LL BE FINE AS LONG AS WE MOVE THAT THIRD CONTROL CENTER TO THE EAST WING. I DON'T--
CA-KOOOM
THE HELL--?
WHAT IS THAT?
MOTHER OF GOD!
NO...
...IT'S NOT ABOUT GOD AT ALL.

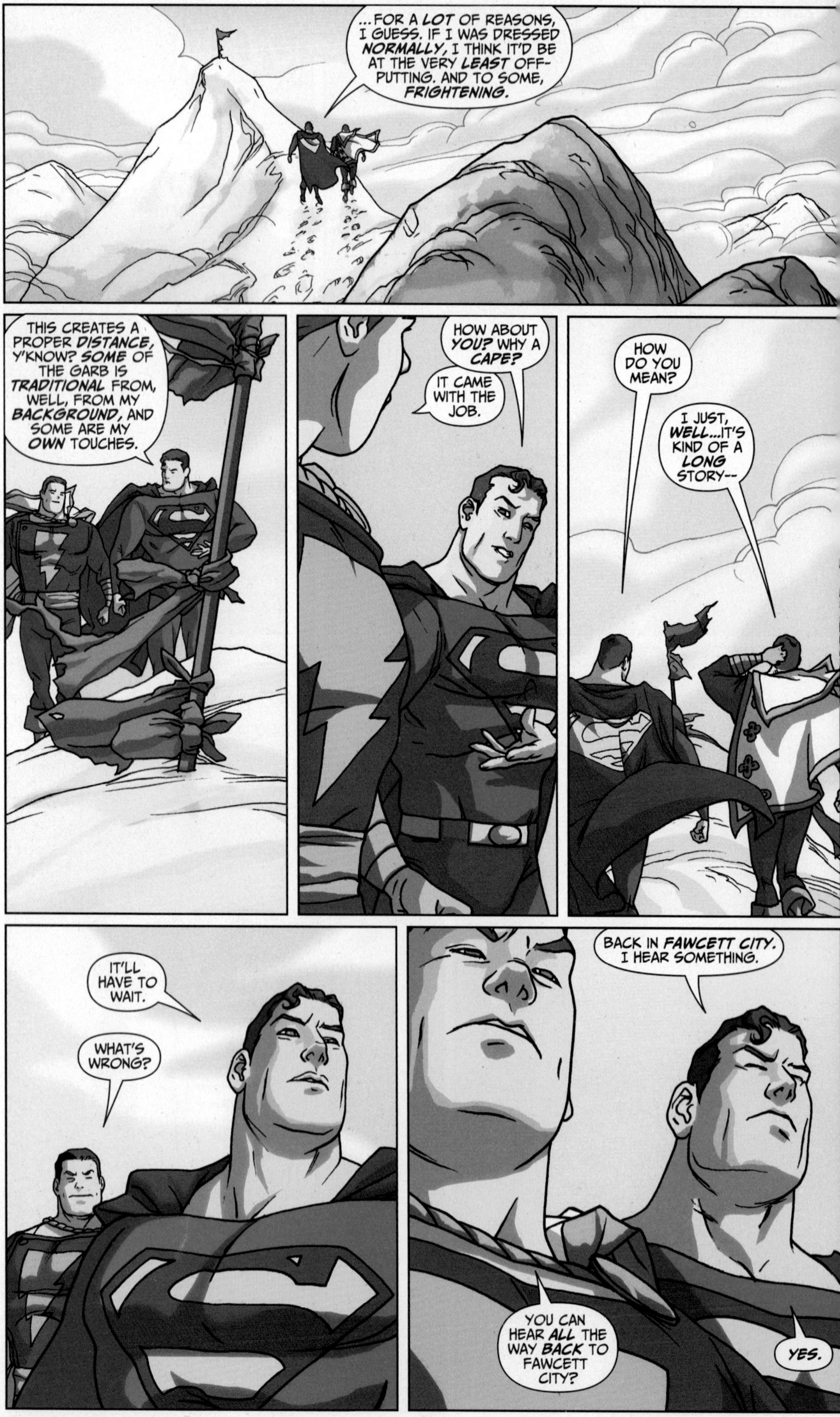
...FOR A LOT OF REASONS, I GUESS. IF I WAS DRESSED NORMALLY, I THINK IT'D BE AT THE VERY LEAST OFF-PUTTING. AND TO SOME, FRIGHTENING.
THIS CREATES A PROPER DISTANCE, Y'KNOW? SOME OF THE GARB IS TRADITIONAL FROM, WELL, FROM MY BACKGROUND, AND SOME ARE MY OWN TOUCHES.
HOW ABOUT YOU? WHY A CAPE?
IT CAME WITH THE JOB.
HOW DO YOU MEAN?
I JUST, WELL...IT'S KIND OF A LONG STORY--
IT'LL HAVE TO WAIT.
WHAT'S WRONG?
BACK IN FAWCETT CITY. I HEAR SOMETHING.
YOU CAN HEAR ALL THE WAY BACK TO FAWCETT CITY?
YES.

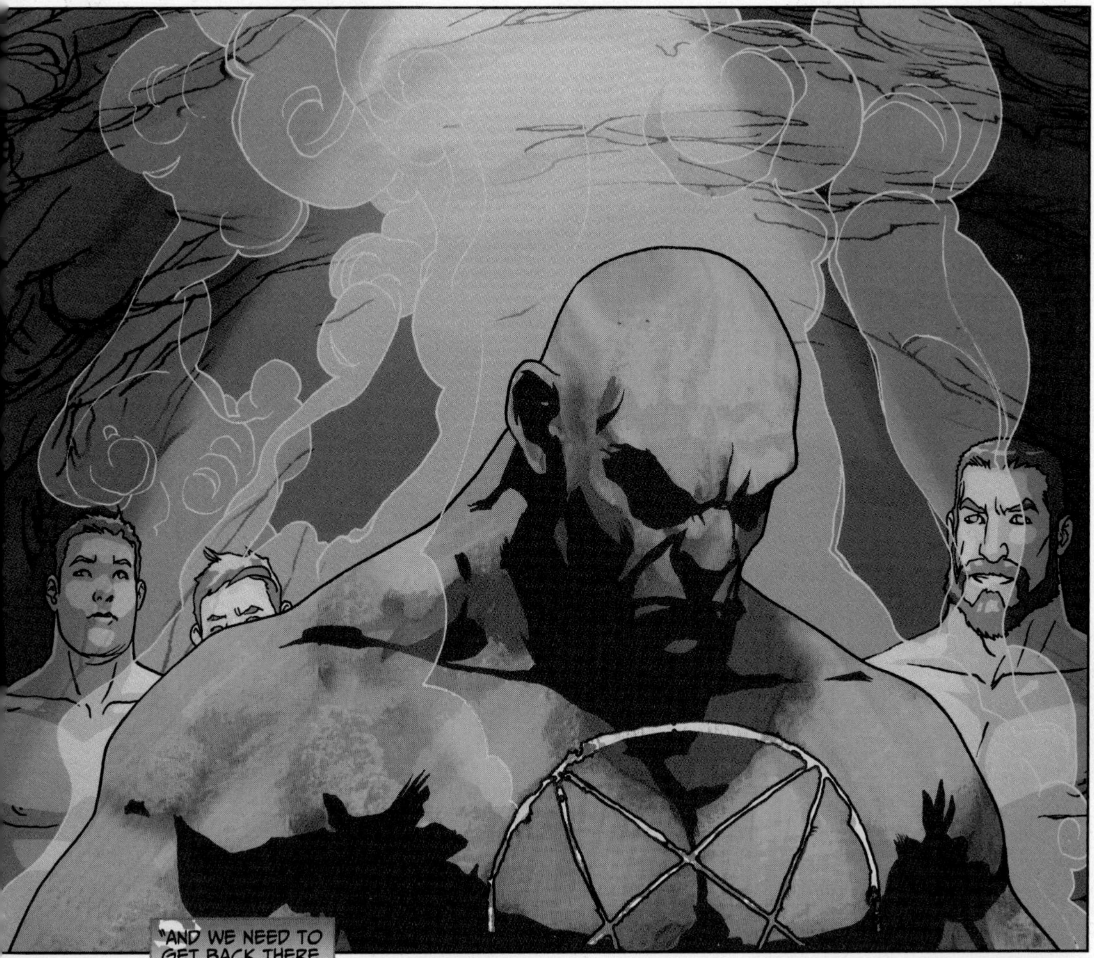
"AND WE NEED TO GET BACK THERE *RIGHT NOW*."

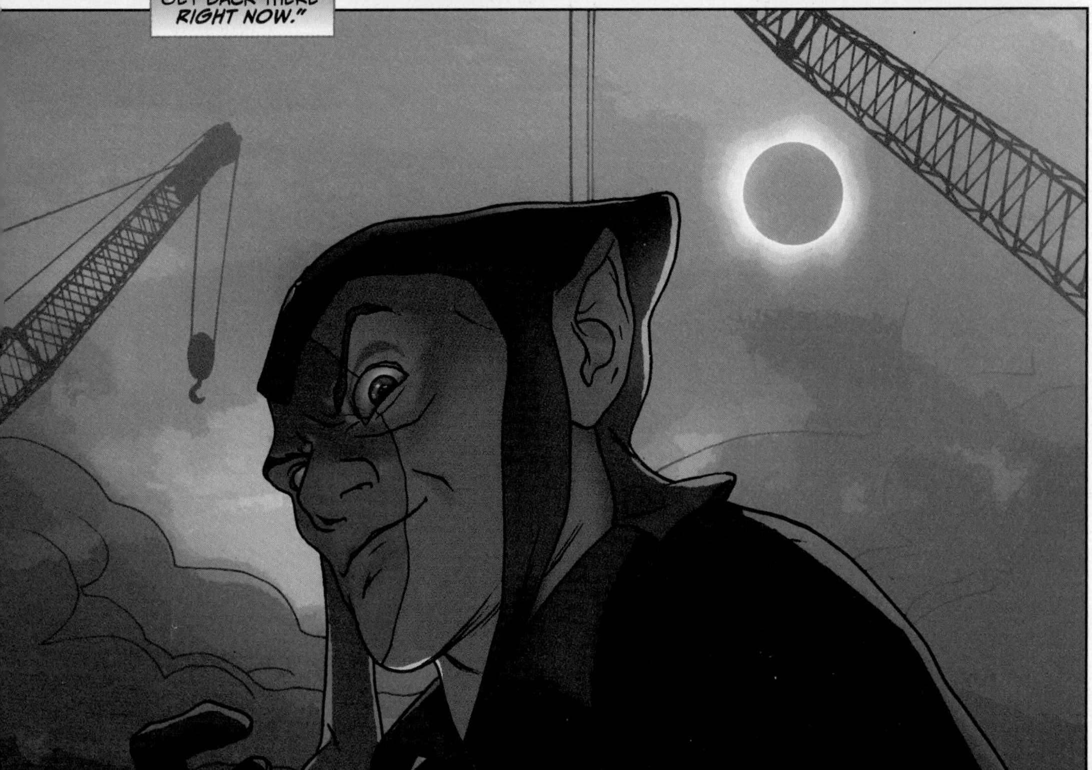

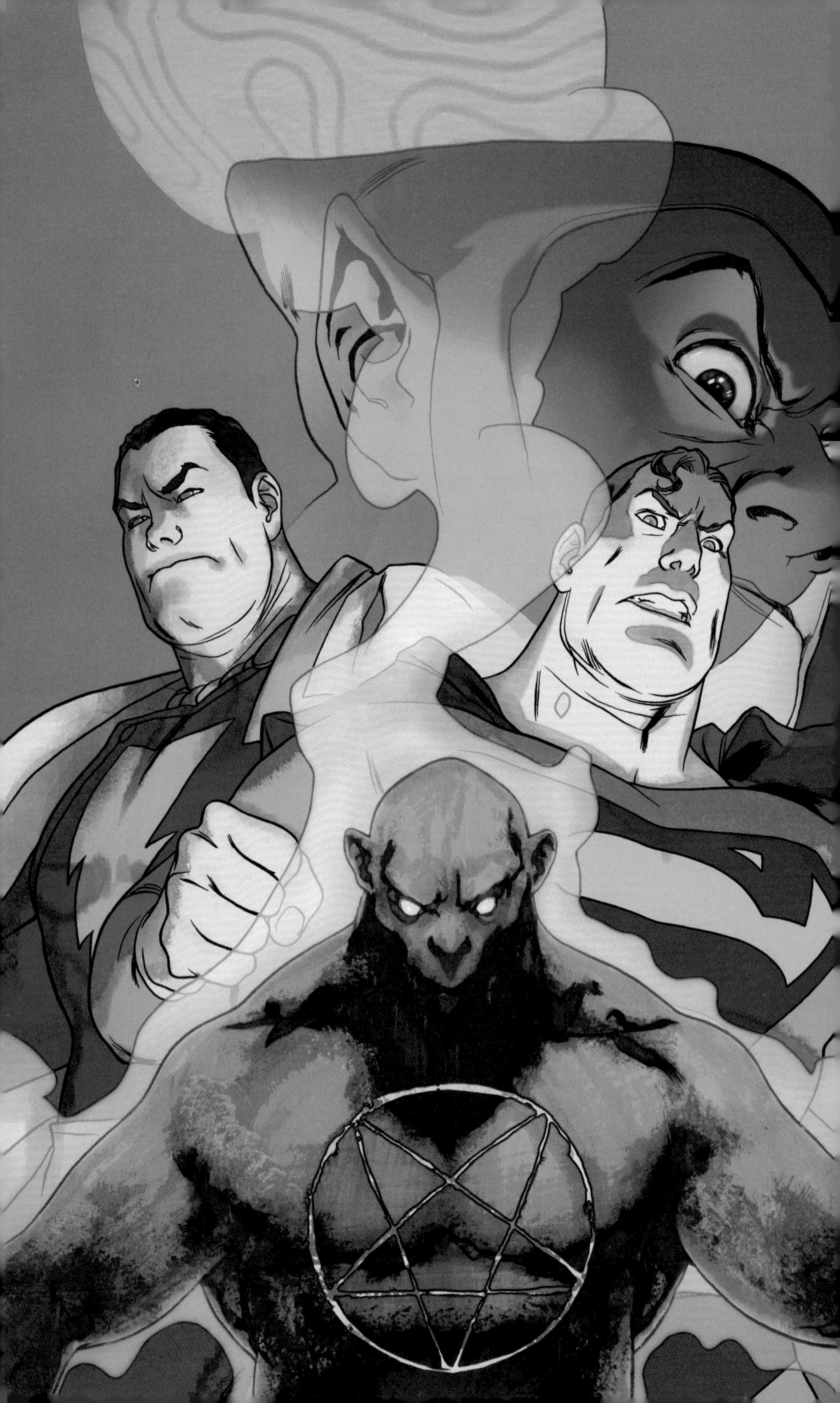

IT BEGAN, THE WAY *MOST* THINGS DO, AS A CREATION OF *NATURE.*

IT WAS THE *SPIRIT OF VENGEANCE.*

BIRTHED TO MAINTAIN *ORDER* IN THE UNIVERSE....TO ADMINISTER *RETRIBUTION...* TO PUNISH THE *WICKED.*

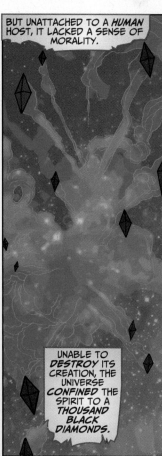

BUT UNATTACHED TO A *HUMAN* HOST, IT LACKED A SENSE OF MORALITY.

UNABLE TO *DESTROY* ITS CREATION, THE UNIVERSE *CONFINED* THE SPIRIT TO A *THOUSAND BLACK DIAMONDS.*

ONE OF WHICH MADE ITS WAY TO EARTH AND TO A REMOTE PACIFIC ISLAND OF *DIABLO.*

THERE, *BRUCE GORDON,* SCIENTIST, WAS AT ODDS WITH THE DIAMOND'S CUSTODIAN.

IN THE END, GORDON WOULD BE LEFT WITH JUST A MINOR INJURY, BUT A NEW *POSSESSION.*

HE NOW POSSESSES THE GEM STONE OF THE DARK SPIRIT *ECLIPSO...* OR RATHER...

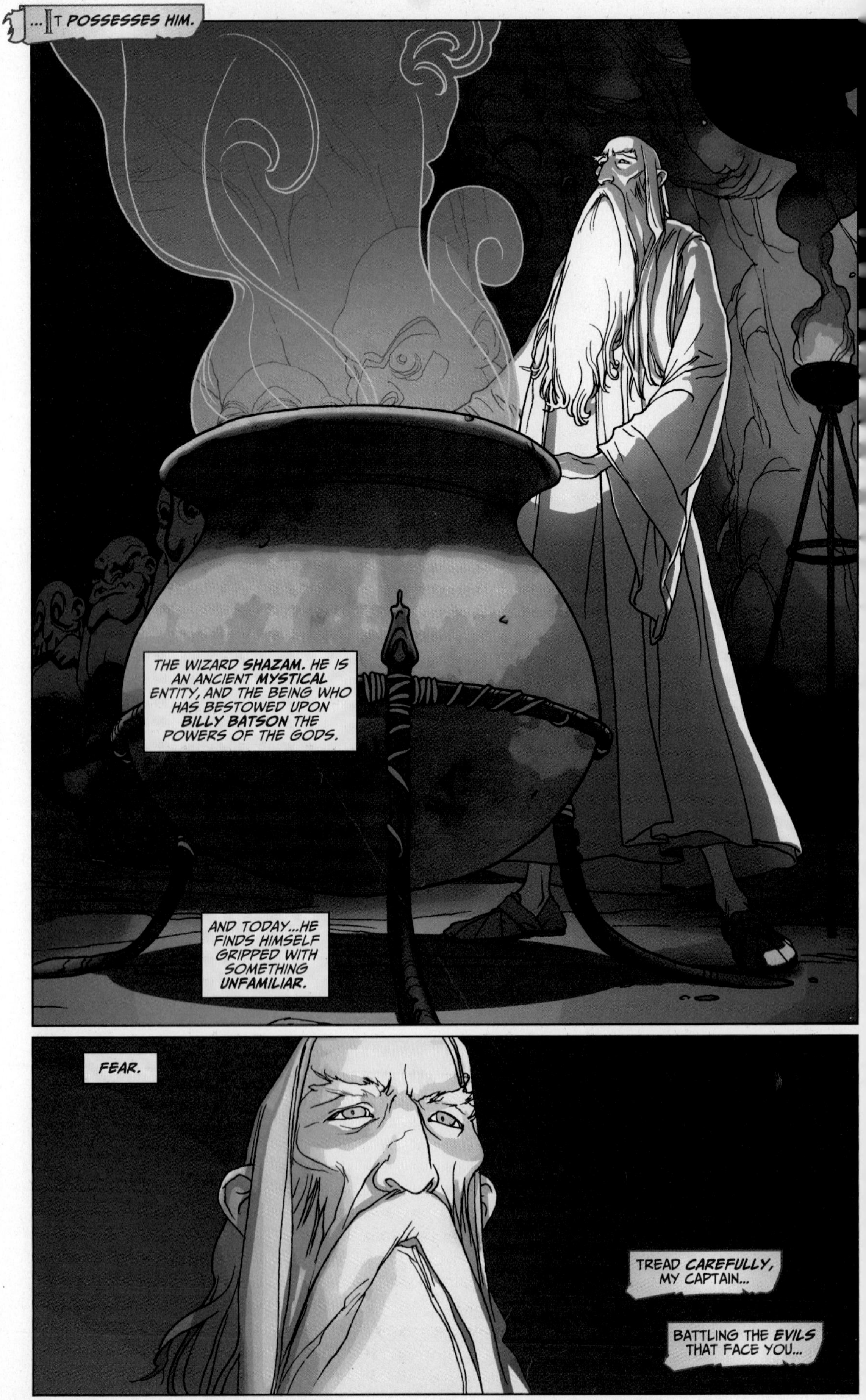
...IT POSSESSES HIM.
THE WIZARD SHAZAM. HE IS AN ANCIENT MYSTICAL ENTITY, AND THE BEING WHO HAS BESTOWED UPON BILLY BATSON THE POWERS OF THE GODS.
AND TODAY...HE FINDS HIMSELF GRIPPED WITH SOMETHING UNFAMILIAR.
FEAR.
TREAD CAREFULLY, MY CAPTAIN...
BATTLING THE EVILS THAT FACE YOU...

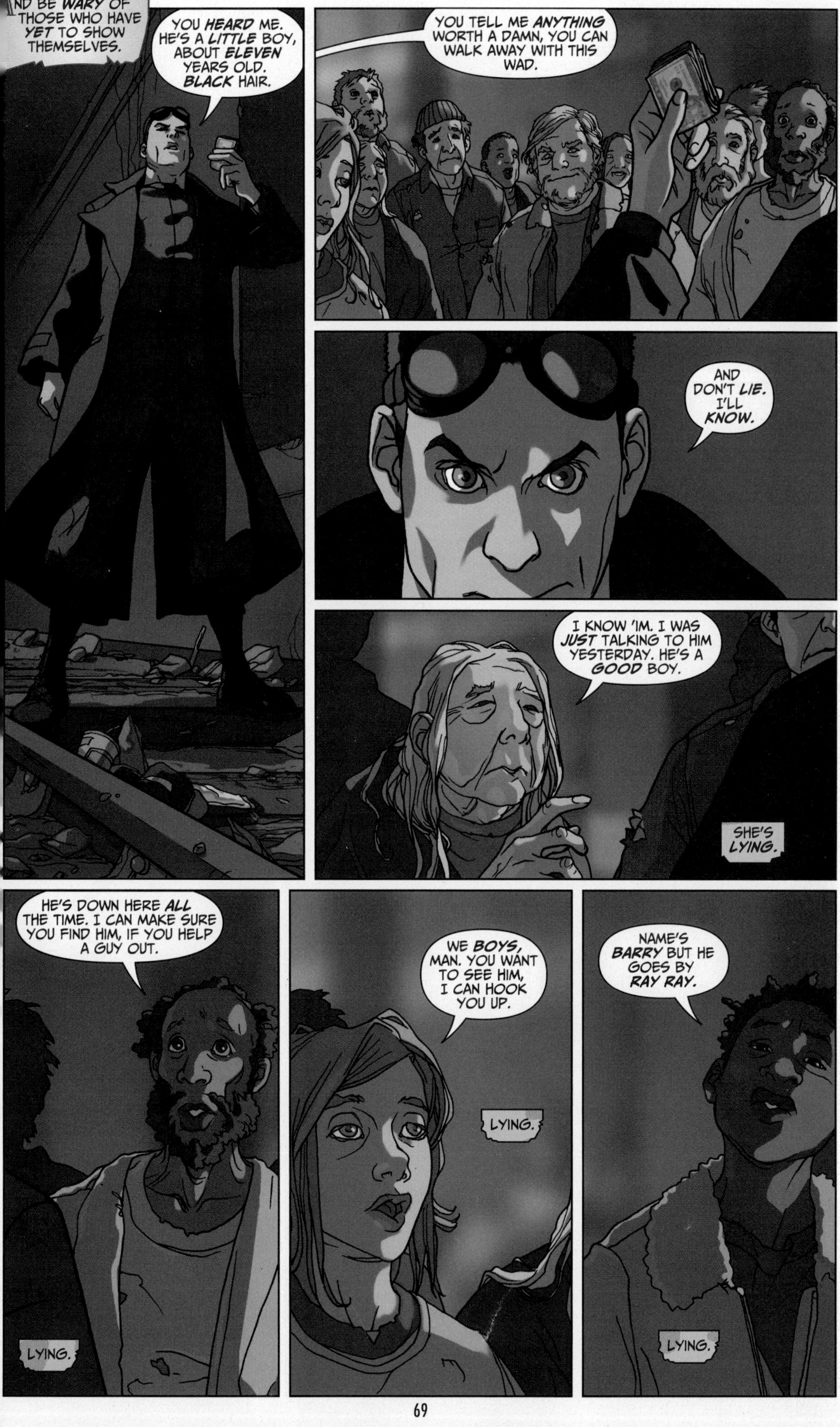
AND BE WARY OF THOSE WHO HAVE YET TO SHOW THEMSELVES.
YOU HEARD ME. HE'S A LITTLE BOY, ABOUT ELEVEN YEARS OLD. BLACK HAIR.
YOU TELL ME ANYTHING WORTH A DAMN, YOU CAN WALK AWAY WITH THIS WAD.
AND DON'T LIE. I'LL KNOW.
I KNOW 'IM. I WAS JUST TALKING TO HIM YESTERDAY. HE'S A GOOD BOY.
SHE'S LYING.
HE'S DOWN HERE ALL THE TIME. I CAN MAKE SURE YOU FIND HIM, IF YOU HELP A GUY OUT.
LYING.
WE BOYS, MAN. YOU WANT TO SEE HIM, I CAN HOOK YOU UP.
LYING.
NAME'S BARRY BUT HE GOES BY RAY RAY.
LYING.

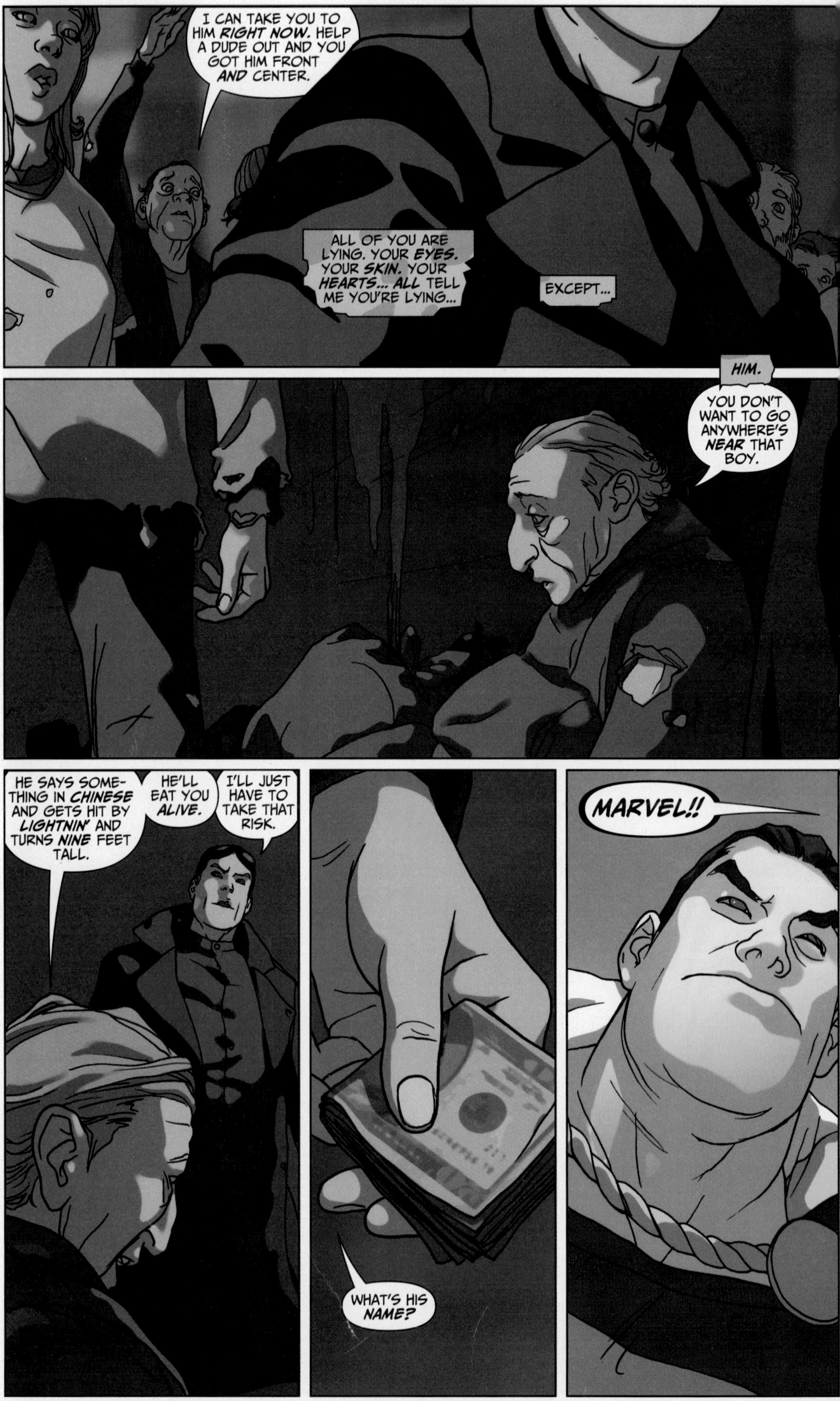
I CAN TAKE YOU TO HIM RIGHT NOW. HELP A DUDE OUT AND YOU GOT HIM FRONT AND CENTER.
ALL OF YOU ARE LYING. YOUR EYES. YOUR SKIN. YOUR HEARTS... ALL TELL ME YOU'RE LYING...
EXCEPT...
HIM.
YOU DON'T WANT TO GO ANYWHERE'S NEAR THAT BOY.
HE SAYS SOME-THING IN CHINESE AND GETS HIT BY LIGHTNIN' AND TURNS NINE FEET TALL.
HE'LL EAT YOU ALIVE.
I'LL JUST HAVE TO TAKE THAT RISK.
WHAT'S HIS NAME?
MARVEL!!

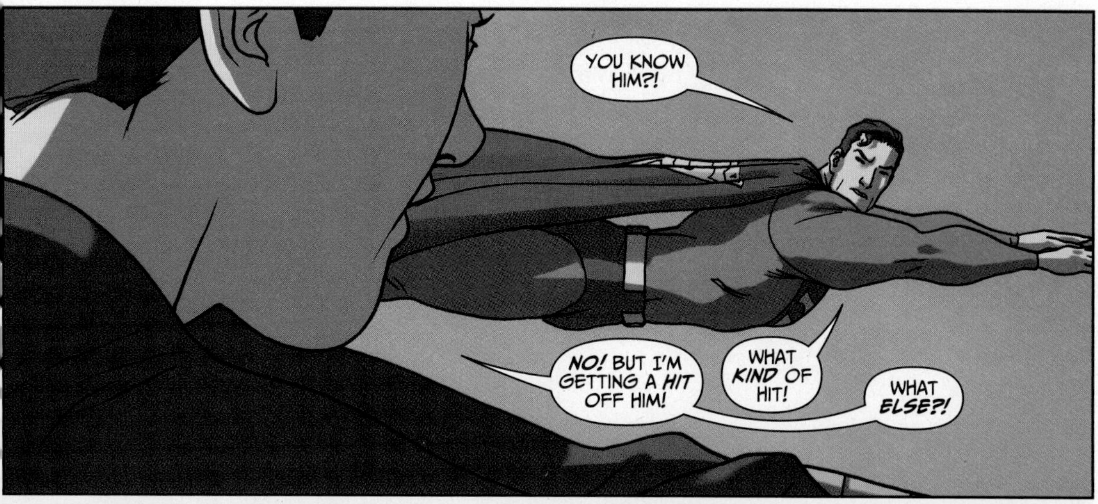
YOU KNOW HIM?!
NO! BUT I'M GETTING A HIT OFF HIM!
WHAT KIND OF HIT!
WHAT ELSE?!

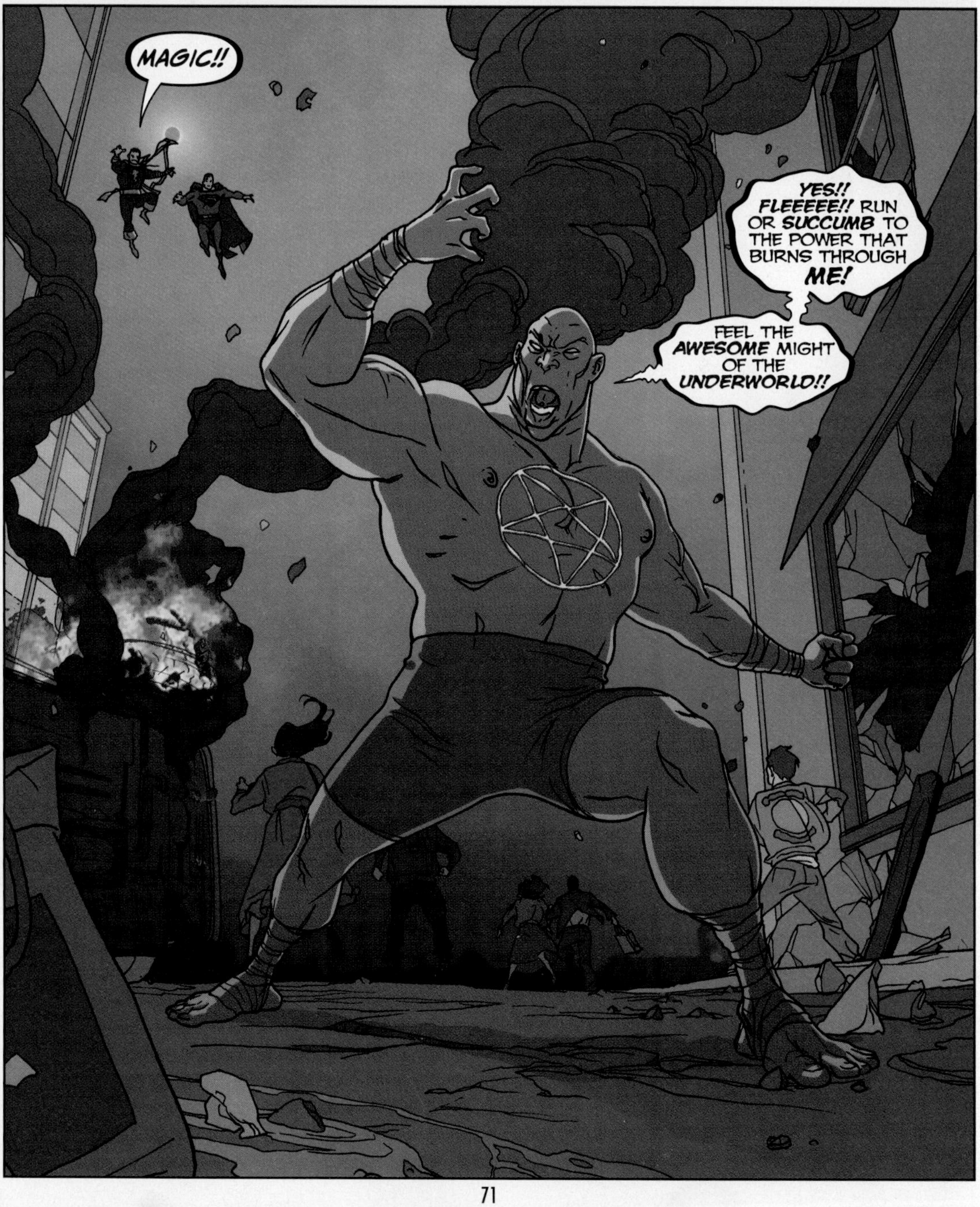
MAGIC!!
YES!! FLEEEEE!! RUN OR SUCCUMB TO THE POWER THAT BURNS THROUGH ME!
FEEL THE AWESOME MIGHT OF THE UNDERWORLD!!

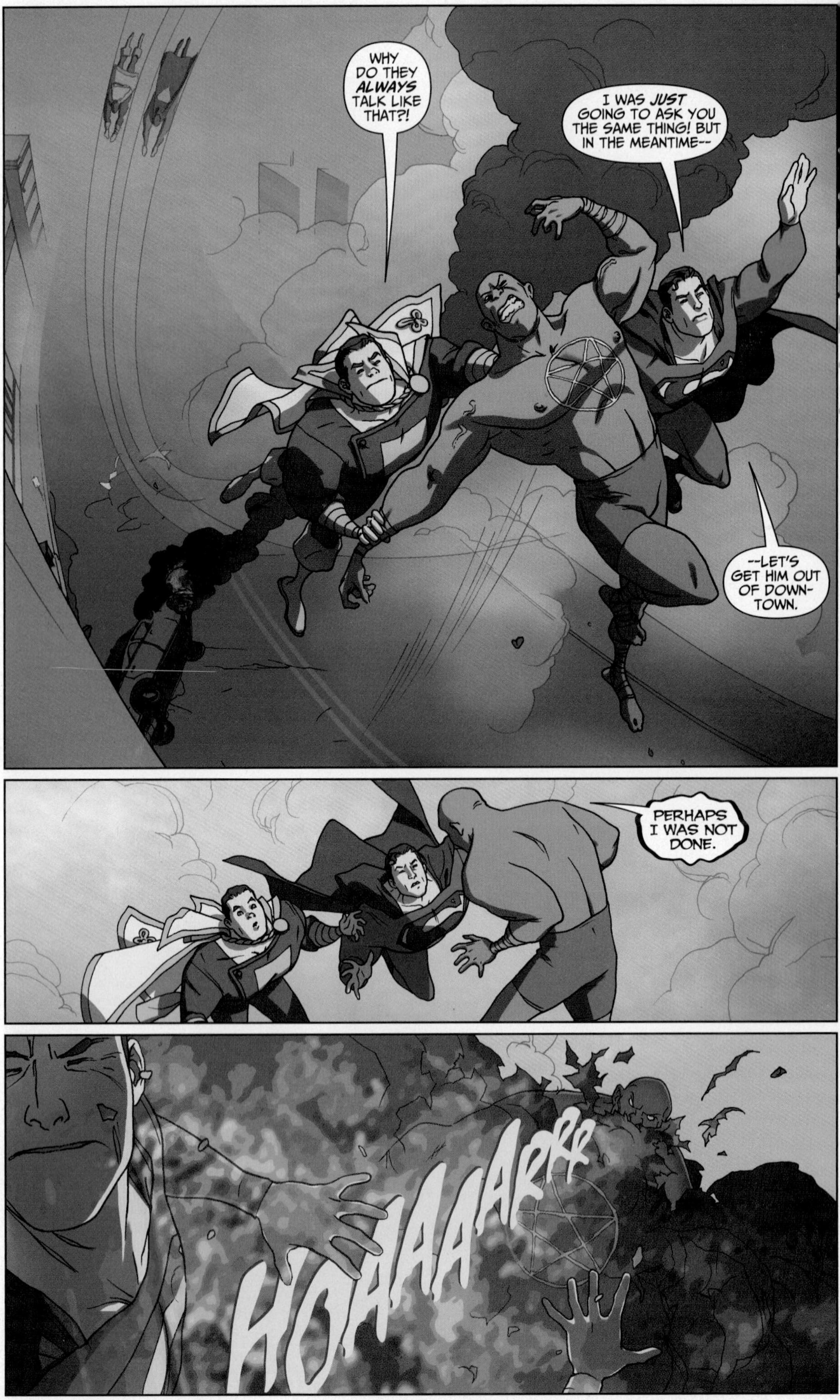

WHY DO THEY *ALWAYS* TALK LIKE THAT?!
I WAS *JUST* GOING TO ASK YOU THE SAME THING! BUT IN THE MEANTIME--
--LET'S GET HIM OUT OF DOWN-TOWN.
PERHAPS I WAS NOT DONE.
HOAAAARRR

AAAH HA HA HA **HA!!!**

HE CAN BREATHE **FIRE.**

AND **FLIES.**

GOING TO HAVE TO WATCH THAT.

I'LL SAY.

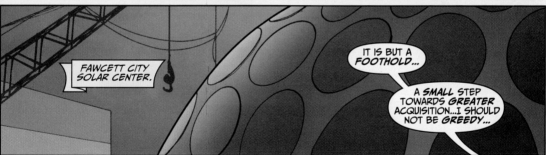

FAWCETT CITY SOLAR CENTER.

IT IS BUT A **FOOTHOLD...**

A **SMALL** STEP TOWARDS **GREATER** ACQUISITION...I SHOULD NOT BE **GREEDY...**

THIS WORLD HAS THAT **ADAGE...** "ROME WAS NOT BUILT IN A **DAY...**" AND OF **COURSE** IT WASN'T...IT TOOK **CENTURIES...**

UNTIL RECENTLY, ITS CONSTRUCTION WAS UNDER THE WATCHFUL EYE OF BRUCE GORDON.

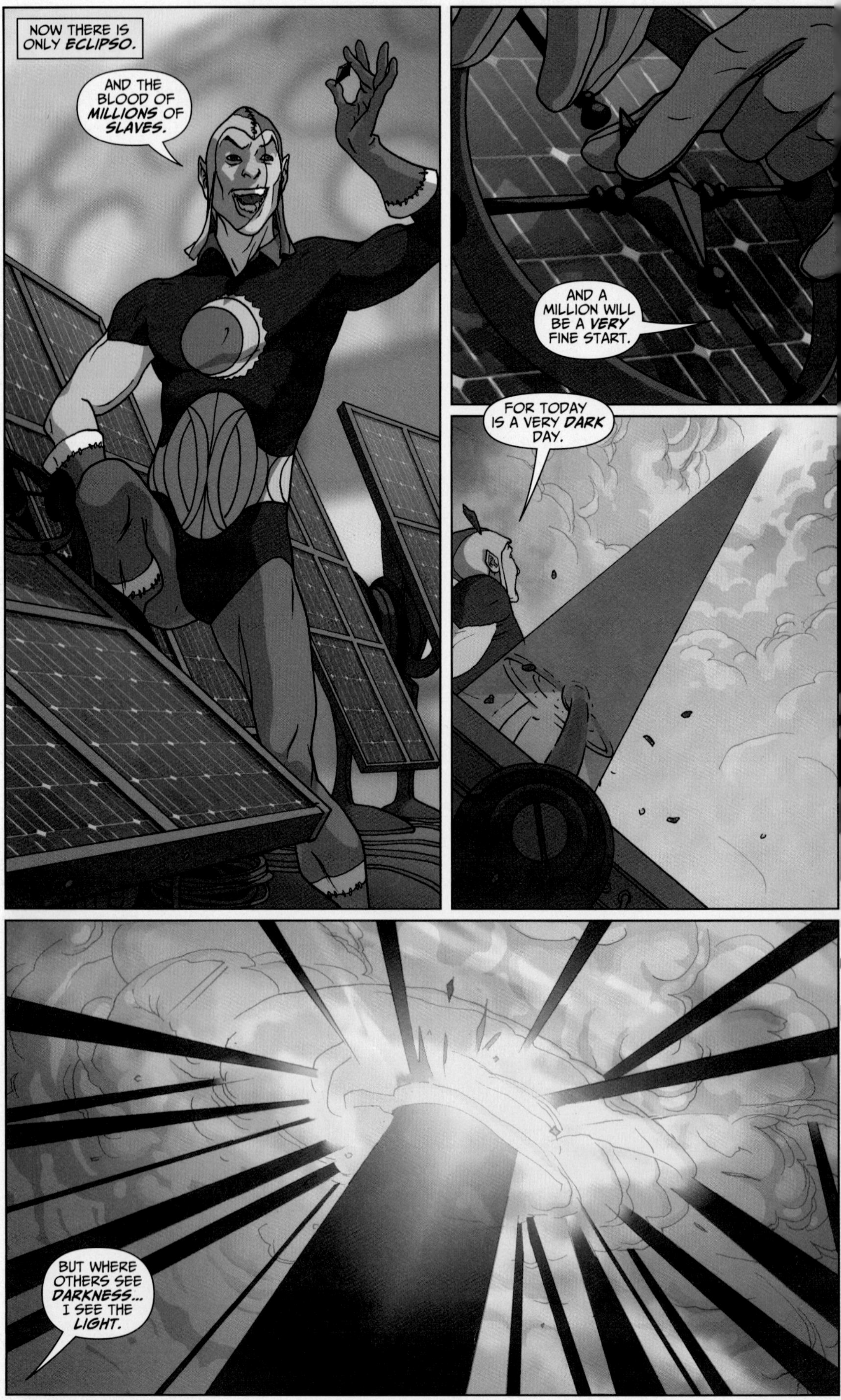
NOW THERE IS ONLY ECLIPSO.
AND THE BLOOD OF MILLIONS OF SLAVES.
AND A MILLION WILL BE A VERY FINE START.
FOR TODAY IS A VERY DARK DAY.
BUT WHERE OTHERS SEE DARKNESS... I SEE THE LIGHT.

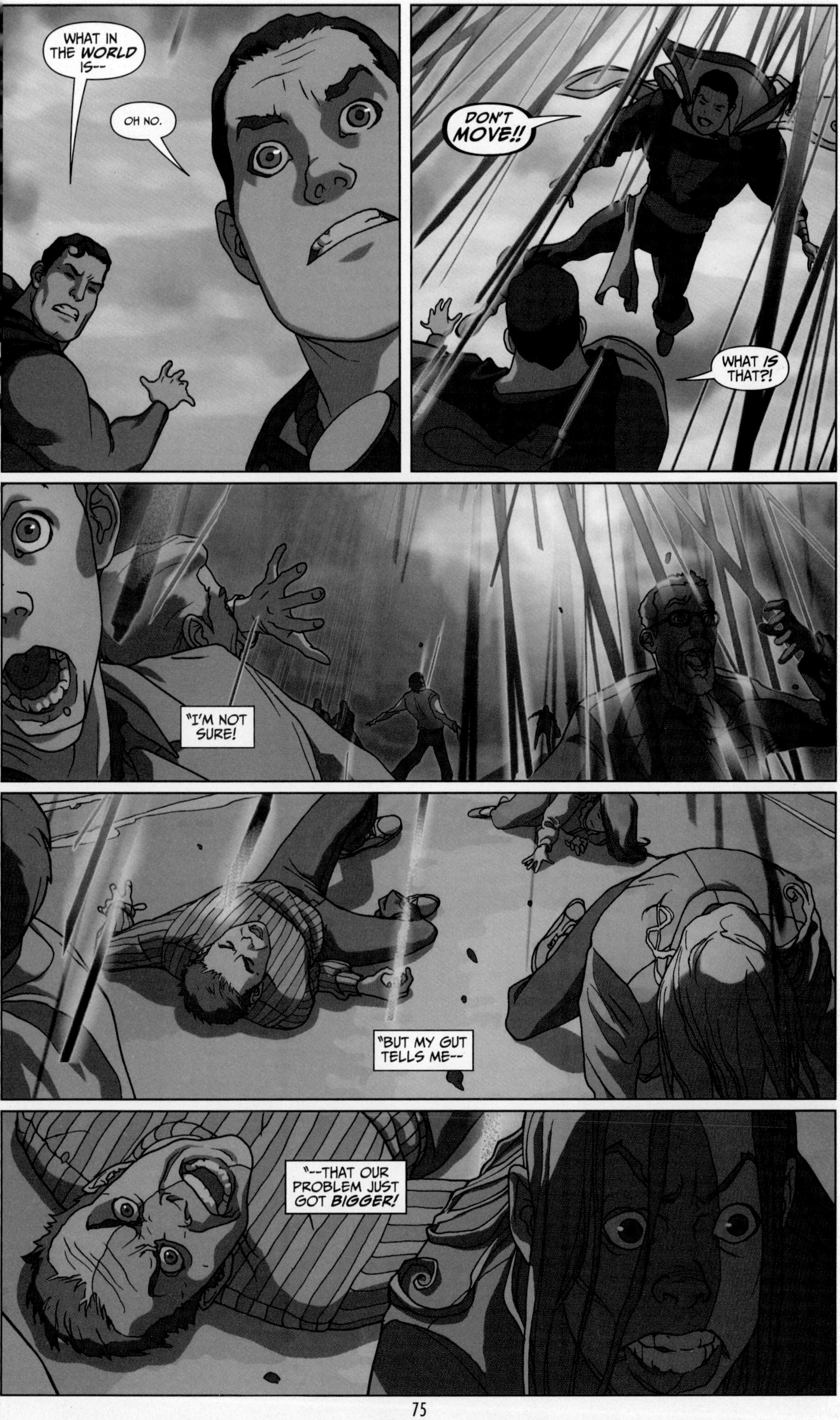
WHAT IN THE *WORLD* IS--
OH NO.
DON'T MOVE!!
WHAT *IS* THAT?!
"I'M NOT SURE!
"BUT MY GUT TELLS ME--
"--THAT OUR PROBLEM JUST GOT *BIGGER*!

"A WHOLE *LOT* BIGGER!"

DR. SIVANA?

WHAT IS IT *NOW*...

I'M *ATTEMPTING* TO ENJOY THE *APOCALYPSE.*

AND *AGAIN,* I QUESTION THE *WISDOM* IN THIS *TRANSACTION.* THERE'RE "DEALS WITH THE *DEVIL*" BUT THIS--

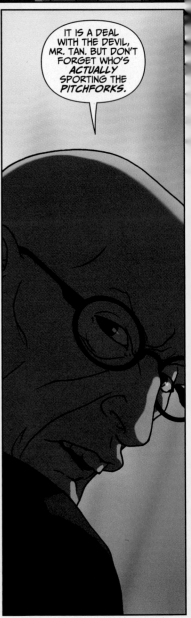

IT IS A DEAL WITH THE DEVIL, MR. TAN. BUT DON'T FORGET WHO'S *ACTUALLY* SPORTING THE *PITCHFORKS.*

MR. SPEC IS HERE.

MY, THAT'S IMPRESSIVE.

HOW DID YOU MANAGE TO DODGE THE FIRE AND BRIMSTONE FALLING FROM THE SKIES.

I'VE ALWAYS BEEN GOOD AT WALKING IN BETWEEN THE RAINDROPS, DOCTOR.

I HAVE THE INFORMATION YOU WANTED.

EXCUSE ME?

YES. WOULD YOU LIKE TO KNOW WHERE CAPTAIN MARVEL LIVES?

AND HOW ABOUT WHEN HE'S AT HIS MOST VULNERABLE?

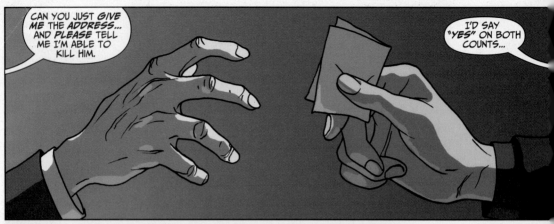

CAN YOU JUST *GIVE* ME THE *ADDRESS*... AND *PLEASE* TELL ME I'M ABLE TO KILL HIM.

I'D SAY *"YES"* ON BOTH COUNTS...

THAT WAS *MUCH* EASIER THAN I THOUGHT...SO MANY CONFUSED, *FRIGHTENED* HEARTS TURNED TO *RAGE*...

NOW, THE *REAL* WORK CAN BEGIN.

EH?

WHAT IS *THIS?* INANE *TRICKERY?!*

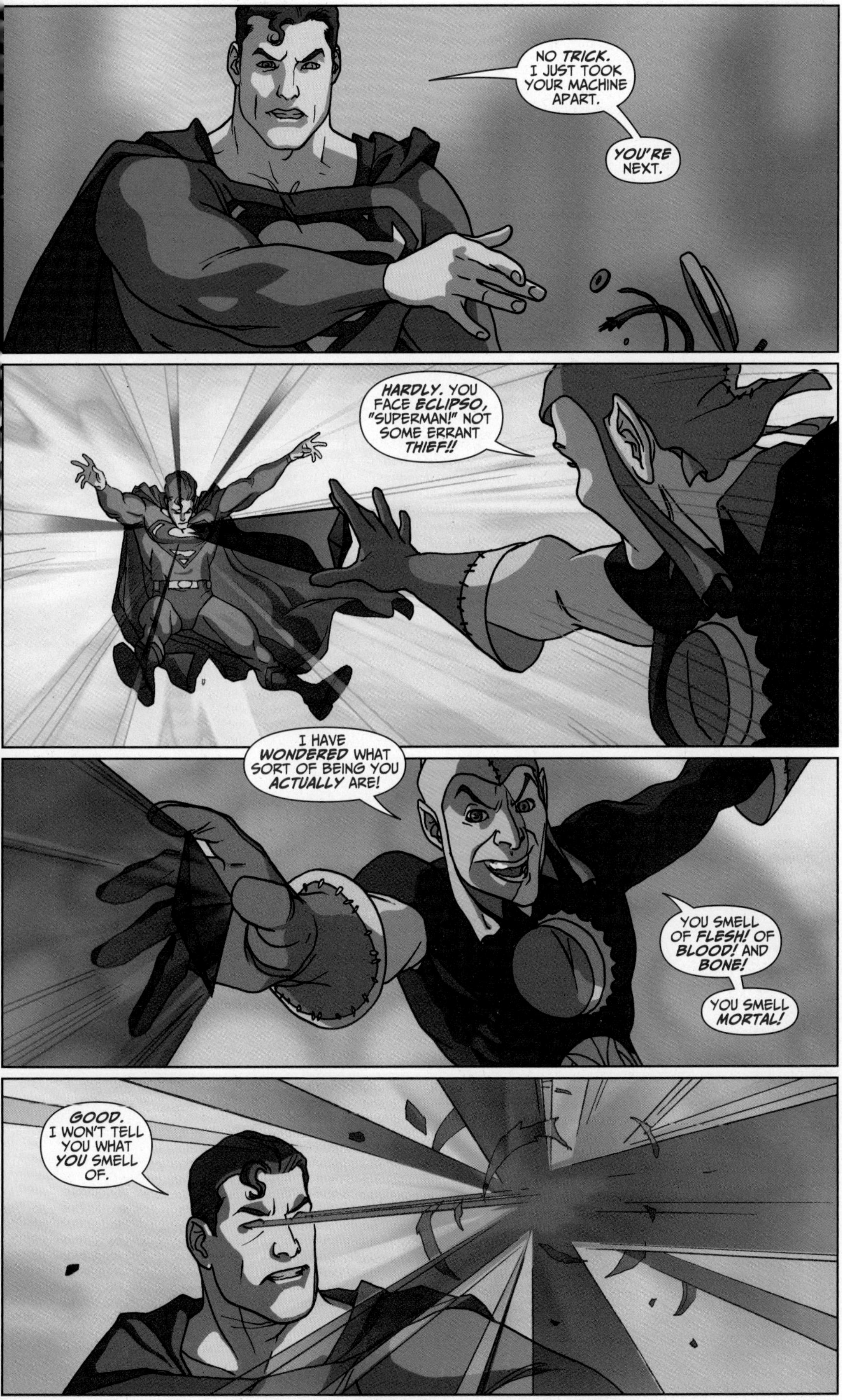

NO TRICK. I JUST TOOK YOUR MACHINE APART.
YOU'RE NEXT.
HARDLY. YOU FACE ECLIPSO, "SUPERMAN!" NOT SOME ERRANT THIEF!!
I HAVE WONDERED WHAT SORT OF BEING YOU ACTUALLY ARE!
YOU SMELL OF FLESH! OF BLOOD! AND BONE!
YOU SMELL MORTAL!
GOOD. I WON'T TELL YOU WHAT YOU SMELL OF.

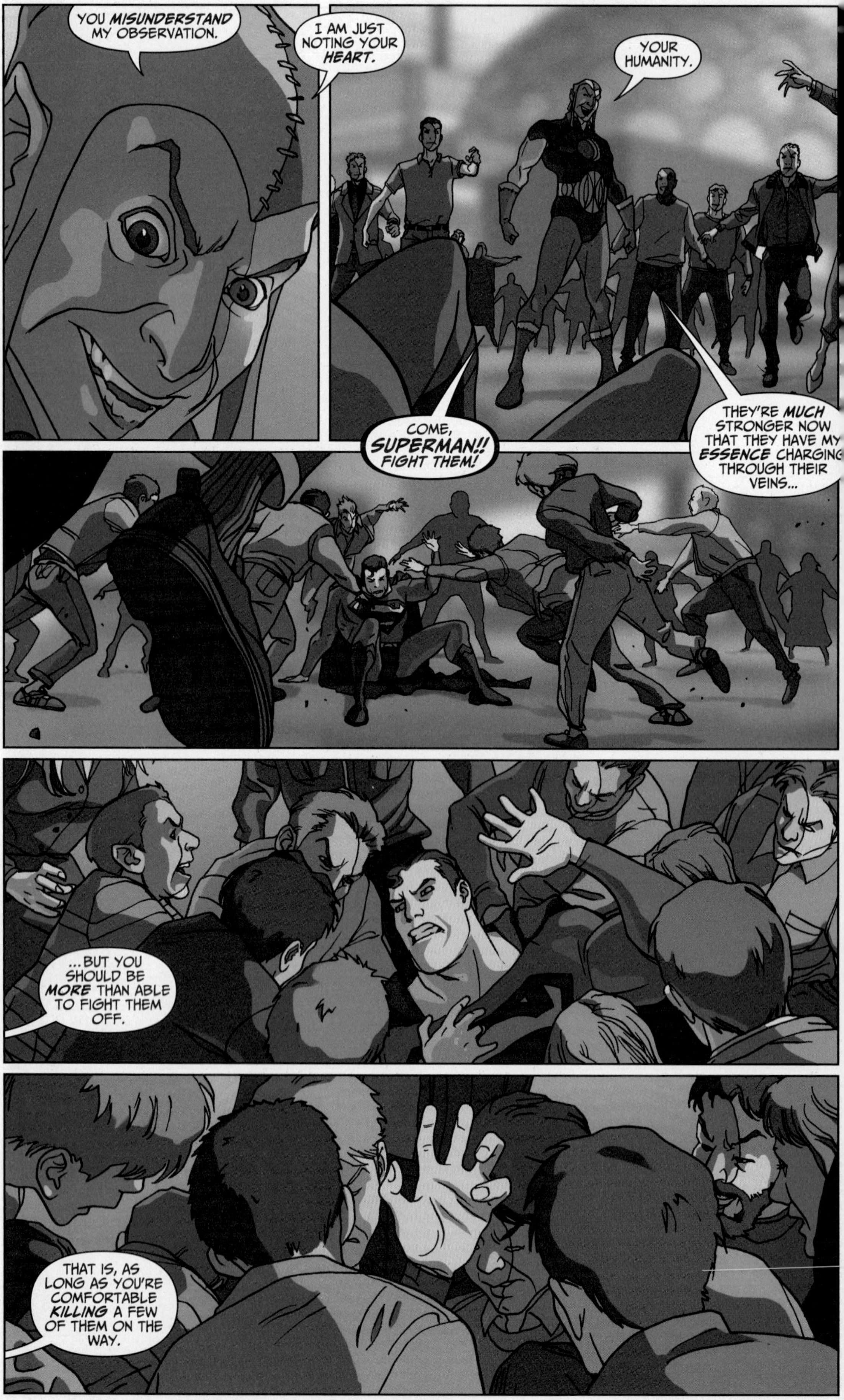
YOU MISUNDERSTAND MY OBSERVATION.
I AM JUST NOTING YOUR HEART.
YOUR HUMANITY.
COME, SUPERMAN!! FIGHT THEM!
THEY'RE MUCH STRONGER NOW THAT THEY HAVE MY ESSENCE CHARGING THROUGH THEIR VEINS...
...BUT YOU SHOULD BE MORE THAN ABLE TO FIGHT THEM OFF.
THAT IS, AS LONG AS YOU'RE COMFORTABLE KILLING A FEW OF THEM ON THE WAY.

IS THAT ALL YOU'VE GOT?!!

NO! I HAVE SO MUCH *MORE*!! I'M SORRY TO SEE THAT *SUPERMAN* IS TOO *COWARDLY* TO FACE ME!!

MORE LIKE HE'S GOT *BIGGER* FISH TO FRY THAN A LOW-RENT, DEMONIC, FORCE-WIELDING *BUTT TROLL!*

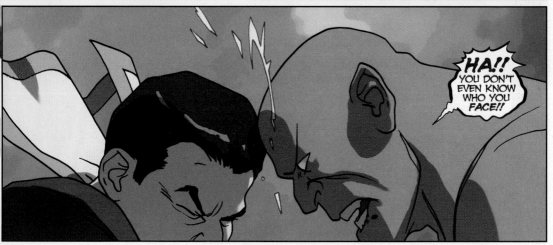

HA!! YOU DON'T EVEN KNOW WHO YOU *FACE!!*

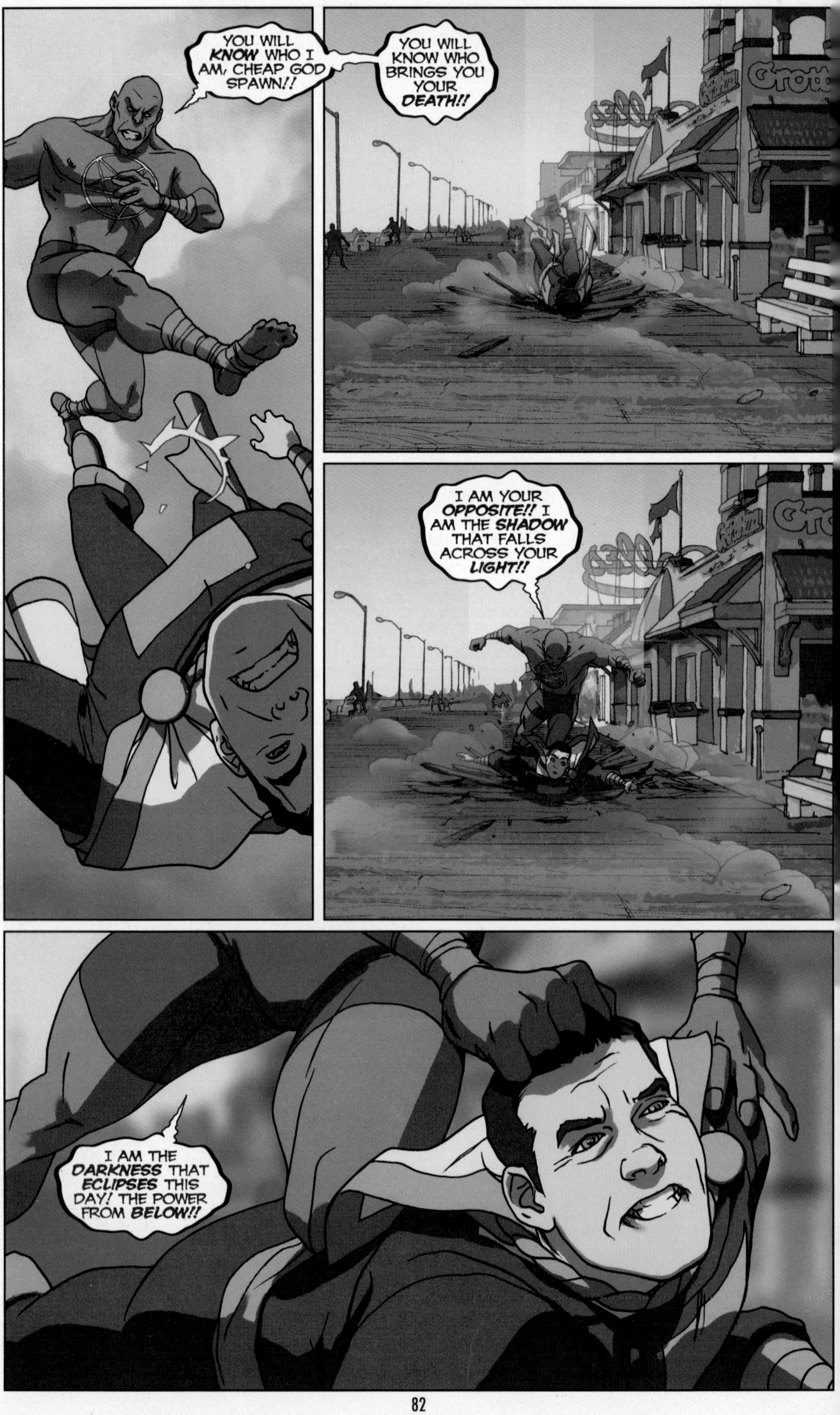
YOU WILL KNOW WHO I AM, CHEAP GOD SPAWN!!
YOU WILL KNOW WHO BRINGS YOU YOUR DEATH!!
I AM YOUR OPPOSITE!! I AM THE SHADOW THAT FALLS ACROSS YOUR LIGHT!!
I AM THE DARKNESS THAT ECLIPSES THIS DAY! THE POWER FROM BELOW!!

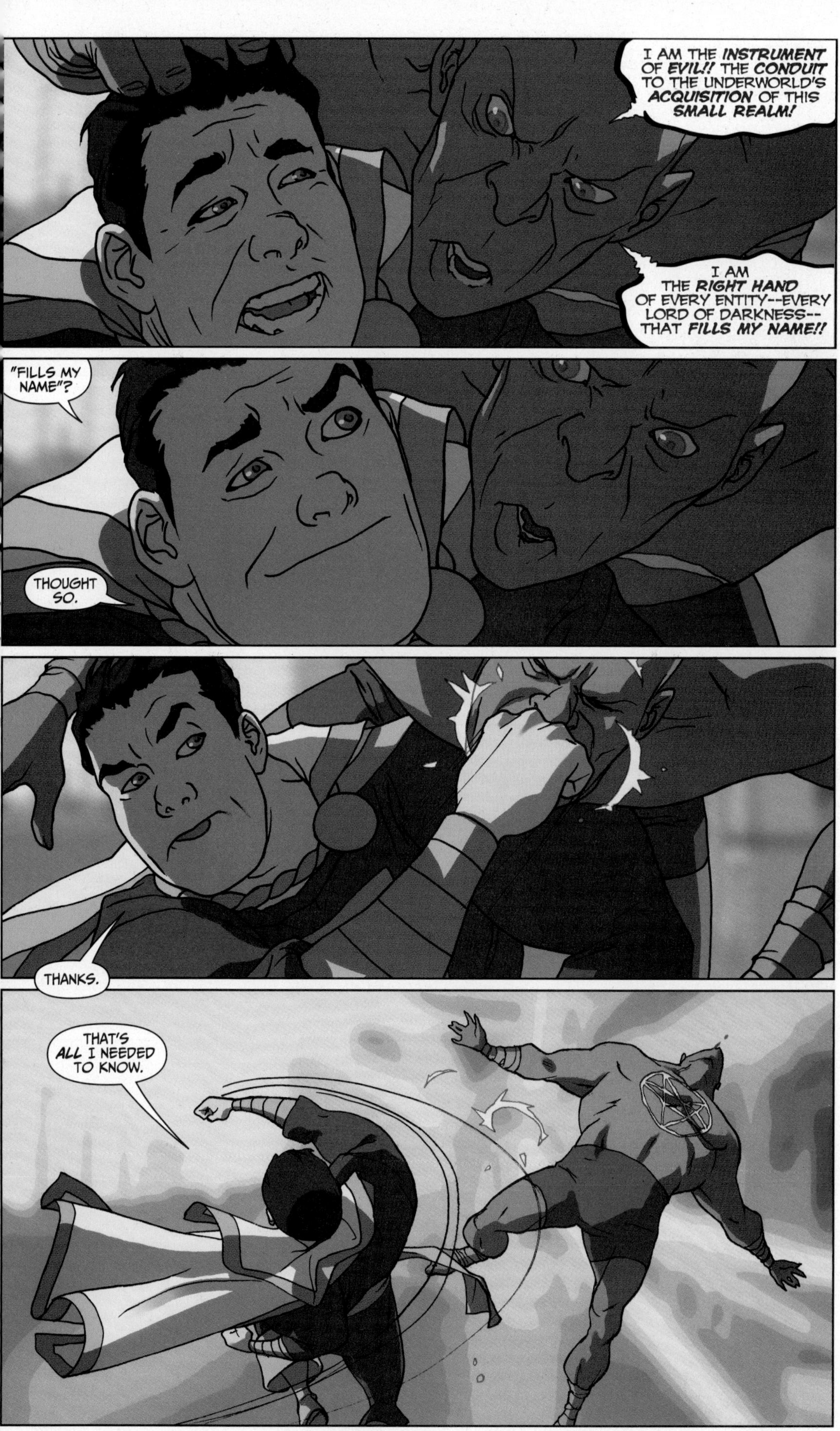
I AM THE INSTRUMENT OF EVIL!! THE CONDUIT TO THE UNDERWORLD'S ACQUISITION OF THIS SMALL REALM!
I AM THE RIGHT HAND OF EVERY ENTITY--EVERY LORD OF DARKNESS--THAT FILLS MY NAME!!
"FILLS MY NAME"?
THOUGHT SO.
THANKS.
THAT'S ALL I NEEDED TO KNOW.

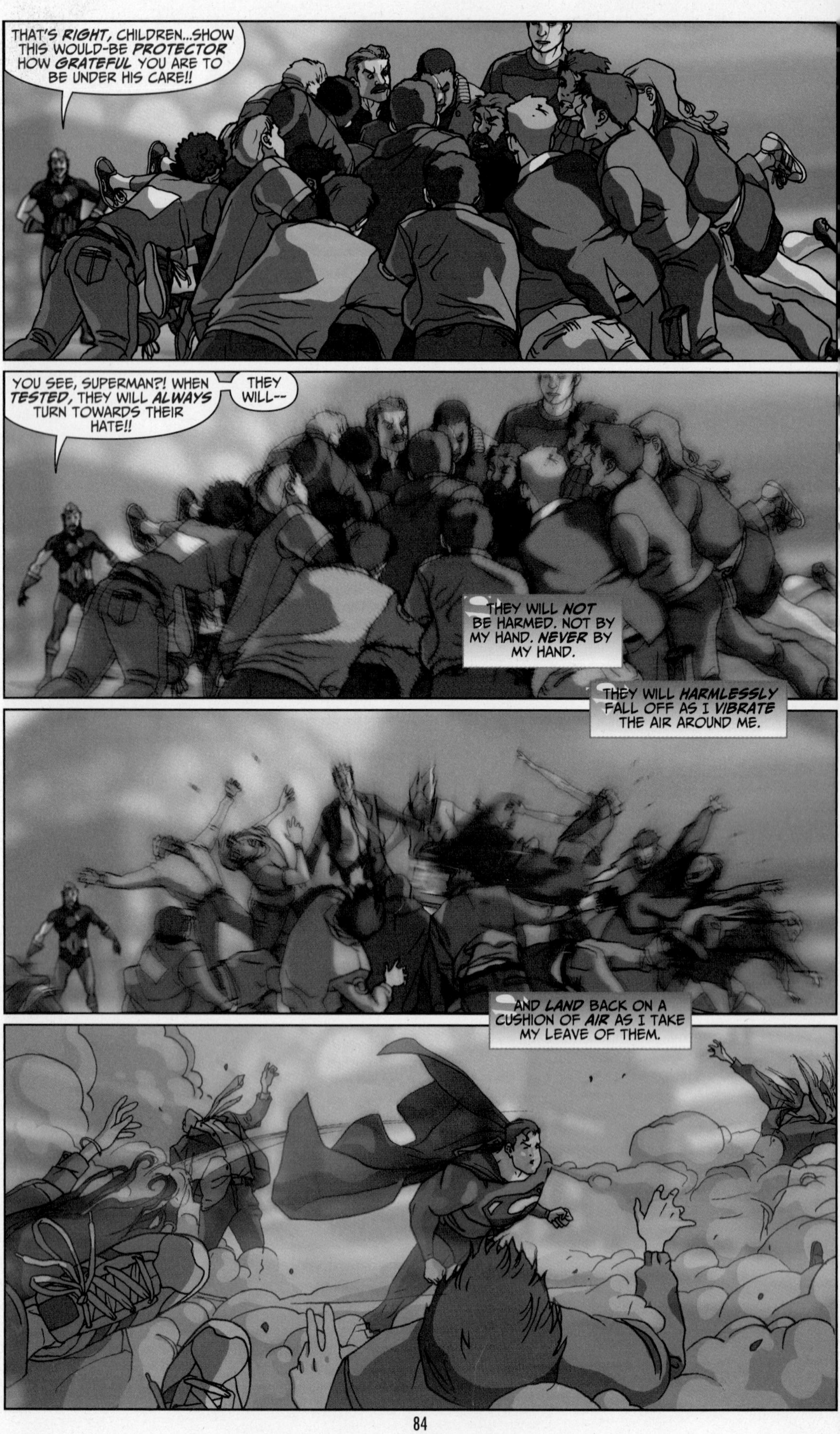
THAT'S RIGHT, CHILDREN...SHOW THIS WOULD-BE PROTECTOR HOW GRATEFUL YOU ARE TO BE UNDER HIS CARE!!
YOU SEE, SUPERMAN?! WHEN TESTED, THEY WILL ALWAYS TURN TOWARDS THEIR HATE!!
THEY WILL--
THEY WILL NOT BE HARMED. NOT BY MY HAND. NEVER BY MY HAND.
THEY WILL HARMLESSLY FALL OFF AS I VIBRATE THE AIR AROUND ME.
AND LAND BACK ON A CUSHION OF AIR AS I TAKE MY LEAVE OF THEM.

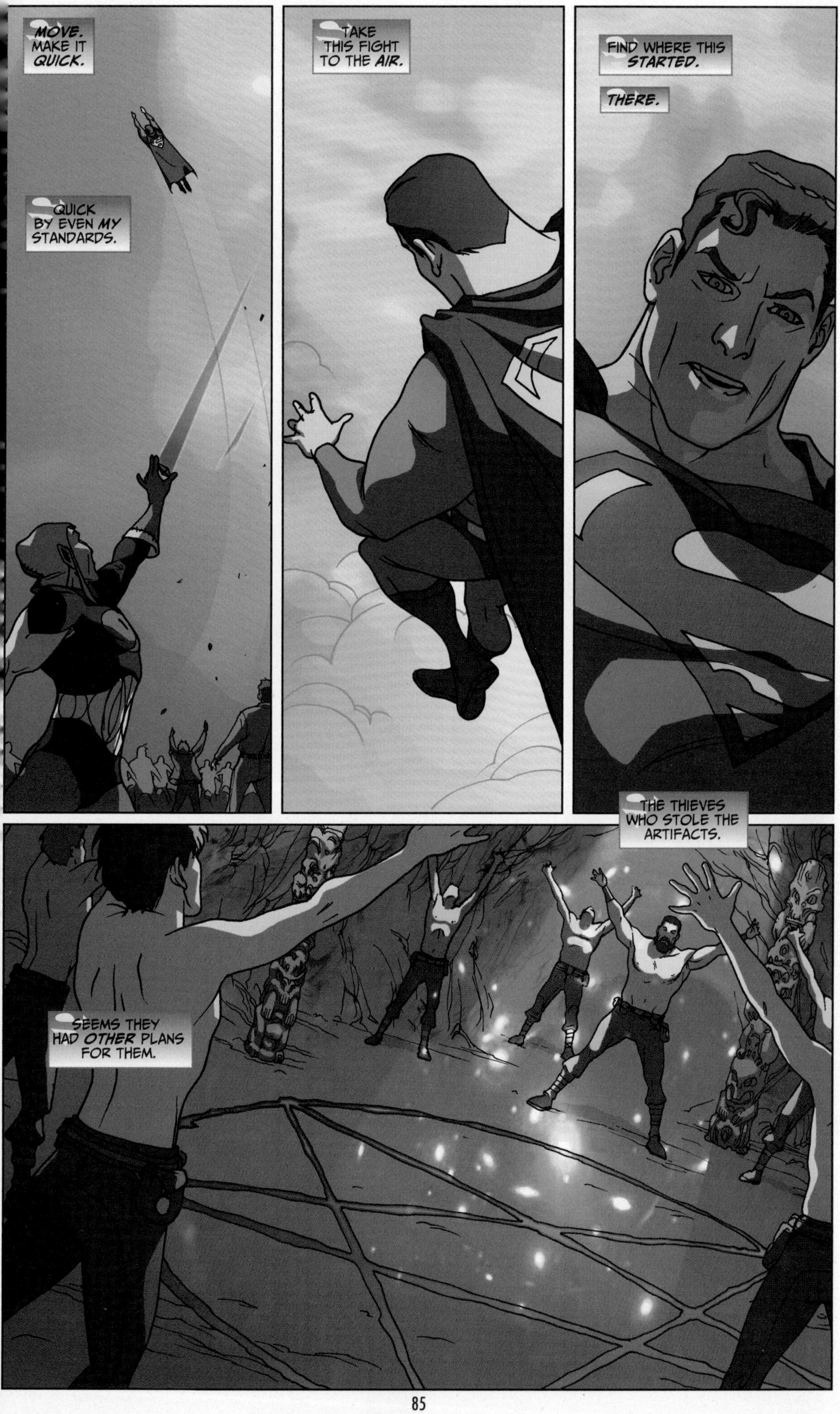
MOVE. MAKE IT QUICK.
QUICK BY EVEN MY STANDARDS.
TAKE THIS FIGHT TO THE AIR.
FIND WHERE THIS STARTED.
THERE.
THE THIEVES WHO STOLE THE ARTIFACTS.
SEEMS THEY HAD OTHER PLANS FOR THEM.

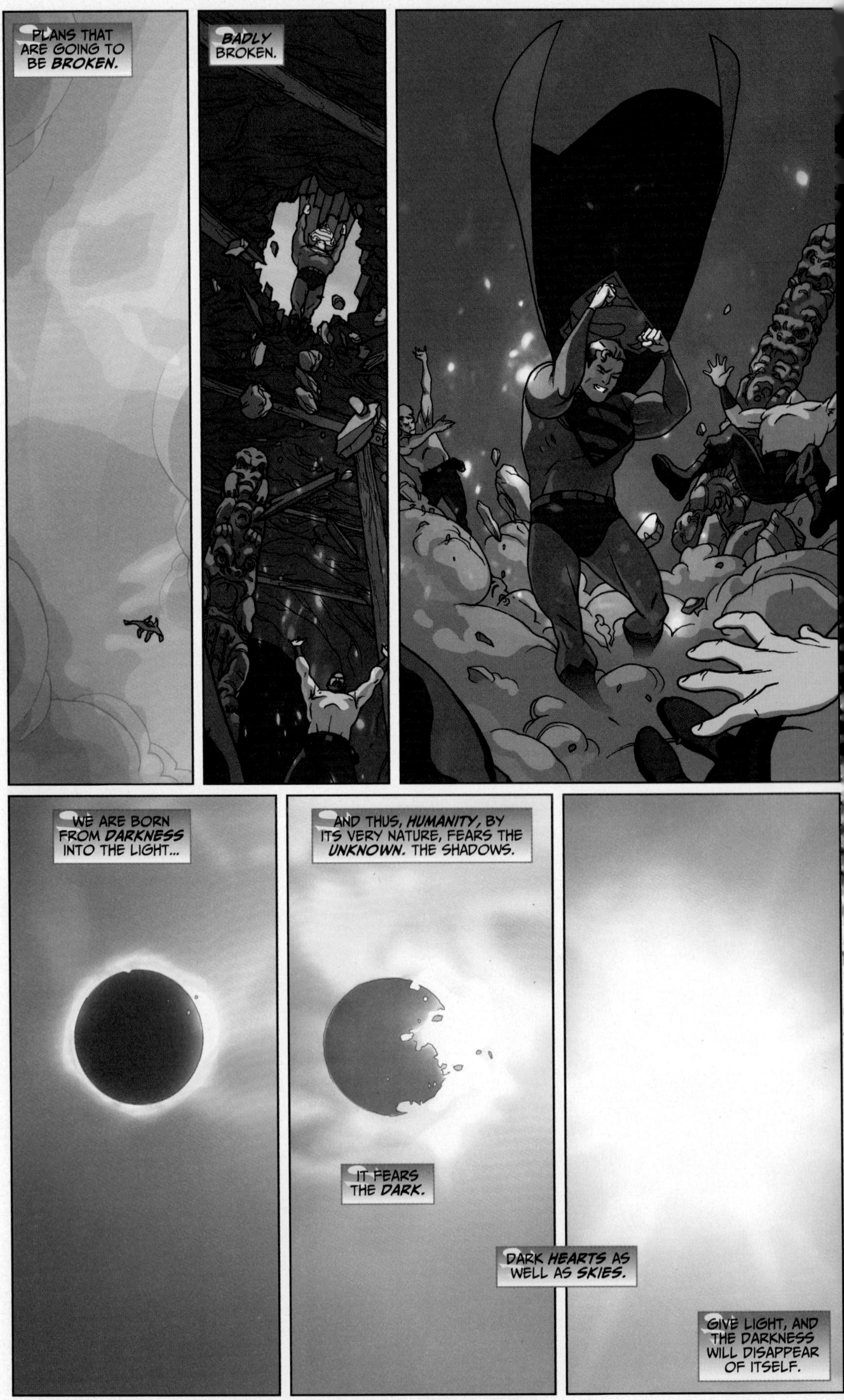
PLANS THAT ARE GOING TO BE *BROKEN.*
BADLY BROKEN.
WE ARE BORN FROM *DARKNESS* INTO THE LIGHT...
AND THUS, *HUMANITY*, BY ITS VERY NATURE, FEARS THE *UNKNOWN.* THE SHADOWS.
IT FEARS THE *DARK.*
DARK *HEARTS* AS WELL AS *SKIES.*
GIVE LIGHT, AND THE DARKNESS WILL DISAPPEAR OF ITSELF.

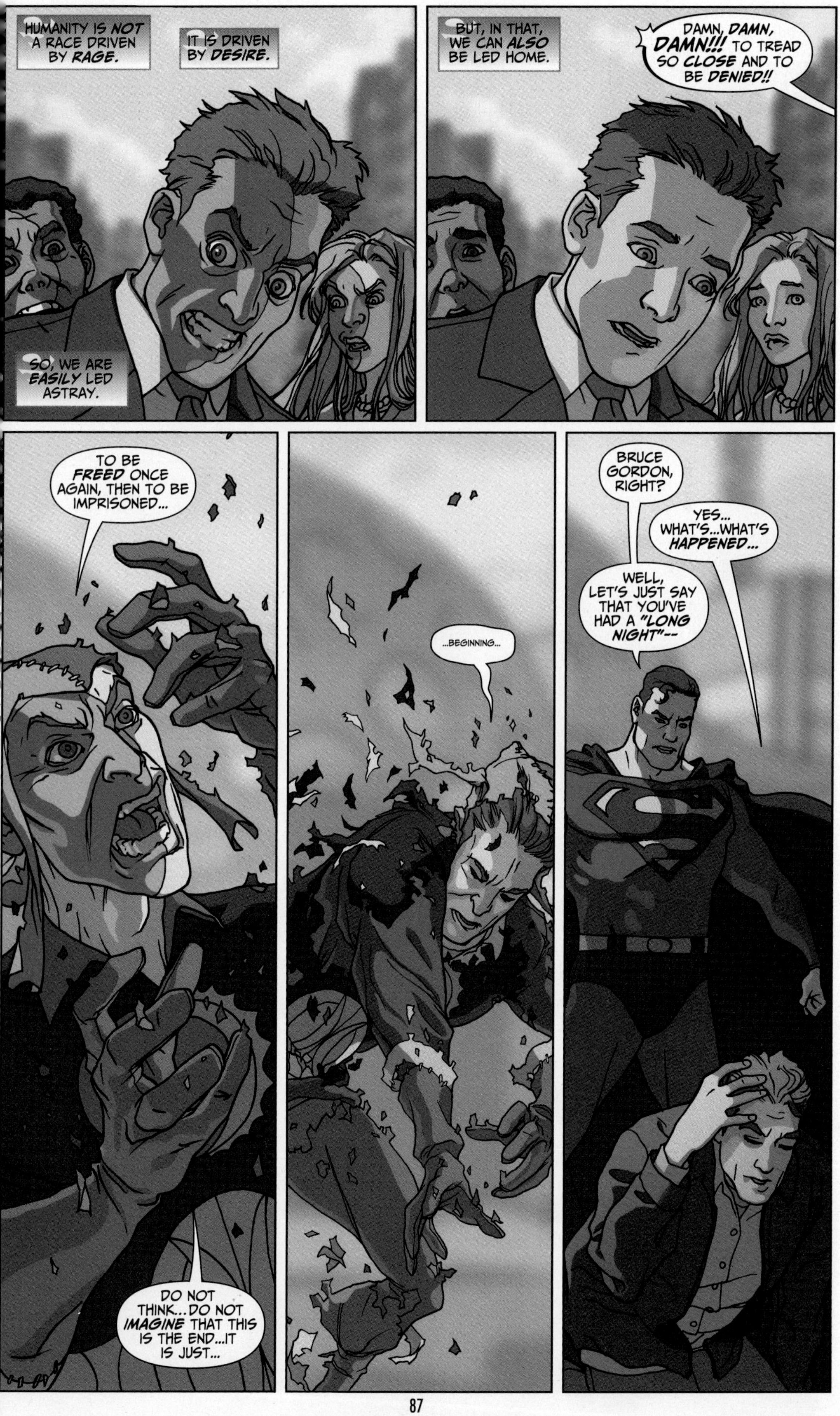
HUMANITY IS NOT A RACE DRIVEN BY RAGE.
IT IS DRIVEN BY DESIRE.
SO, WE ARE EASILY LED ASTRAY.
BUT, IN THAT, WE CAN ALSO BE LED HOME.
DAMN, DAMN, DAMN!!! TO TREAD SO CLOSE AND TO BE DENIED!!
TO BE FREED ONCE AGAIN, THEN TO BE IMPRISONED...
DO NOT THINK...DO NOT IMAGINE THAT THIS IS THE END...IT IS JUST...
...BEGINNING...
BRUCE GORDON, RIGHT?
YES... WHAT'S...WHAT'S HAPPENED...
WELL, LET'S JUST SAY THAT YOU'VE HAD A "LONG NIGHT"--

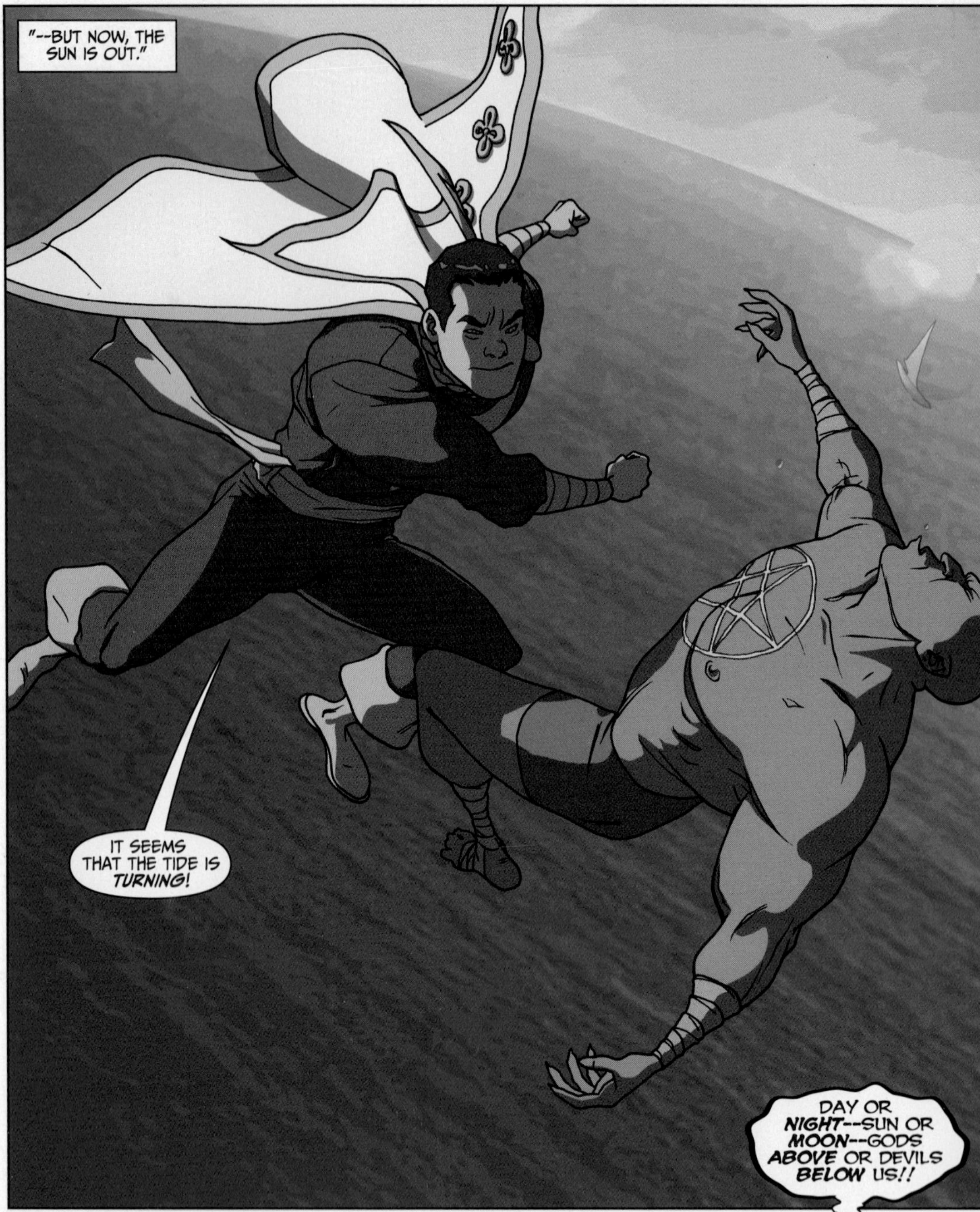
"--BUT NOW, THE SUN IS OUT."
IT SEEMS THAT THE TIDE IS TURNING!
DAY OR NIGHT--SUN OR MOON--GODS ABOVE OR DEVILS BELOW US!!

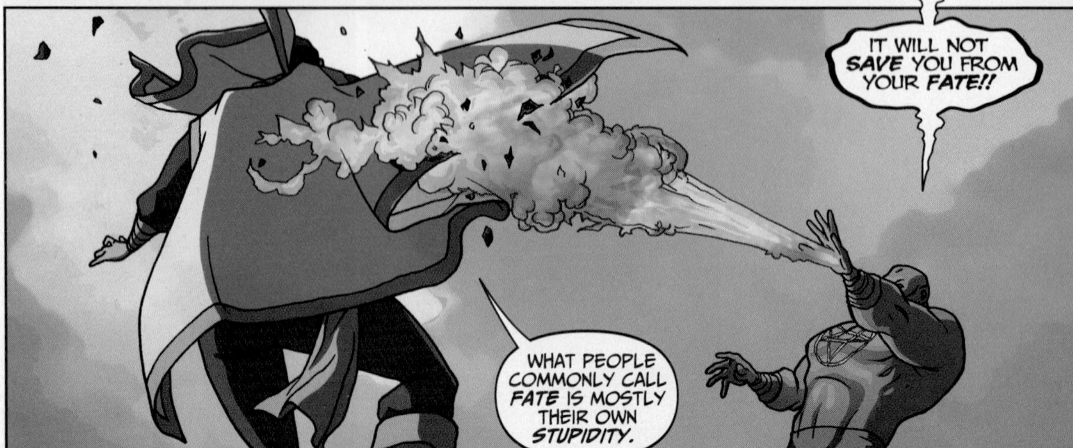
IT WILL NOT SAVE YOU FROM YOUR FATE!!
WHAT PEOPLE COMMONLY CALL FATE IS MOSTLY THEIR OWN STUPIDITY.

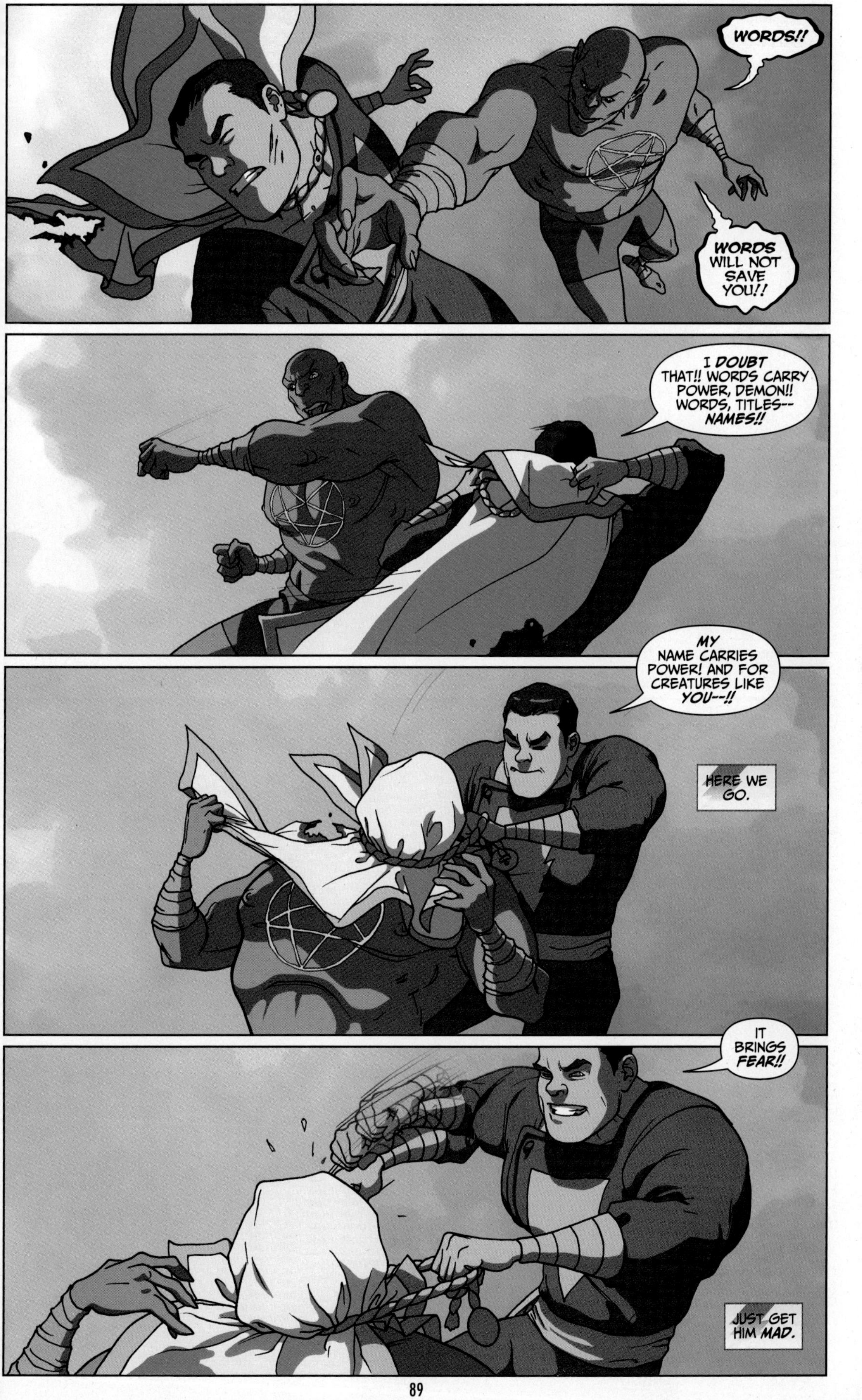
WORDS!!
WORDS WILL NOT SAVE YOU!!
I DOUBT THAT!! WORDS CARRY POWER, DEMON!! WORDS, TITLES-- NAMES!!
MY NAME CARRIES POWER! AND FOR CREATURES LIKE YOU--!!
HERE WE GO.
IT BRINGS FEAR!!
JUST GET HIM MAD.

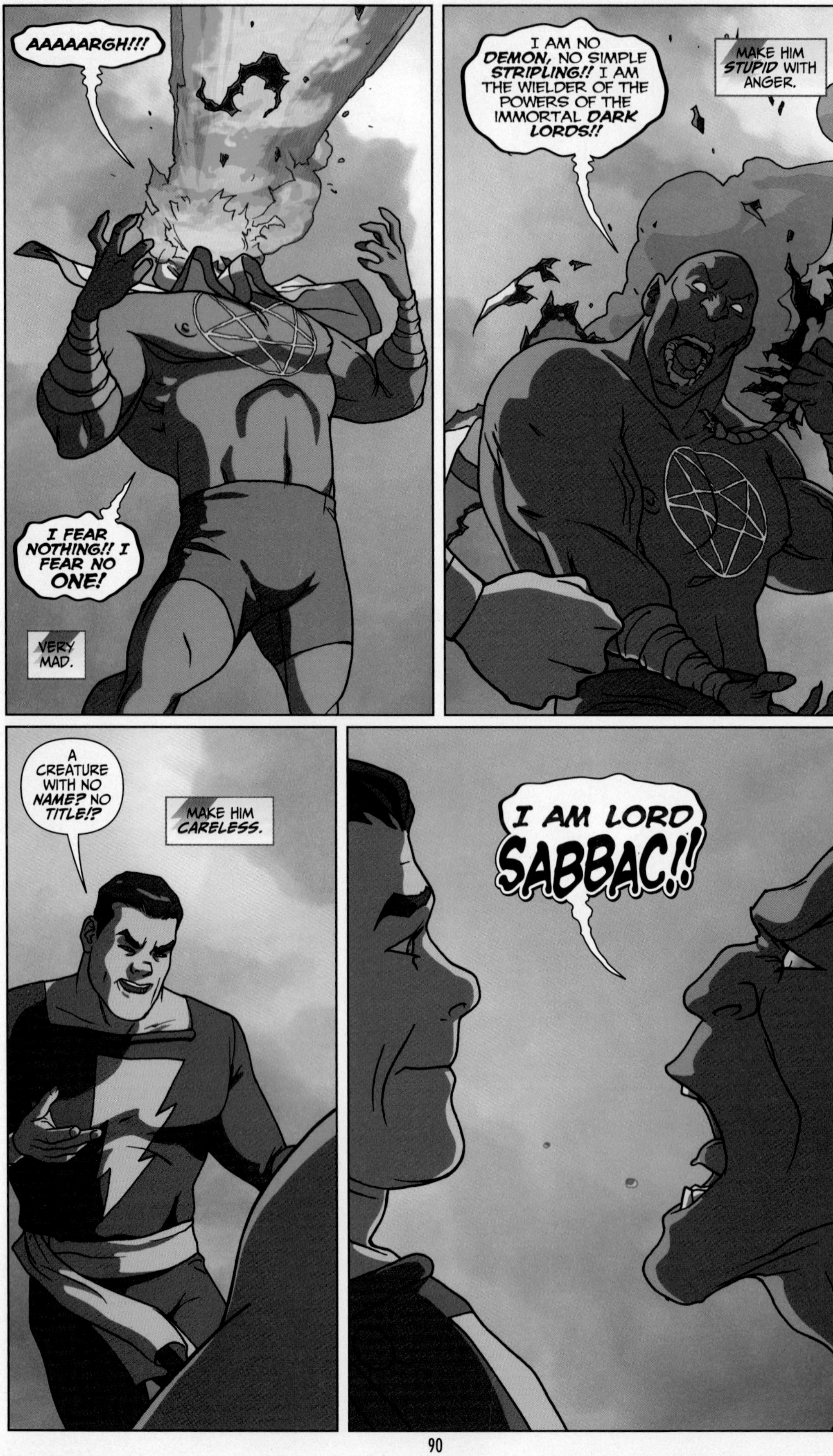
AAAAARGH!!!
I FEAR NOTHING!! I FEAR NO ONE!
VERY MAD.
I AM NO DEMON, NO SIMPLE STRIPLING!! I AM THE WIELDER OF THE POWERS OF THE IMMORTAL DARK LORDS!!
MAKE HIM STUPID WITH ANGER.
A CREATURE WITH NO NAME? NO TITLE!?
MAKE HIM CARELESS.
I AM LORD SABBAC!!

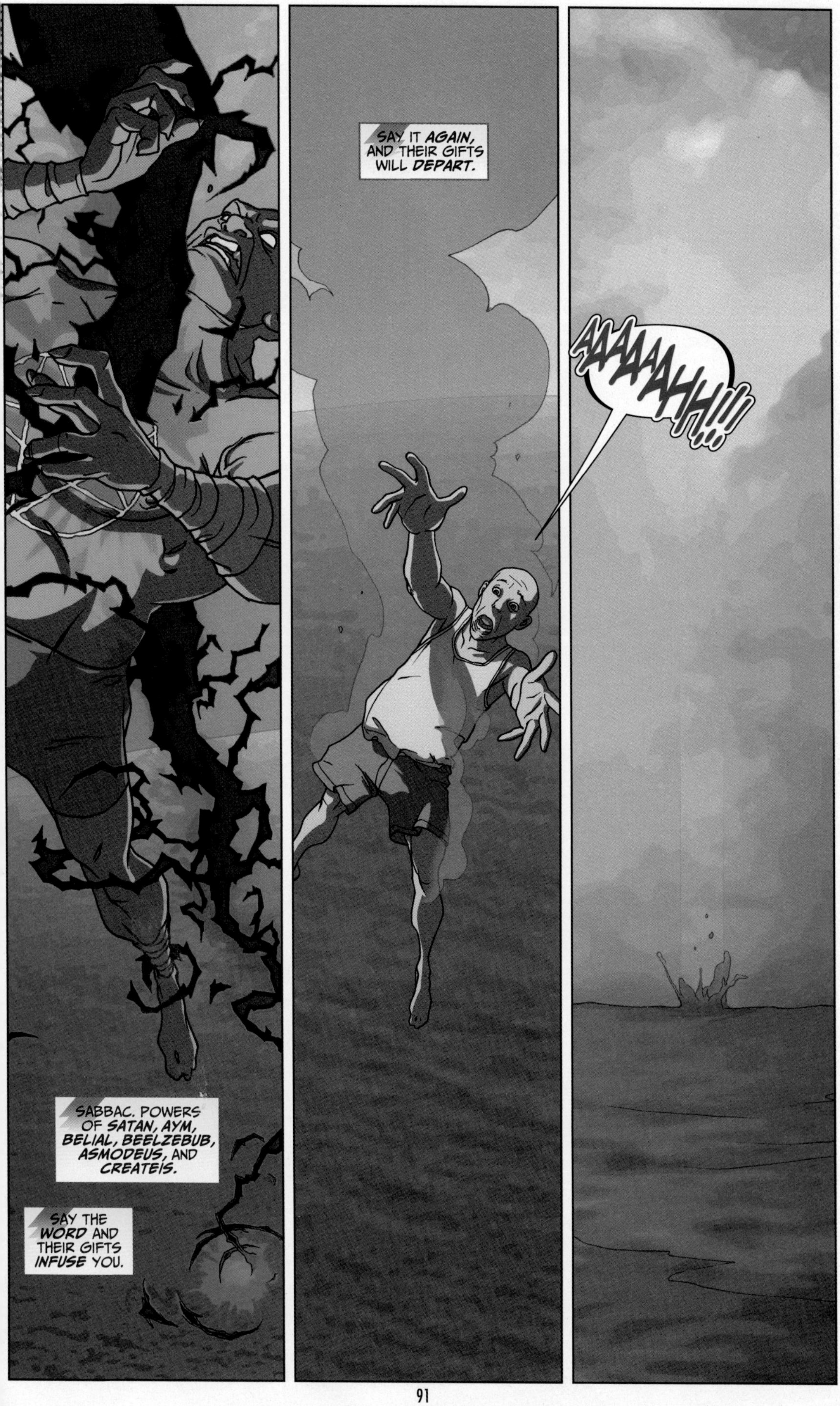
SABBAC. POWERS OF SATAN, AYM, BELIAL, BEELZEBUB, ASMODEUS, AND CREATEIS.
SAY THE WORD AND THEIR GIFTS INFUSE YOU.
SAY IT AGAIN, AND THEIR GIFTS WILL DEPART.
AAAAAAHH!!!

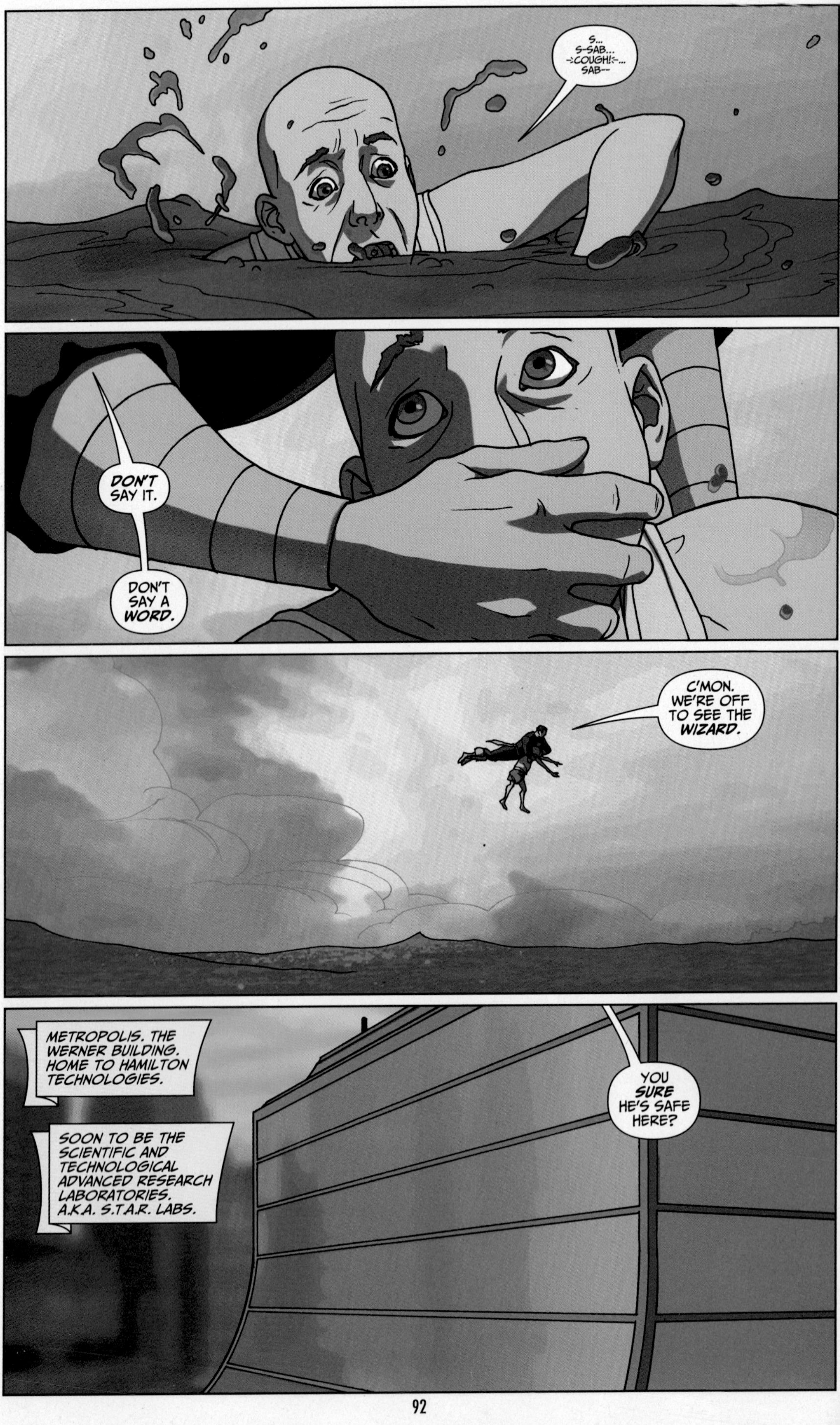
S...
S-SAB...
-COUGH!-...
SAB--
DON'T SAY IT.
DON'T SAY A WORD.
C'MON. WE'RE OFF TO SEE THE WIZARD.
METROPOLIS. THE WERNER BUILDING. HOME TO HAMILTON TECHNOLOGIES.
SOON TO BE THE SCIENTIFIC AND TECHNOLOGICAL ADVANCED RESEARCH LABORATORIES. A.K.A. S.T.A.R. LABS.
YOU SURE HE'S SAFE HERE?

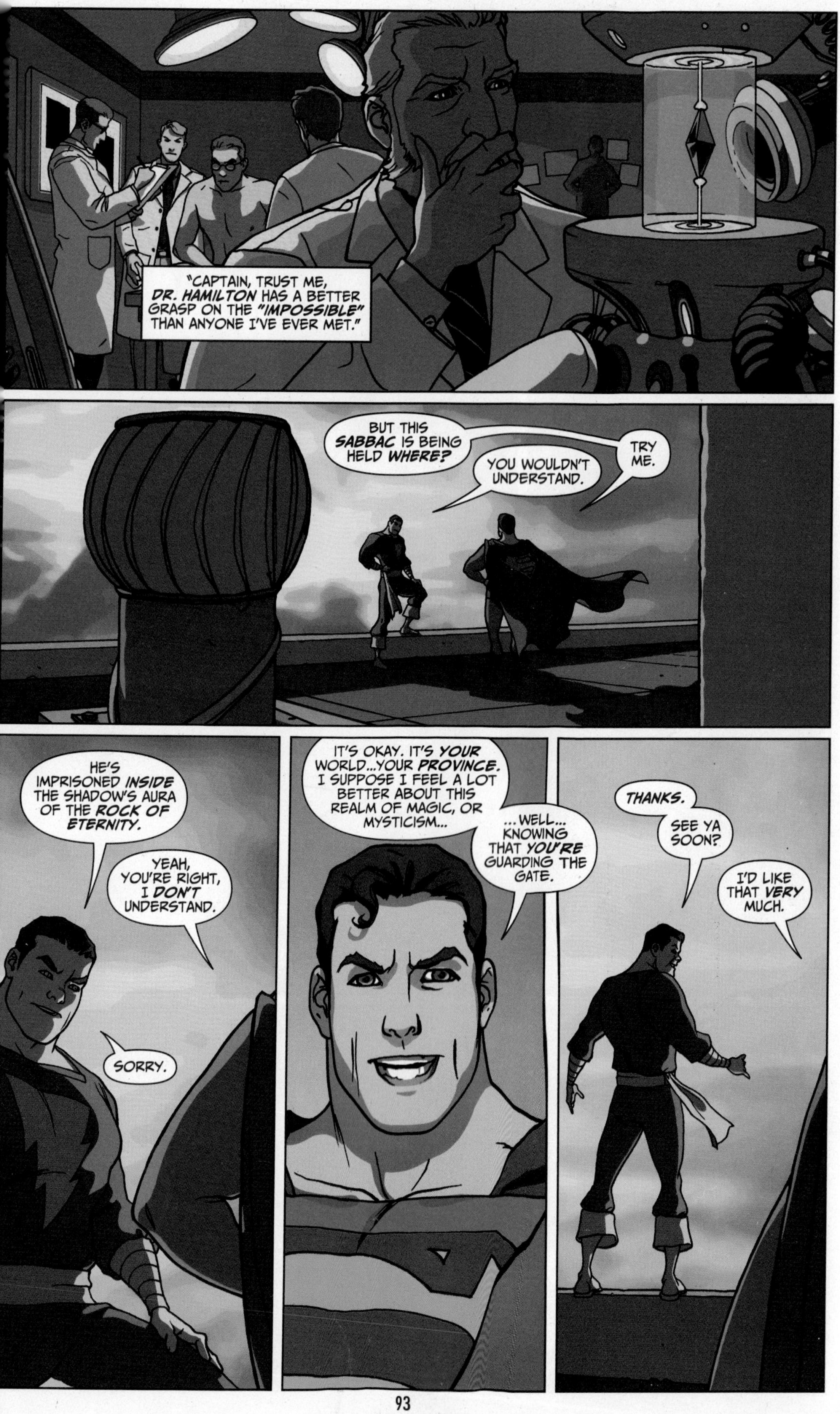
"CAPTAIN, TRUST ME, DR. HAMILTON HAS A BETTER GRASP ON THE "IMPOSSIBLE" THAN ANYONE I'VE EVER MET."
BUT THIS SABBAC IS BEING HELD WHERE?
YOU WOULDN'T UNDERSTAND.
TRY ME.
HE'S IMPRISONED INSIDE THE SHADOW'S AURA OF THE ROCK OF ETERNITY.
YEAH, YOU'RE RIGHT, I DON'T UNDERSTAND.
SORRY.
IT'S OKAY. IT'S YOUR WORLD...YOUR PROVINCE. I SUPPOSE I FEEL A LOT BETTER ABOUT THIS REALM OF MAGIC, OR MYSTICISM...
...WELL... KNOWING THAT YOU'RE GUARDING THE GATE.
THANKS.
SEE YA SOON?
I'D LIKE THAT VERY MUCH.

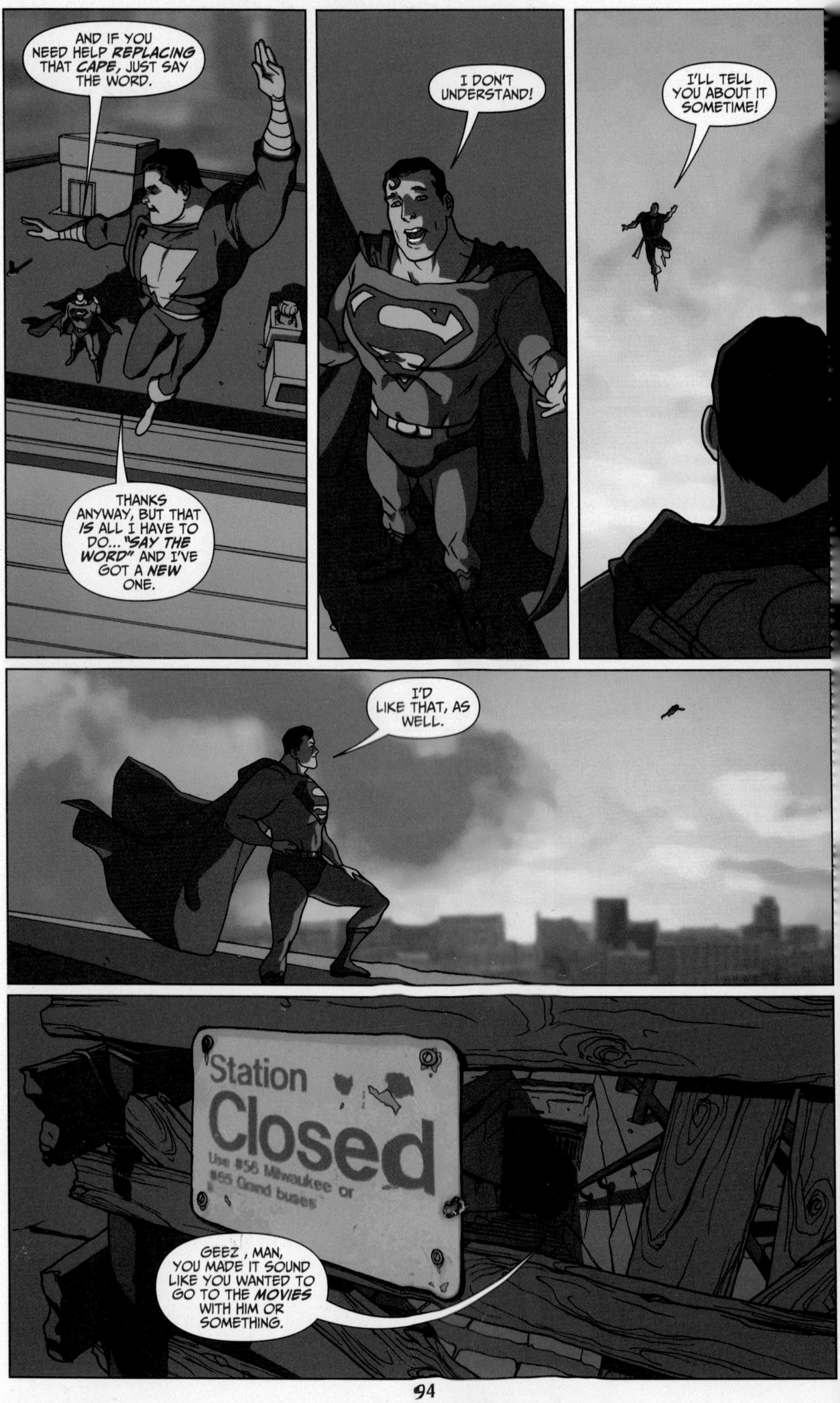
AND IF YOU NEED HELP *REPLACING* THAT *CAPE*, JUST SAY THE WORD.
THANKS ANYWAY, BUT THAT *IS* ALL I HAVE TO DO... *"SAY THE WORD"* AND I'VE GOT A *NEW* ONE.
I DON'T UNDERSTAND!
I'LL TELL YOU ABOUT IT SOMETIME!
I'D LIKE THAT, AS WELL.
Station
Closed
Use #56 Milwaukee or
#65 Grand buses
GEEZ , MAN, YOU MADE IT SOUND LIKE YOU WANTED TO GO TO THE *MOVIES* WITH HIM OR SOMETHING.

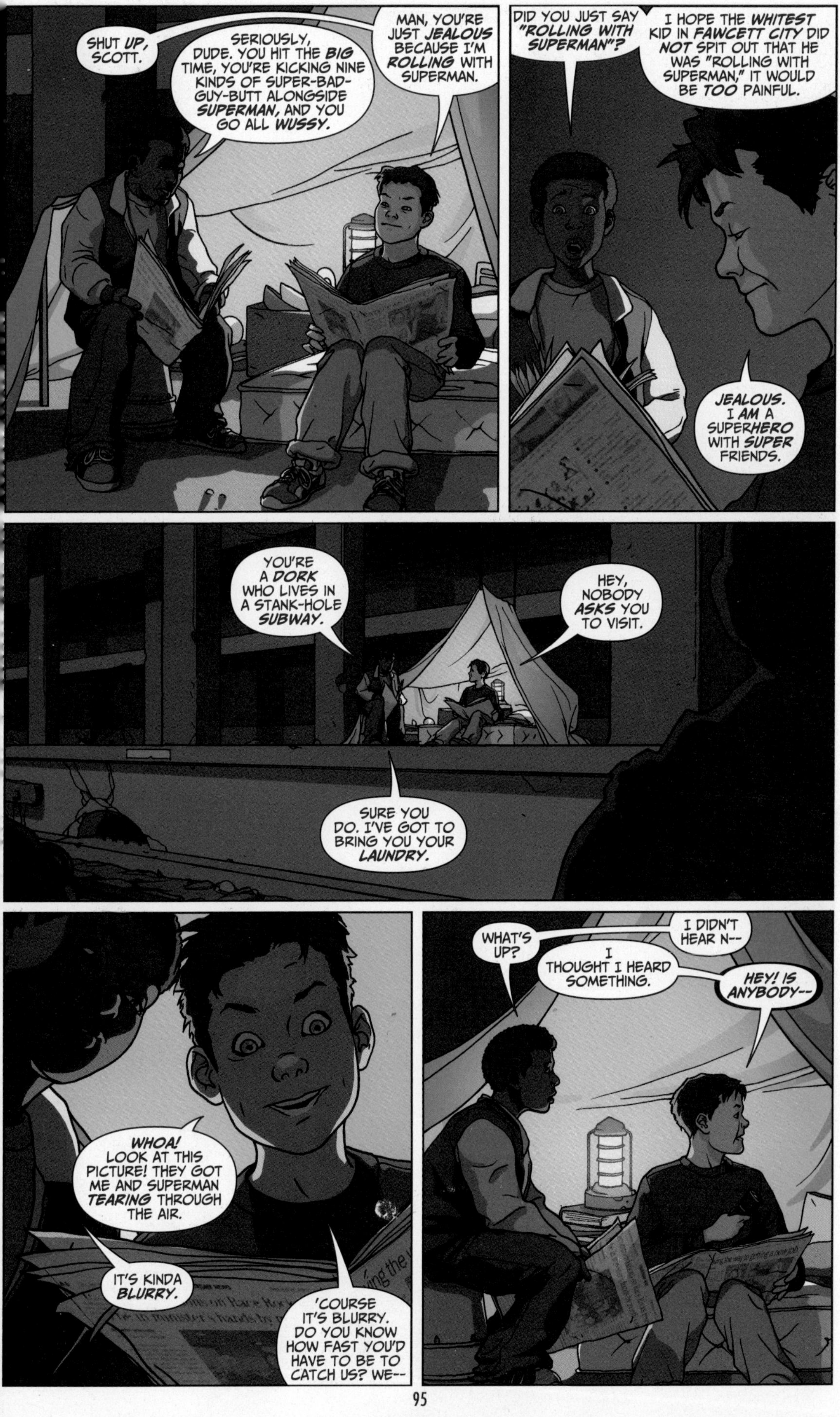
SHUT UP, SCOTT.
SERIOUSLY, DUDE. YOU HIT THE BIG TIME, YOU'RE KICKING NINE KINDS OF SUPER-BAD-GUY-BUTT ALONGSIDE SUPERMAN, AND YOU GO ALL WUSSY.
MAN, YOU'RE JUST JEALOUS BECAUSE I'M ROLLING WITH SUPERMAN.
DID YOU JUST SAY "ROLLING WITH SUPERMAN"?
I HOPE THE WHITEST KID IN FAWCETT CITY DID NOT SPIT OUT THAT HE WAS "ROLLING WITH SUPERMAN," IT WOULD BE TOO PAINFUL.
JEALOUS. I AM A SUPERHERO WITH SUPER FRIENDS.
YOU'RE A DORK WHO LIVES IN A STANK-HOLE SUBWAY.
HEY, NOBODY ASKS YOU TO VISIT.
SURE YOU DO. I'VE GOT TO BRING YOU YOUR LAUNDRY.
WHOA! LOOK AT THIS PICTURE! THEY GOT ME AND SUPERMAN TEARING THROUGH THE AIR.
IT'S KINDA BLURRY.
'COURSE IT'S BLURRY. DO YOU KNOW HOW FAST YOU'D HAVE TO BE TO CATCH US? WE--
WHAT'S UP?
I DIDN'T HEAR N--
I THOUGHT I HEARD SOMETHING.
HEY! IS ANYBODY--

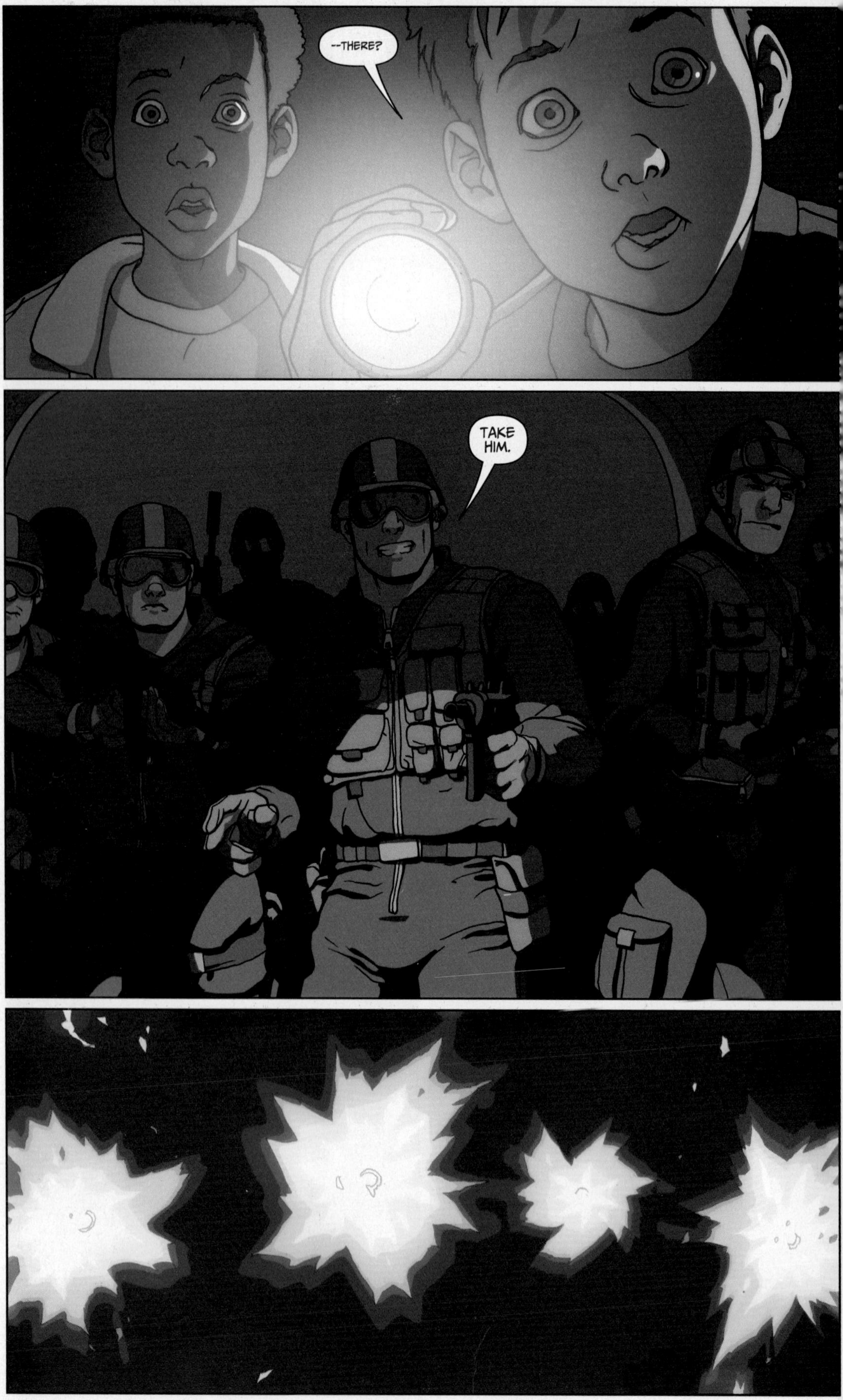
--THERE?
TAKE HIM.

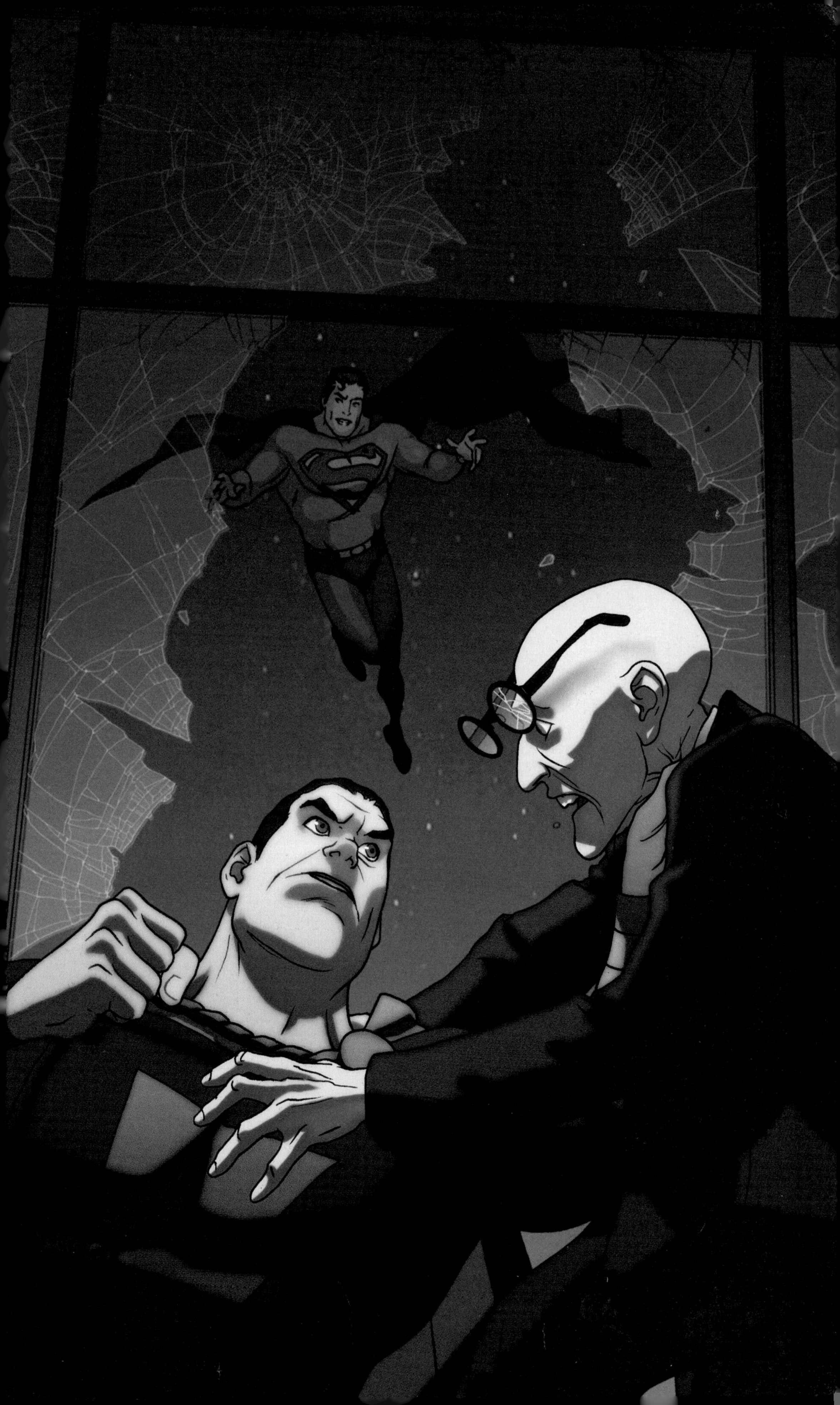

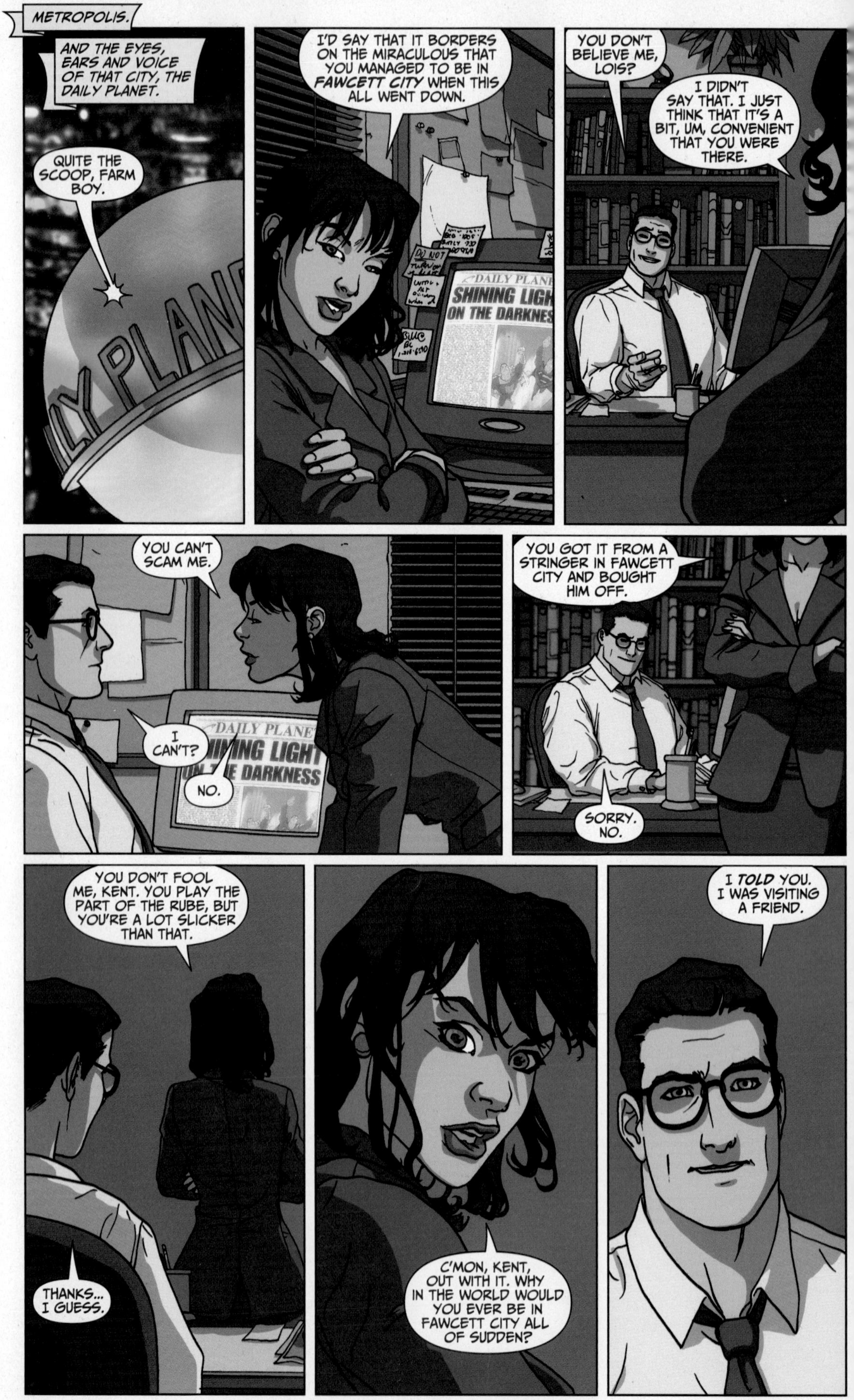
METROPOLIS.
AND THE EYES, EARS AND VOICE OF THAT CITY, THE DAILY PLANET.
QUITE THE SCOOP, FARM BOY.
I'D SAY THAT IT BORDERS ON THE MIRACULOUS THAT YOU MANAGED TO BE IN FAWCETT CITY WHEN THIS ALL WENT DOWN.
DAILY PLANET
SHINING LIGHT ON THE DARKNESS
YOU DON'T BELIEVE ME, LOIS?
I DIDN'T SAY THAT. I JUST THINK THAT IT'S A BIT, UM, CONVENIENT THAT YOU WERE THERE.
YOU CAN'T SCAM ME.
I CAN'T?
NO.
YOU GOT IT FROM A STRINGER IN FAWCETT CITY AND BOUGHT HIM OFF.
SORRY. NO.
YOU DON'T FOOL ME, KENT. YOU PLAY THE PART OF THE RUBE, BUT YOU'RE A LOT SLICKER THAN THAT.
THANKS... I GUESS.
C'MON, KENT, OUT WITH IT. WHY IN THE WORLD WOULD YOU EVER BE IN FAWCETT CITY ALL OF SUDDEN?
I TOLD YOU. I WAS VISITING A FRIEND.

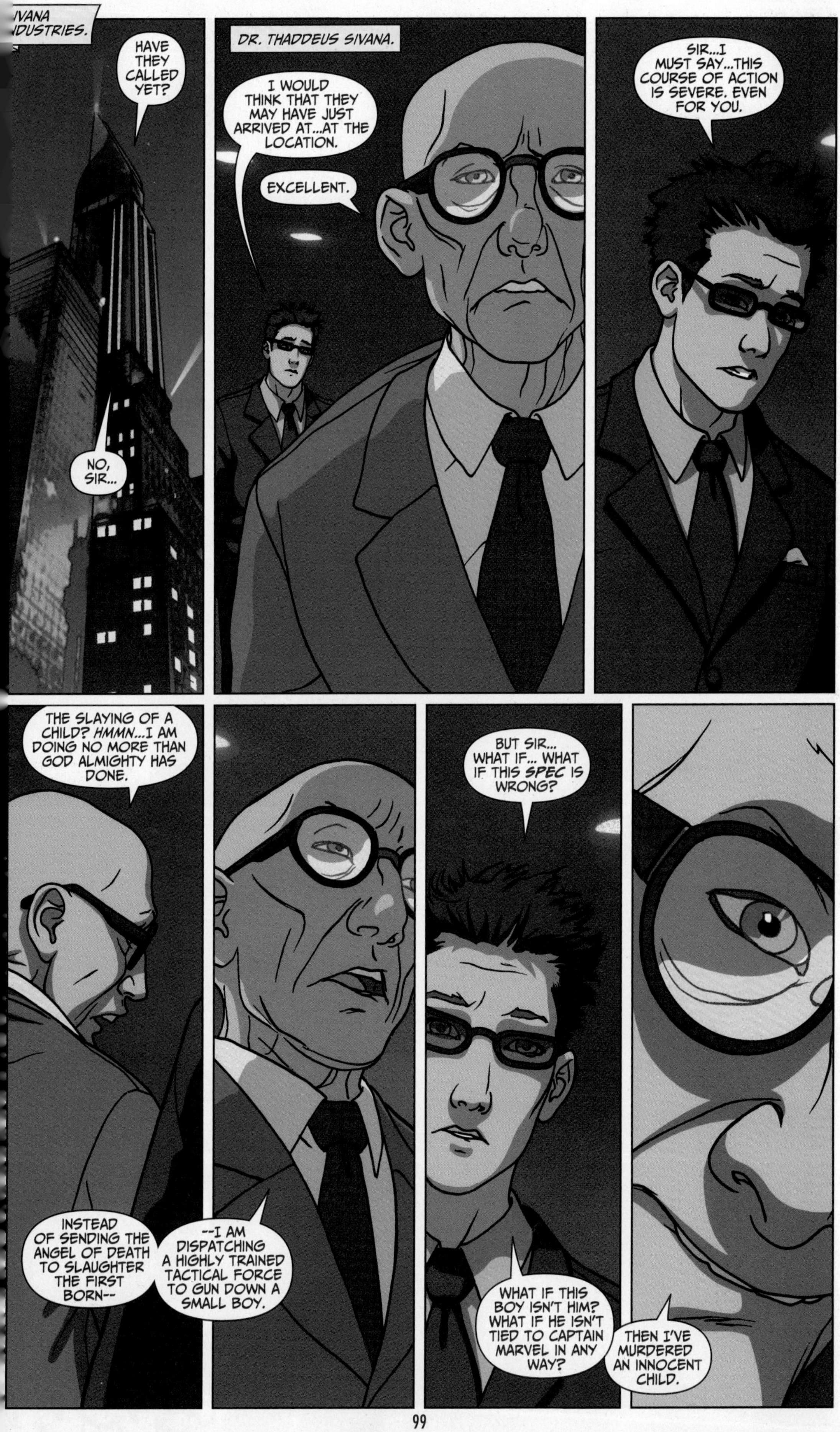
SIVANA INDUSTRIES.
HAVE THEY CALLED YET?
NO, SIR...
DR. THADDEUS SIVANA.
I WOULD THINK THAT THEY MAY HAVE JUST ARRIVED AT...AT THE LOCATION.
EXCELLENT.
SIR...I MUST SAY...THIS COURSE OF ACTION IS SEVERE. EVEN FOR YOU.
THE SLAYING OF A CHILD? HMMN...I AM DOING NO MORE THAN GOD ALMIGHTY HAS DONE.
INSTEAD OF SENDING THE ANGEL OF DEATH TO SLAUGHTER THE FIRST BORN--
--I AM DISPATCHING A HIGHLY TRAINED TACTICAL FORCE TO GUN DOWN A SMALL BOY.
BUT SIR... WHAT IF... WHAT IF THIS SPEC IS WRONG?
WHAT IF THIS BOY ISN'T HIM? WHAT IF HE ISN'T TIED TO CAPTAIN MARVEL IN ANY WAY?
THEN I'VE MURDERED AN INNOCENT CHILD.

"I'LL GET OVER IT."

HE HEARD ONE OF THEM COCK A GUN BEFORE THEY OPENED FIRE.

TWO WEEKS AFTER HE BEGAN THIS ADVENTURE HE STOPPED A BANK ROBBERY.

ONE OF THE GUNMEN OPENED FIRE ON HIM.

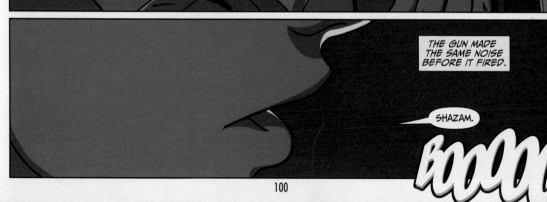

THE GUN MADE THE SAME NOISE BEFORE IT FIRED.

SHAZAM.

BOOOO

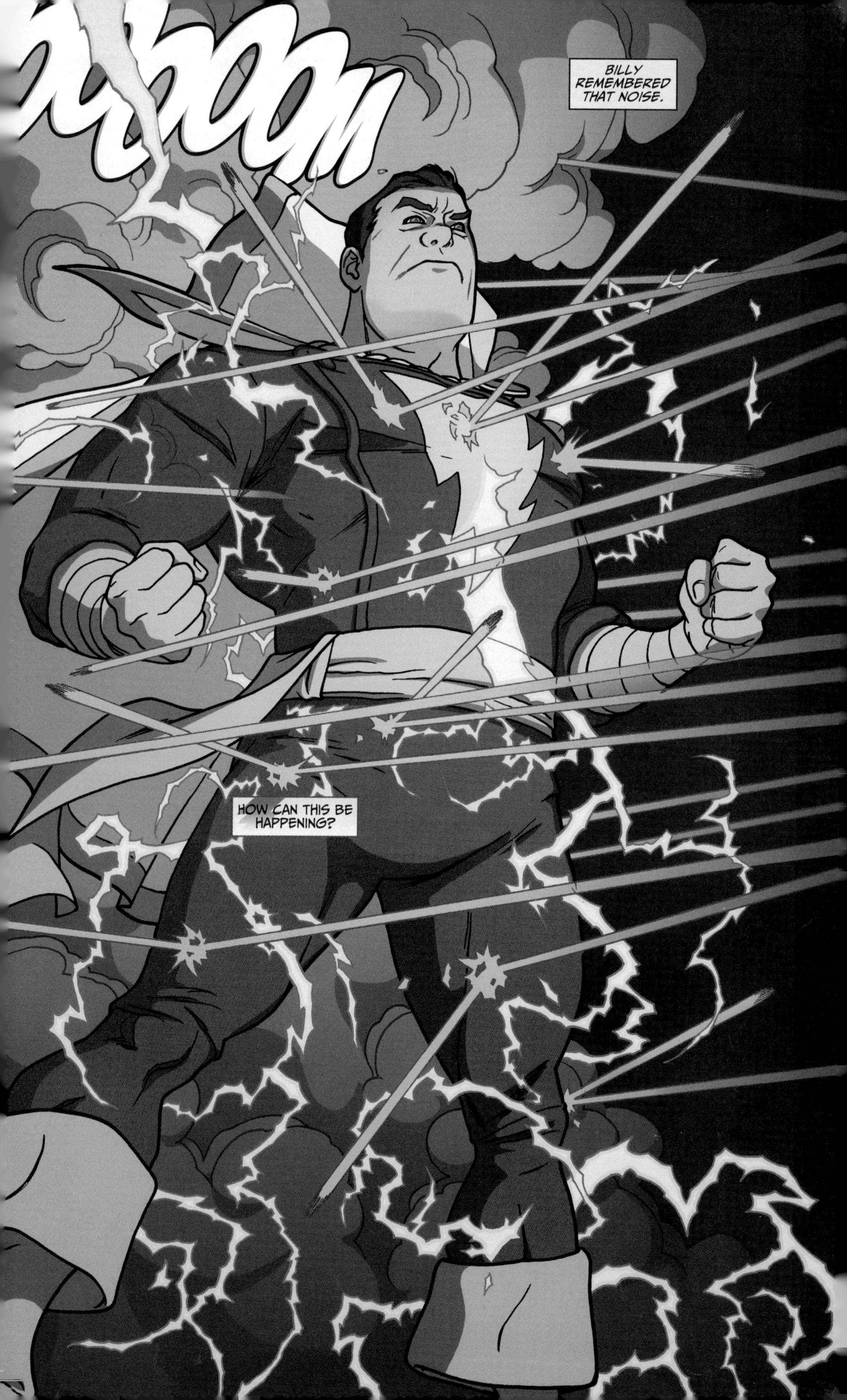
BILLY REMEMBERED THAT NOISE.
HOW CAN THIS BE HAPPENING?

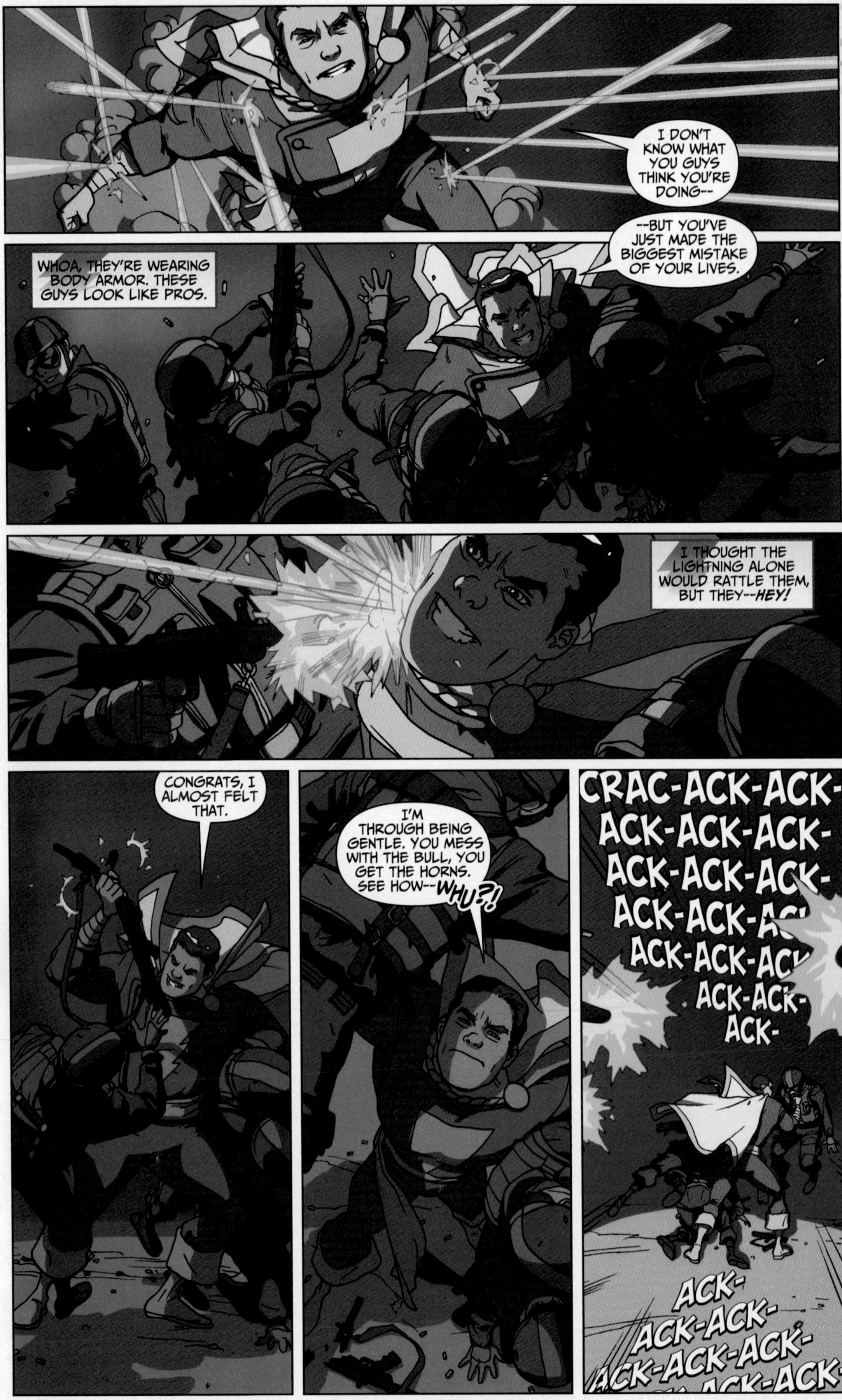
I DON'T KNOW WHAT YOU GUYS THINK YOU'RE DOING--
--BUT YOU'VE JUST MADE THE BIGGEST MISTAKE OF YOUR LIVES.
WHOA, THEY'RE WEARING BODY ARMOR. THESE GUYS LOOK LIKE PROS.
I THOUGHT THE LIGHTNING ALONE WOULD RATTLE THEM, BUT THEY--HEY!
CONGRATS, I ALMOST FELT THAT.
I'M THROUGH BEING GENTLE. YOU MESS WITH THE BULL, YOU GET THE HORNS. SEE HOW--WHU?!
CRAC-ACK-ACK-ACK-ACK-ACK-ACK-ACK-ACK-ACK-ACK-ACK-ACK-ACK-ACK-ACK-ACK-
ACK-ACK-ACK-ACK-ACK-ACK-ACK-ACK-

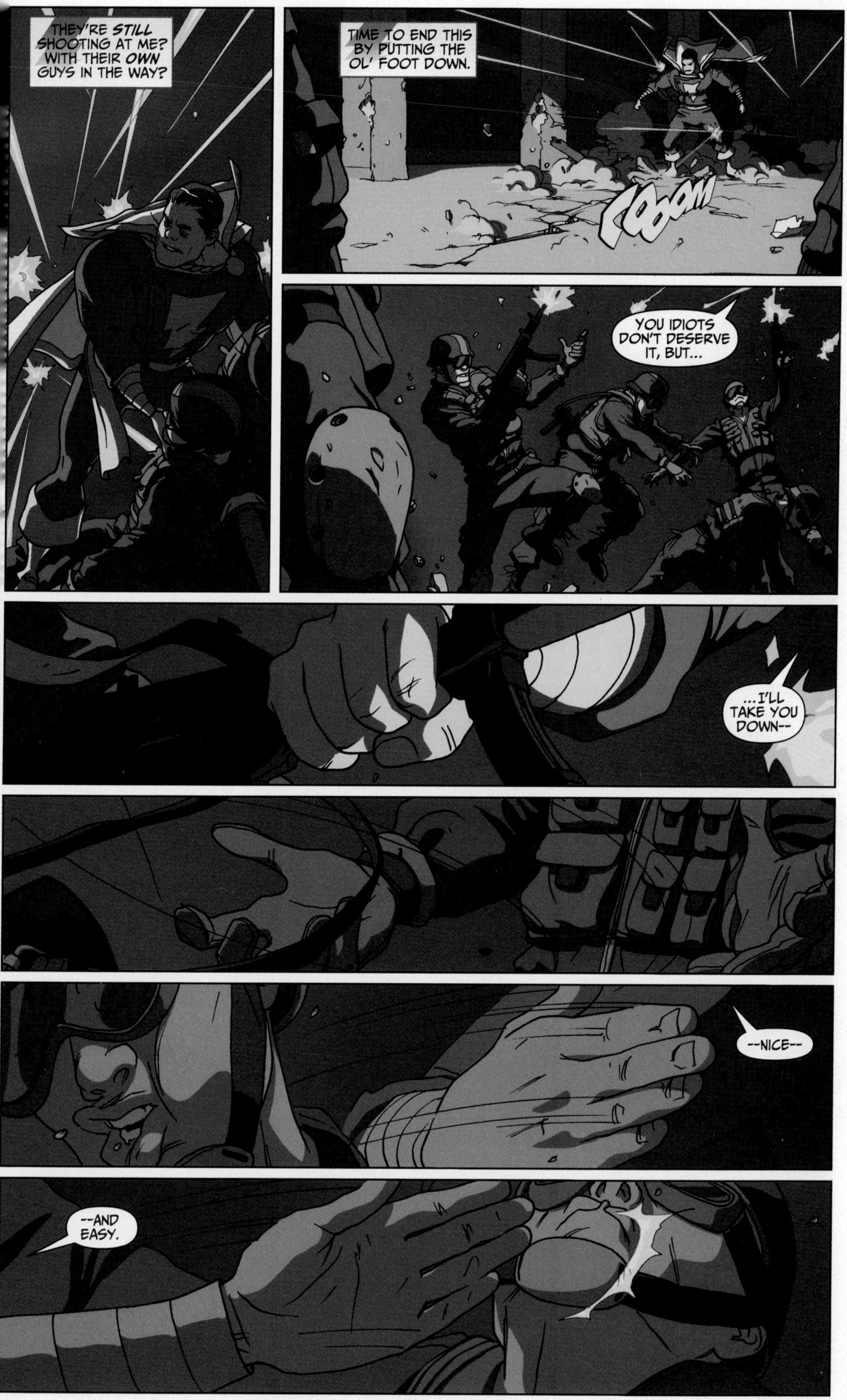
THEY'RE STILL SHOOTING AT ME? WITH THEIR OWN GUYS IN THE WAY?
TIME TO END THIS BY PUTTING THE OL' FOOT DOWN.
KOOOM
YOU IDIOTS DON'T DESERVE IT, BUT...
...I'LL TAKE YOU DOWN--
--NICE--
--AND EASY.

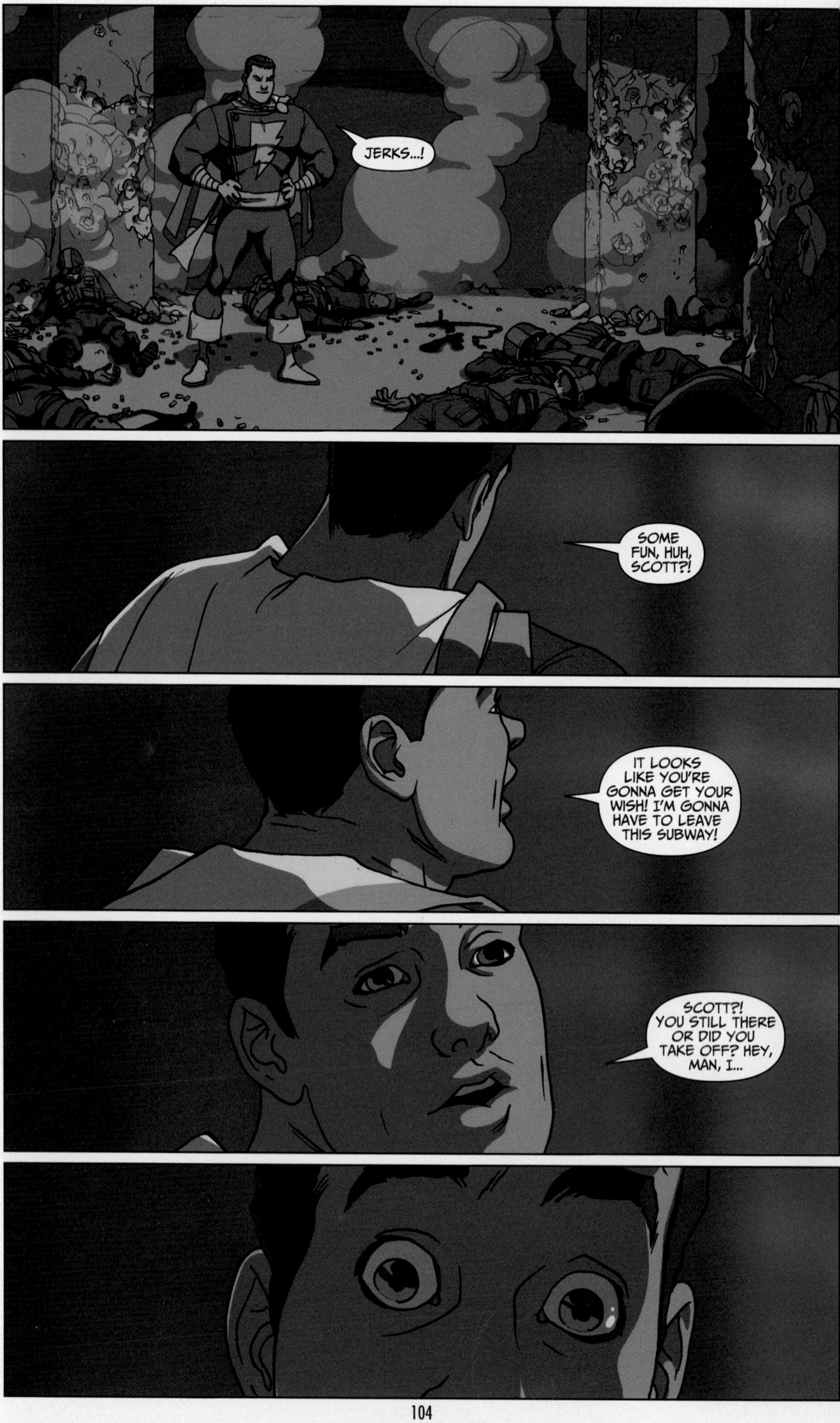
JERKS...!
SOME FUN, HUH, SCOTT?!
IT LOOKS LIKE YOU'RE GONNA GET YOUR WISH! I'M GONNA HAVE TO LEAVE THIS SUBWAY!
SCOTT?! YOU STILL THERE OR DID YOU TAKE OFF? HEY, MAN, I...

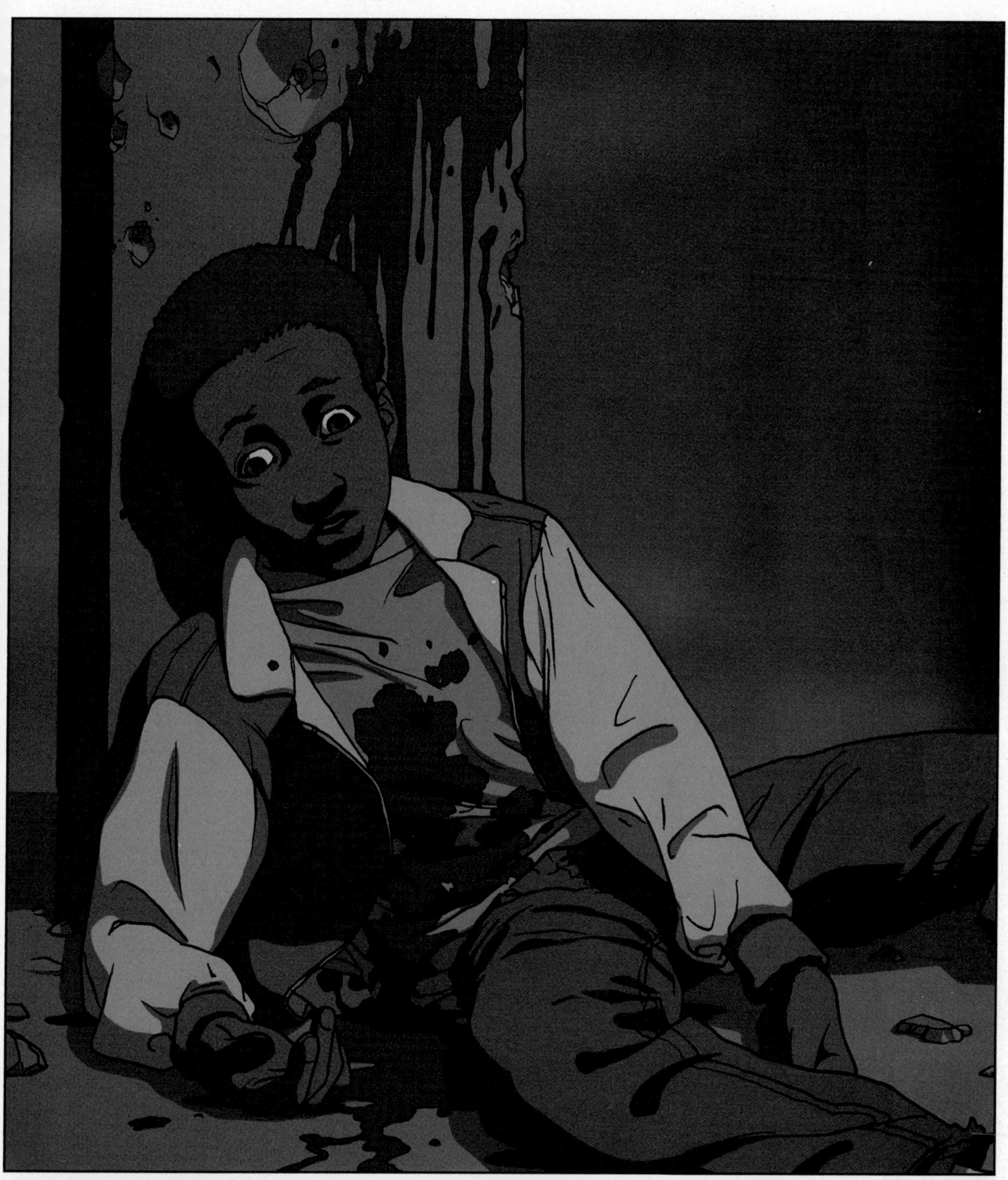

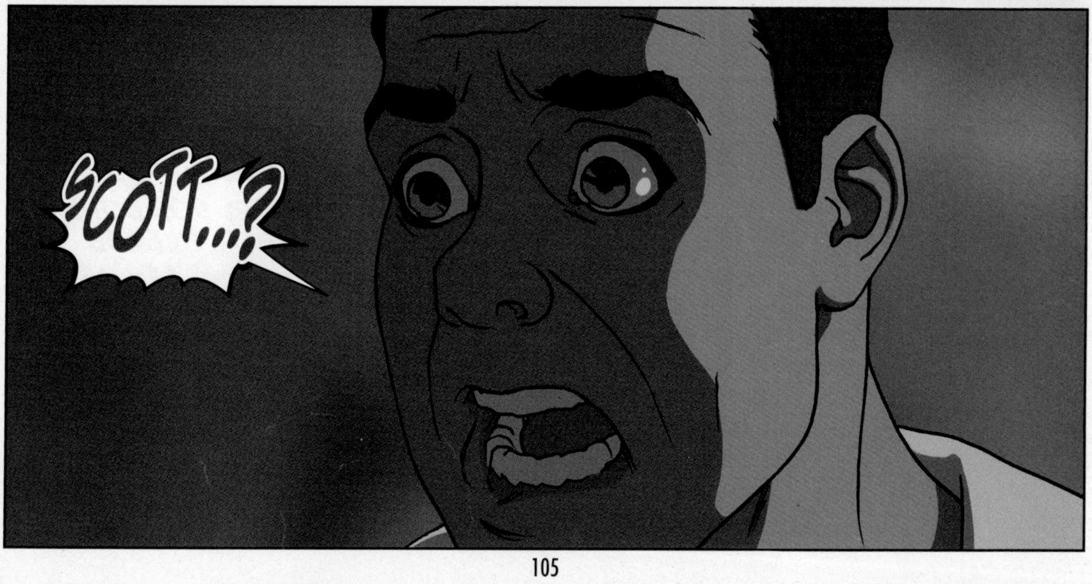
SCOTT...?

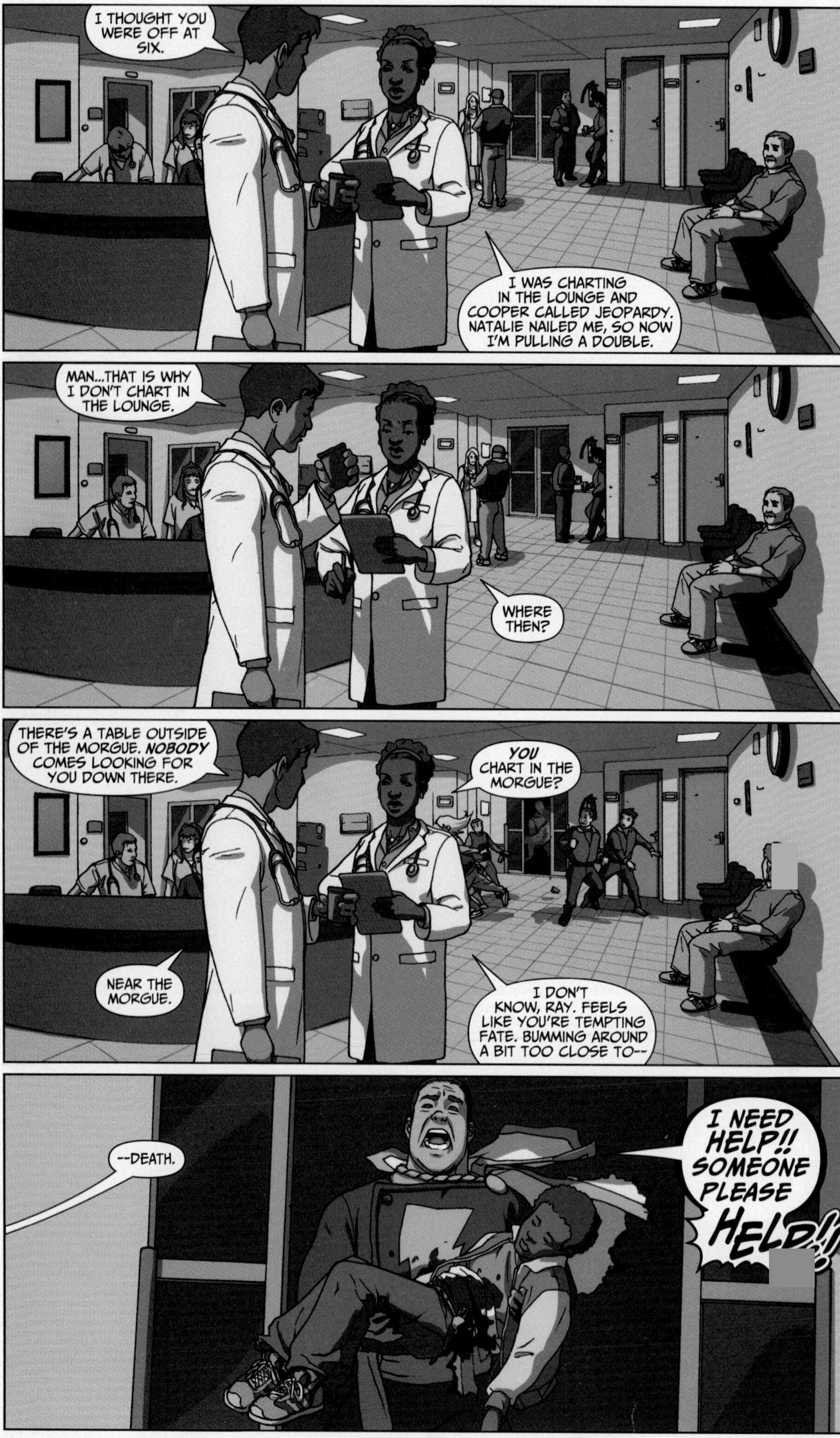
I THOUGHT YOU WERE OFF AT SIX.
I WAS CHARTING IN THE LOUNGE AND COOPER CALLED JEOPARDY. NATALIE NAILED ME, SO NOW I'M PULLING A DOUBLE.
MAN...THAT IS WHY I DON'T CHART IN THE LOUNGE.
WHERE THEN?
THERE'S A TABLE OUTSIDE OF THE MORGUE. *NOBODY* COMES LOOKING FOR YOU DOWN THERE.
YOU CHART IN THE MORGUE?
NEAR THE MORGUE.
I DON'T KNOW, RAY. FEELS LIKE YOU'RE TEMPTING FATE. BUMMING AROUND A BIT TOO CLOSE TO--
--DEATH.
I NEED HELP!! SOMEONE PLEASE HELP!!

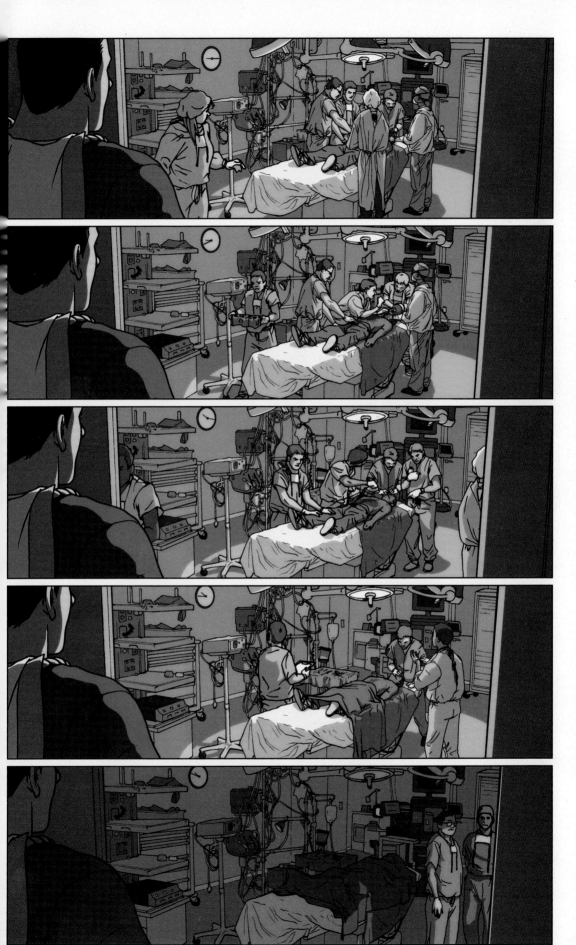

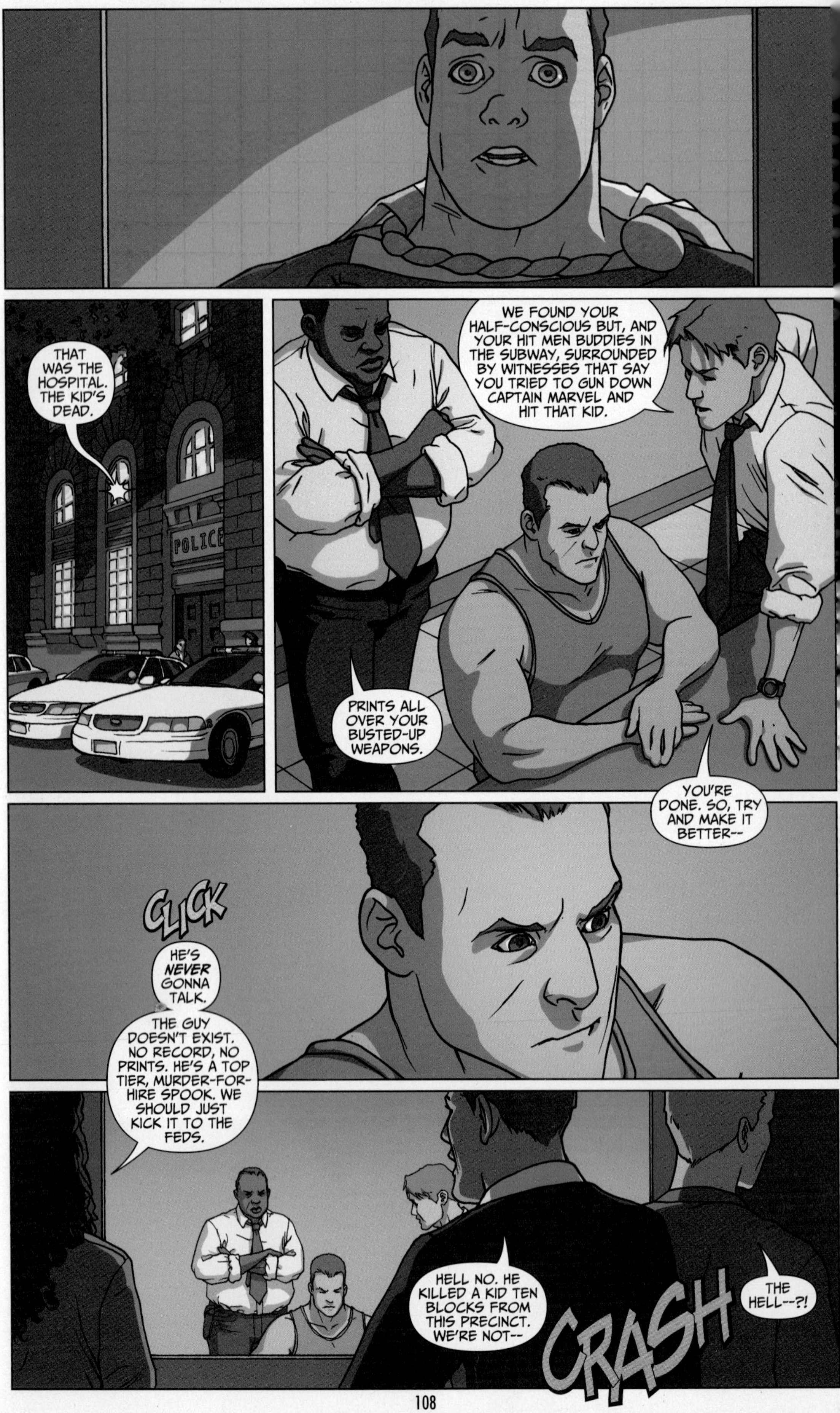
THAT WAS THE HOSPITAL. THE KID'S DEAD.
WE FOUND YOUR HALF-CONSCIOUS BUT, AND YOUR HIT MEN BUDDIES IN THE SUBWAY, SURROUNDED BY WITNESSES THAT SAY YOU TRIED TO GUN DOWN CAPTAIN MARVEL AND HIT THAT KID.
PRINTS ALL OVER YOUR BUSTED-UP WEAPONS.
YOU'RE DONE. SO, TRY AND MAKE IT BETTER--
CLICK
HE'S NEVER GONNA TALK.
THE GUY DOESN'T EXIST. NO RECORD, NO PRINTS. HE'S A TOP TIER, MURDER-FOR-HIRE SPOOK. WE SHOULD JUST KICK IT TO THE FEDS.
HELL NO. HE KILLED A KID TEN BLOCKS FROM THIS PRECINCT. WE'RE NOT--
CRASH
THE HELL--?!

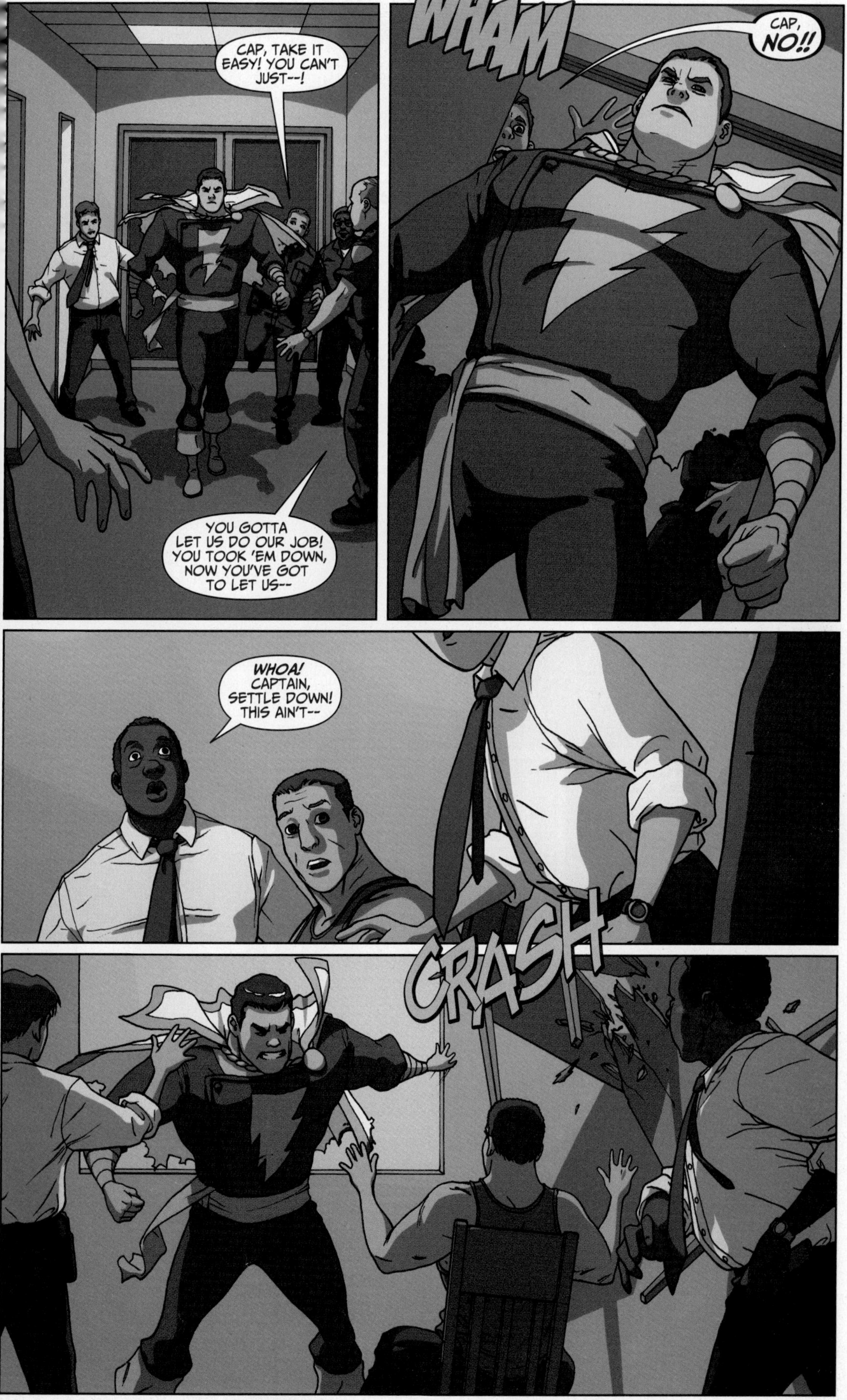

CAP, TAKE IT EASY! YOU CAN'T JUST--!
YOU GOTTA LET US DO OUR JOB! YOU TOOK 'EM DOWN, NOW YOU'VE GOT TO LET US--
WHAM
CAP, NO!!
WHOA! CAPTAIN, SETTLE DOWN! THIS AIN'T--
CRASH

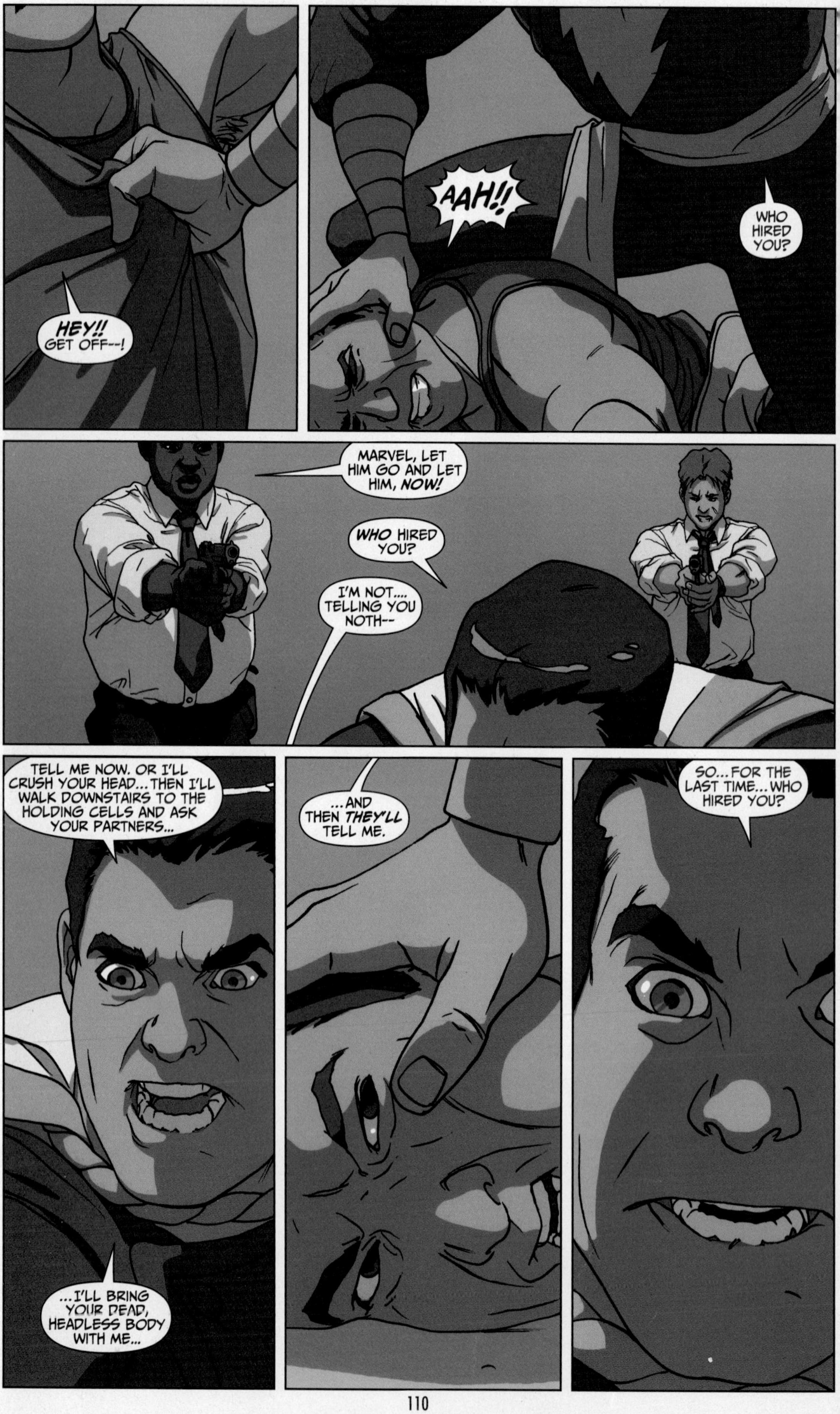
HEY!! GET OFF--!
AAH!!
WHO HIRED YOU?
MARVEL, LET HIM GO AND LET HIM, NOW!
WHO HIRED YOU?
I'M NOT.... TELLING YOU NOTH--
TELL ME NOW. OR I'LL CRUSH YOUR HEAD... THEN I'LL WALK DOWNSTAIRS TO THE HOLDING CELLS AND ASK YOUR PARTNERS...
...I'LL BRING YOUR DEAD, HEADLESS BODY WITH ME...
...AND THEN THEY'LL TELL ME.
SO...FOR THE LAST TIME...WHO HIRED YOU?

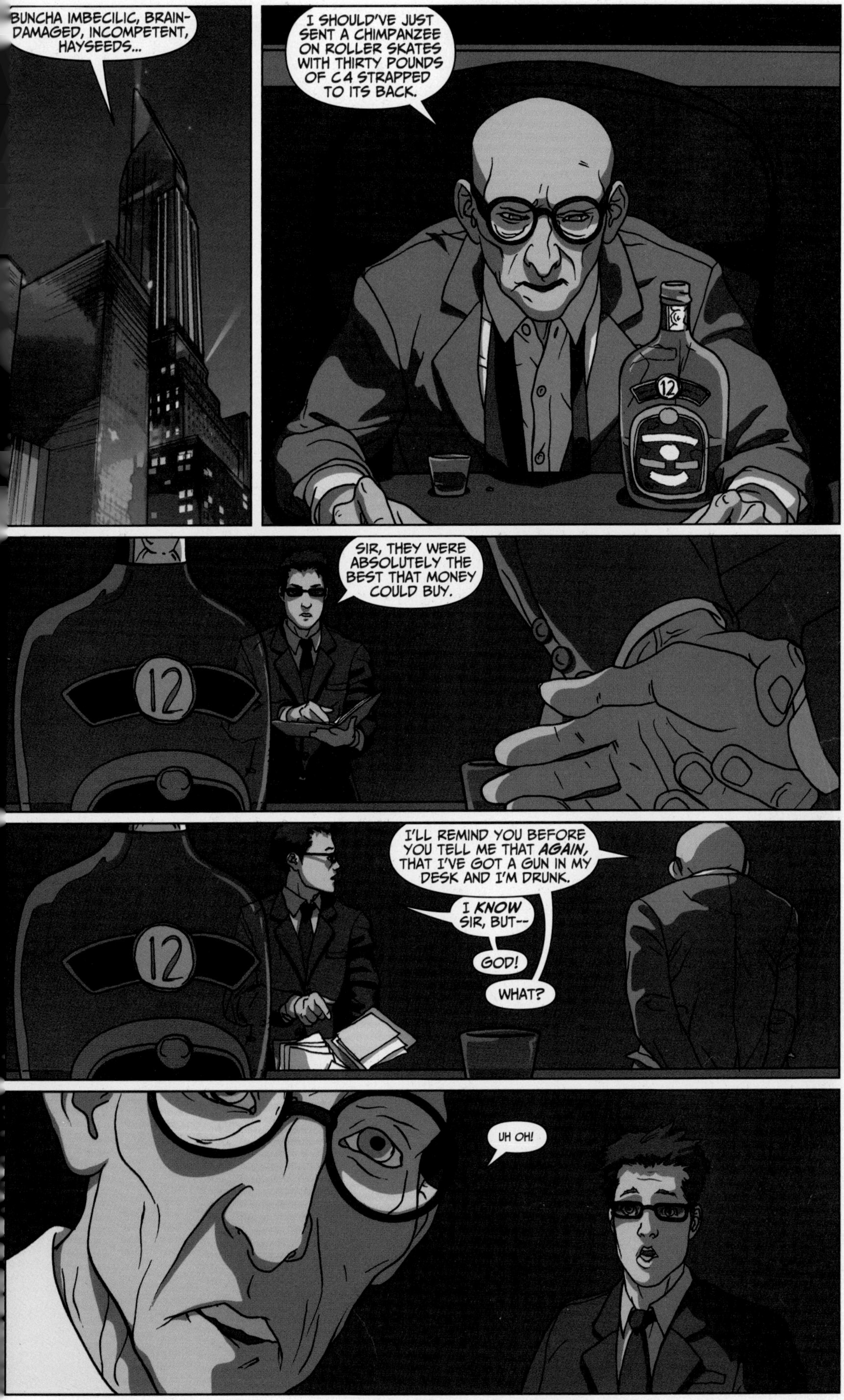

BUNCHA IMBECILIC, BRAIN-DAMAGED, INCOMPETENT, HAYSEEDS...
I SHOULD'VE JUST SENT A CHIMPANZEE ON ROLLER SKATES WITH THIRTY POUNDS OF C4 STRAPPED TO ITS BACK.
SIR, THEY WERE ABSOLUTELY THE BEST THAT MONEY COULD BUY.
I'LL REMIND YOU BEFORE YOU TELL ME THAT AGAIN, THAT I'VE GOT A GUN IN MY DESK AND I'M DRUNK.
I KNOW SIR, BUT--
GOD!
WHAT?
UH OH!

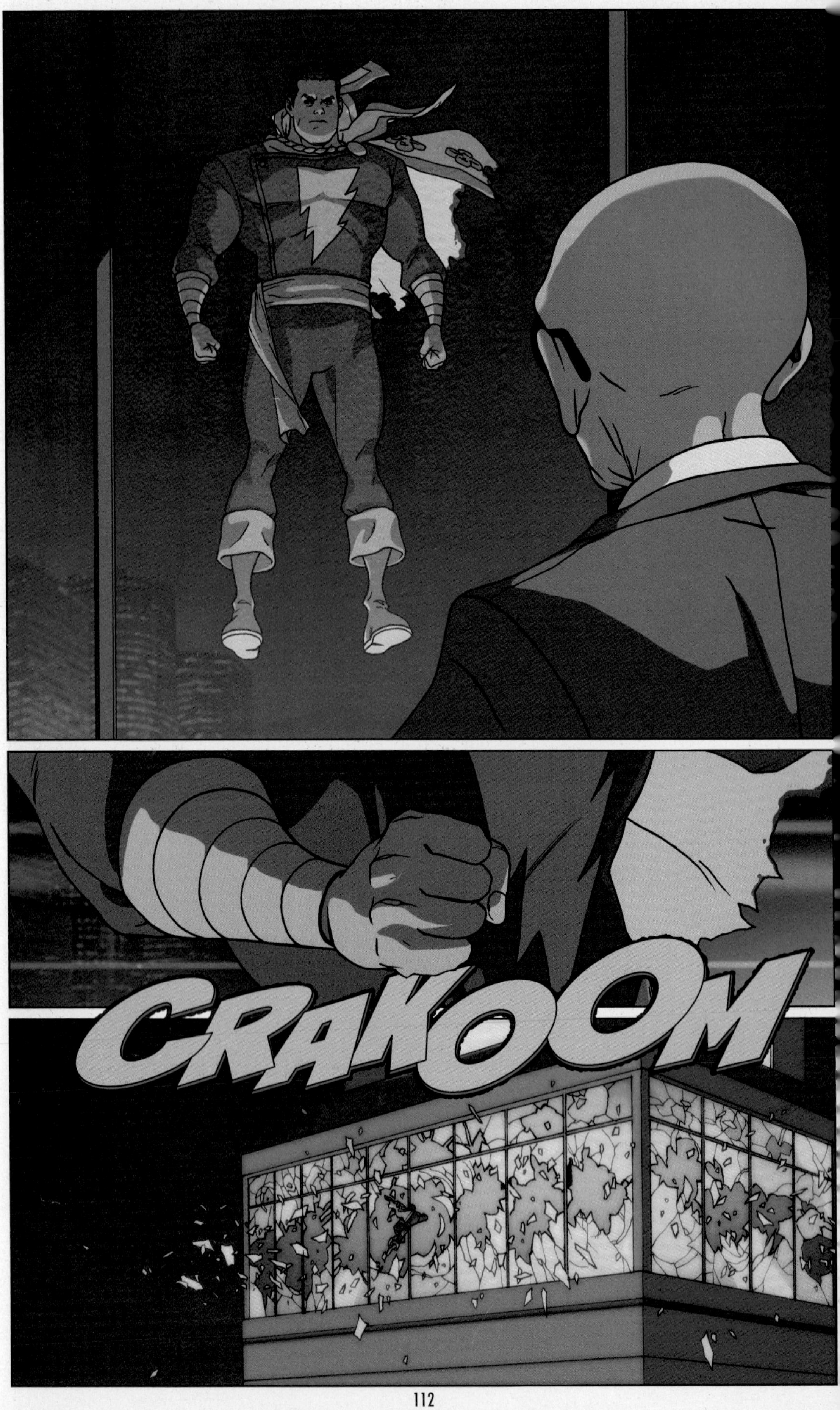
CRAKOOM

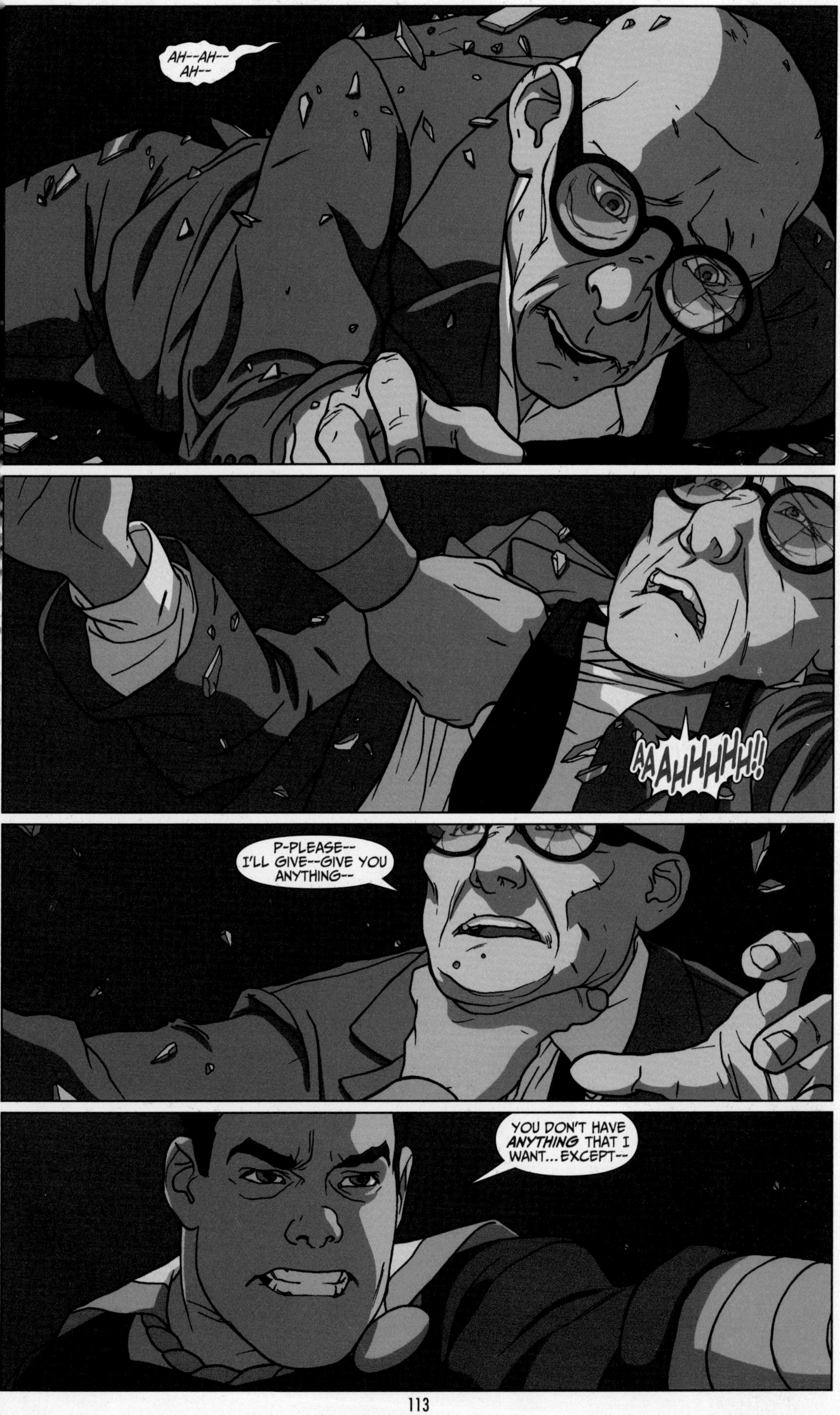
AH--AH--
AH--
AAAHHHHH!!
P-PLEASE--
I'LL GIVE--GIVE YOU
ANYTHING--
YOU DON'T HAVE
ANYTHING THAT I
WANT...EXCEPT--

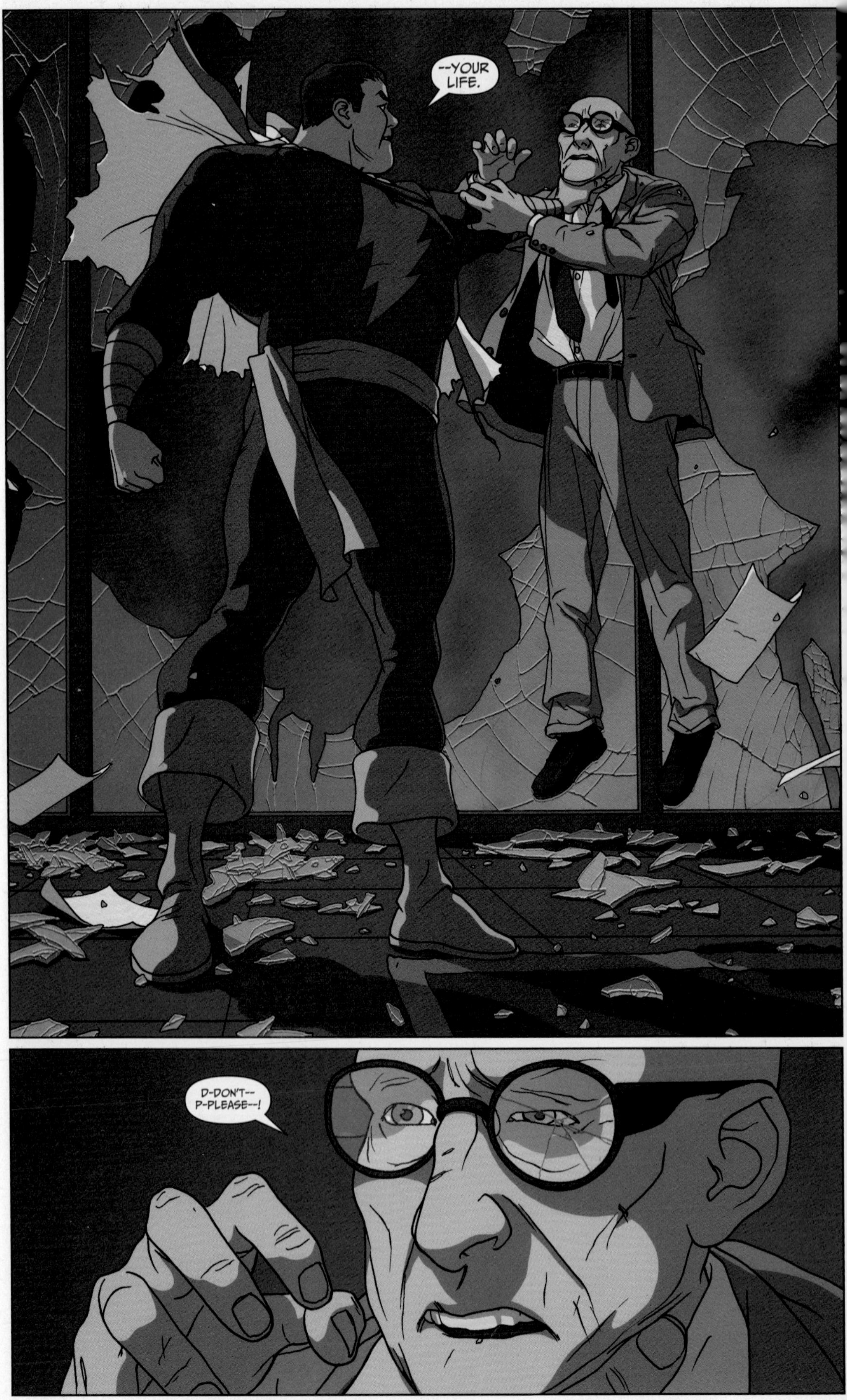
--YOUR LIFE.
D-DON'T-- P-PLEASE--!

DON'T *WHAT?* HURT YOU?

DON'T YOU UNDERSTAND, DOCTOR? THAT'S ALL YOU'VE LEFT ME WITH.

I'M TRYING TO FIND SOME REASON TO LET YOU LIVE.

BUT I CAN'T.

I KNOW IF I LET YOU GO, YOU'RE JUST GOING TO KEEP HURTING...KEEP *MURDERING* PEOPLE...

I'M NOT... I'M NOT SURE I CAN LIVE WITH THAT...

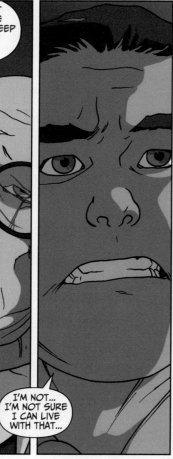

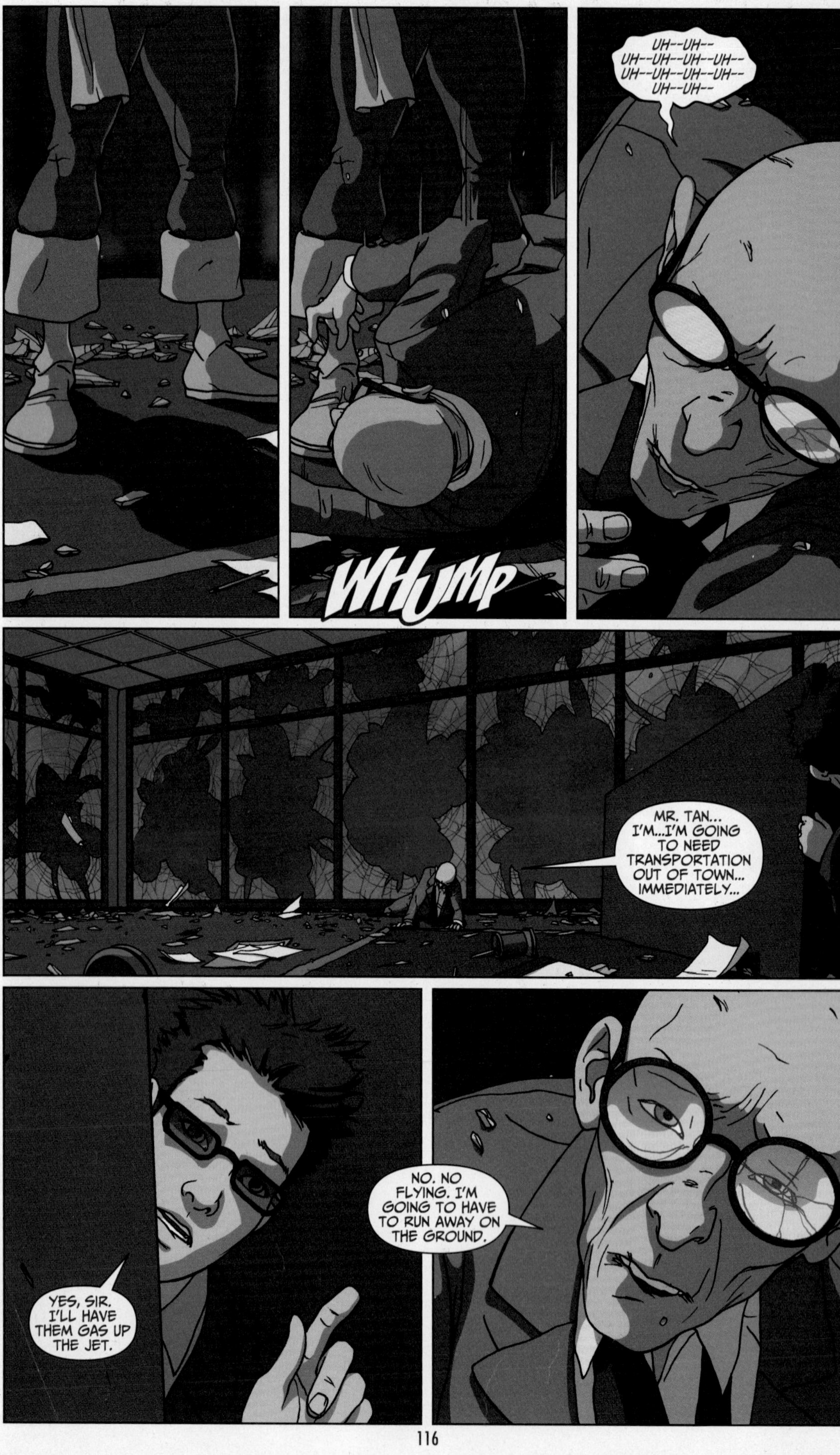
UH--UH-- UH--UH--UH--UH-- UH--UH--UH--UH-- UH--UH--
WHUMP
MR. TAN... I'M...I'M GOING TO NEED TRANSPORTATION OUT OF TOWN... IMMEDIATELY...
YES, SIR. I'LL HAVE THEM GAS UP THE JET.
NO. NO FLYING. I'M GOING TO HAVE TO RUN AWAY ON THE GROUND.

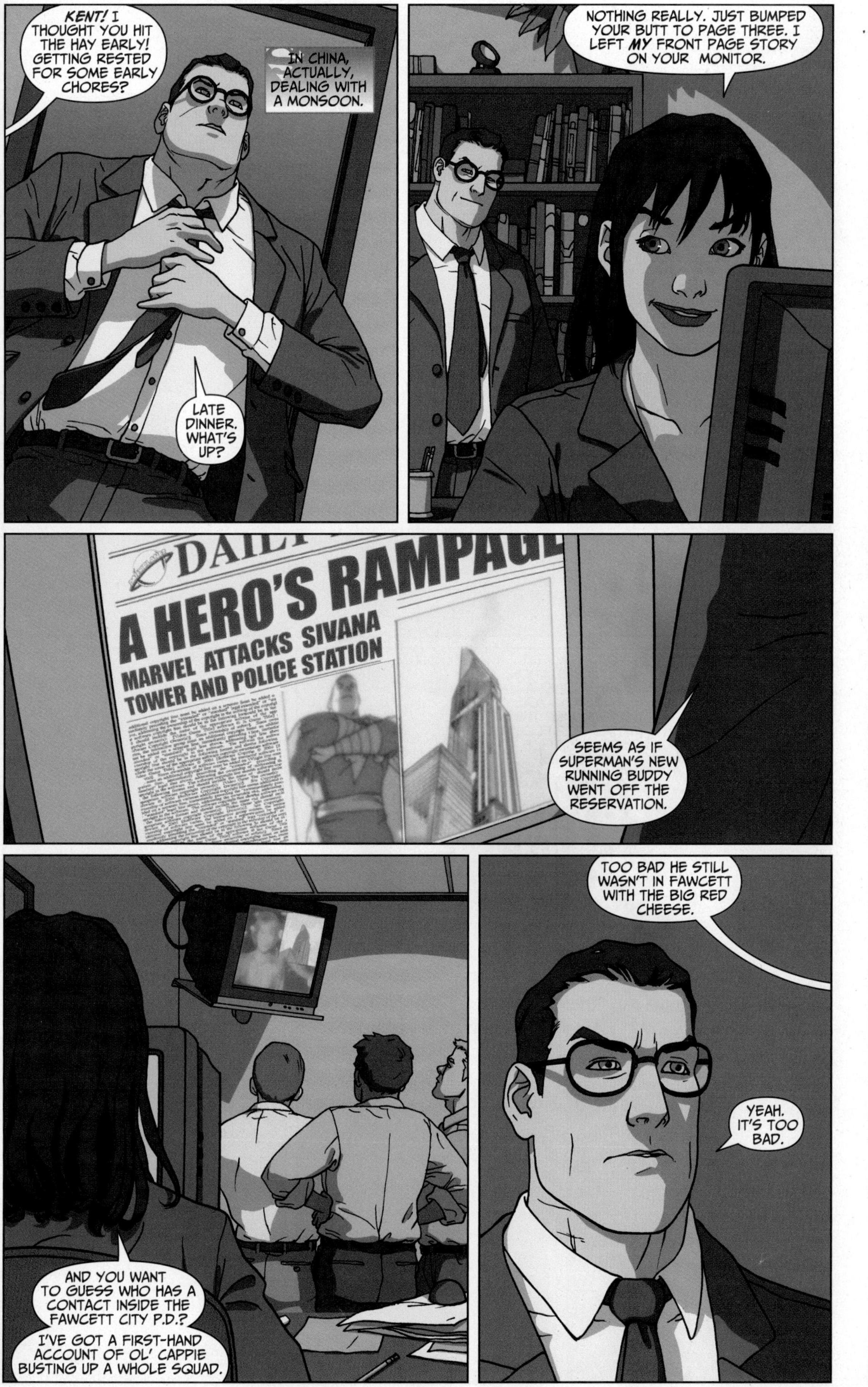
KENT! I THOUGHT YOU HIT THE HAY EARLY! GETTING RESTED FOR SOME EARLY CHORES?
IN CHINA, ACTUALLY, DEALING WITH A MONSOON.
LATE DINNER. WHAT'S UP?
NOTHING REALLY. JUST BUMPED YOUR BUTT TO PAGE THREE. I LEFT MY FRONT PAGE STORY ON YOUR MONITOR.
A HERO'S RAMPAGE
MARVEL ATTACKS SIVANA TOWER AND POLICE STATION
SEEMS AS IF SUPERMAN'S NEW RUNNING BUDDY WENT OFF THE RESERVATION.
AND YOU WANT TO GUESS WHO HAS A CONTACT INSIDE THE FAWCETT CITY P.D.?
I'VE GOT A FIRST-HAND ACCOUNT OF OL' CAPPIE BUSTING UP A WHOLE SQUAD.
TOO BAD HE STILL WASN'T IN FAWCETT WITH THE BIG RED CHEESE.
YEAH. IT'S TOO BAD.

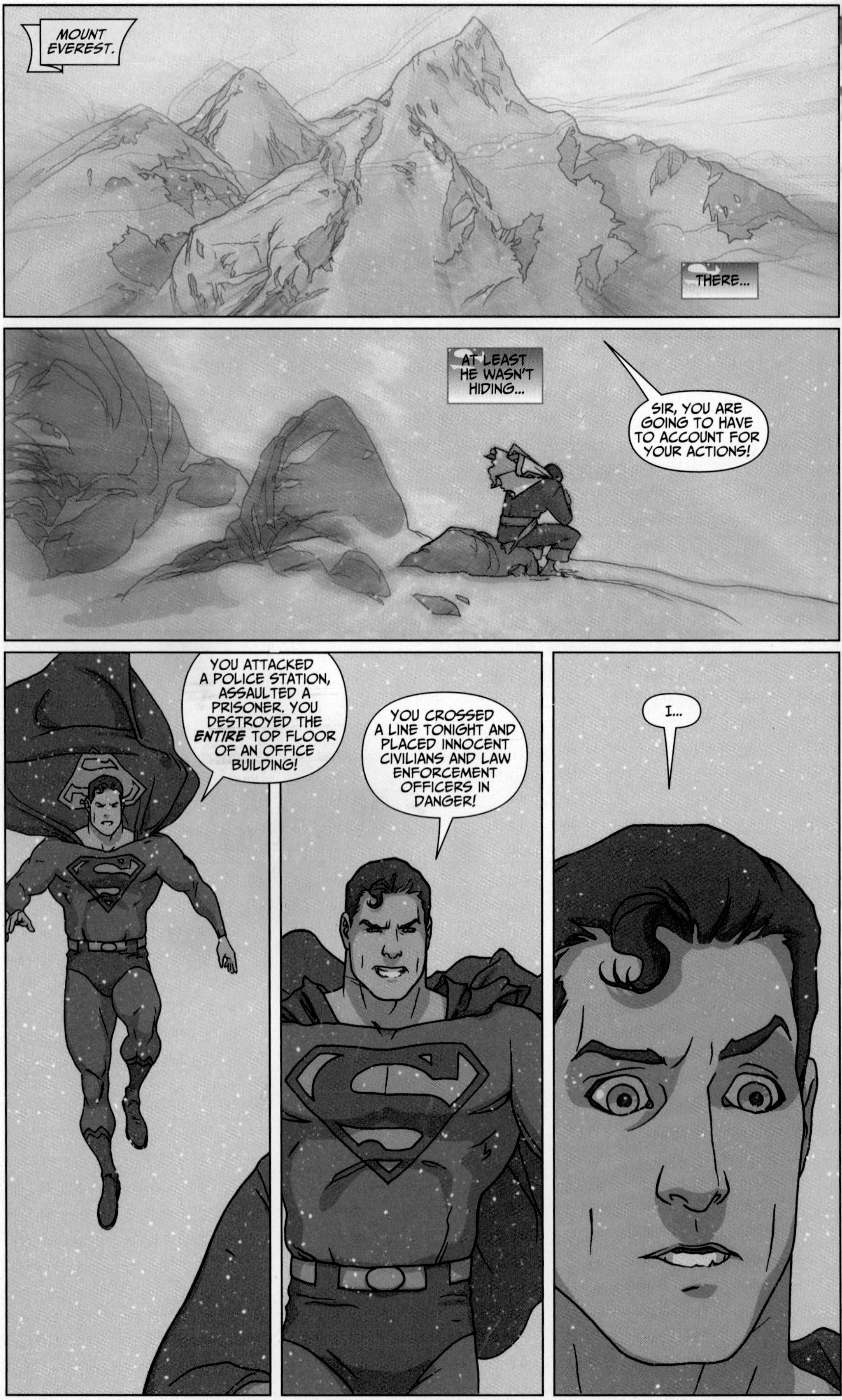
MOUNT EVEREST.
THERE...
AT LEAST HE WASN'T HIDING...
SIR, YOU ARE GOING TO HAVE TO ACCOUNT FOR YOUR ACTIONS!
YOU ATTACKED A POLICE STATION, ASSAULTED A PRISONER. YOU DESTROYED THE ENTIRE TOP FLOOR OF AN OFFICE BUILDING!
YOU CROSSED A LINE TONIGHT AND PLACED INNOCENT CIVILIANS AND LAW ENFORCEMENT OFFICERS IN DANGER!
I...

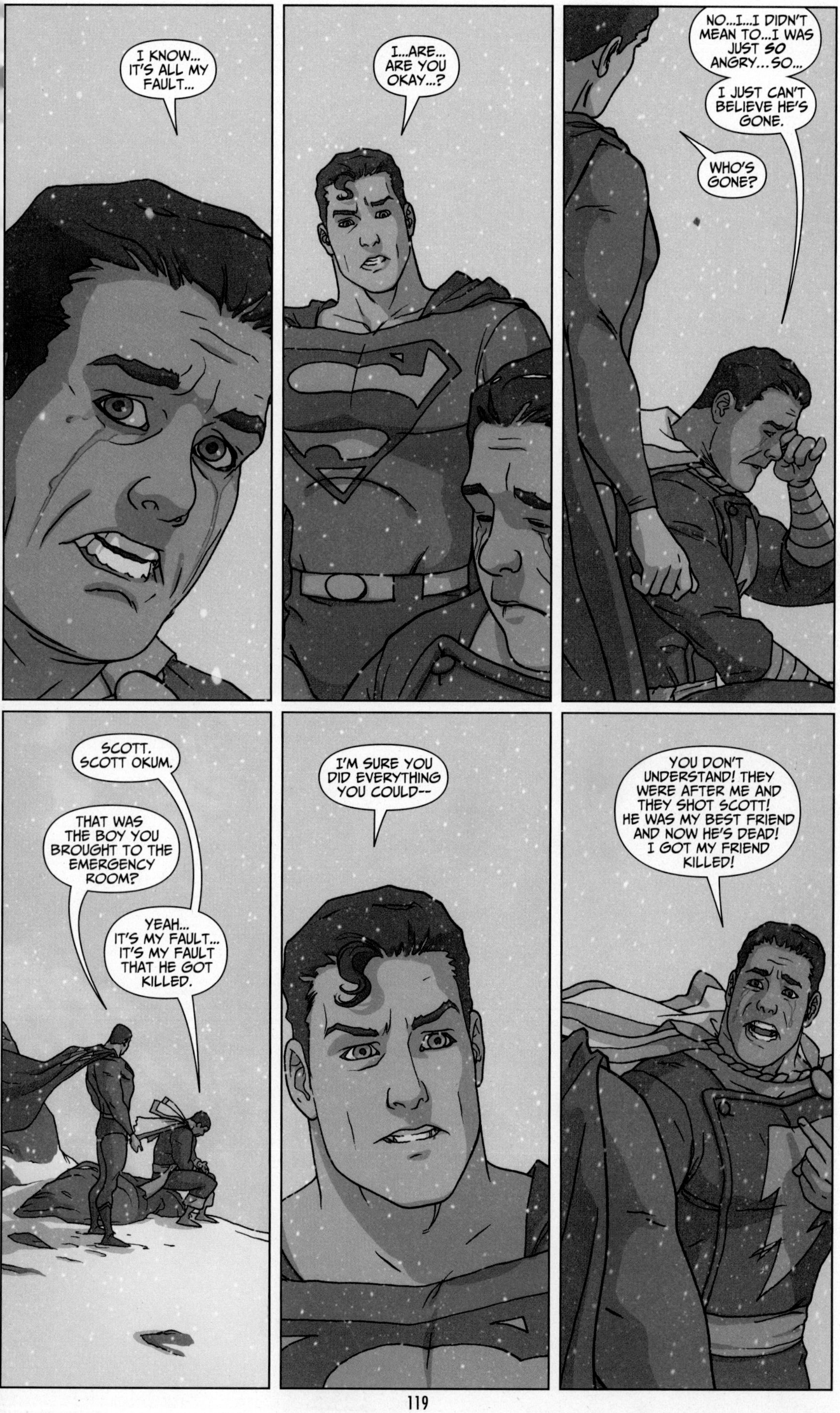
I KNOW...
IT'S ALL MY FAULT...
I...ARE... ARE YOU OKAY...?
NO...I...I DIDN'T MEAN TO...I WAS JUST SO ANGRY... SO...
I JUST CAN'T BELIEVE HE'S GONE.
WHO'S GONE?
SCOTT. SCOTT OKUM.
THAT WAS THE BOY YOU BROUGHT TO THE EMERGENCY ROOM?
YEAH... IT'S MY FAULT... IT'S MY FAULT THAT HE GOT KILLED.
I'M SURE YOU DID EVERYTHING YOU COULD--
YOU DON'T UNDERSTAND! THEY WERE AFTER ME AND THEY SHOT SCOTT! HE WAS MY BEST FRIEND AND NOW HE'S DEAD! I GOT MY FRIEND KILLED!

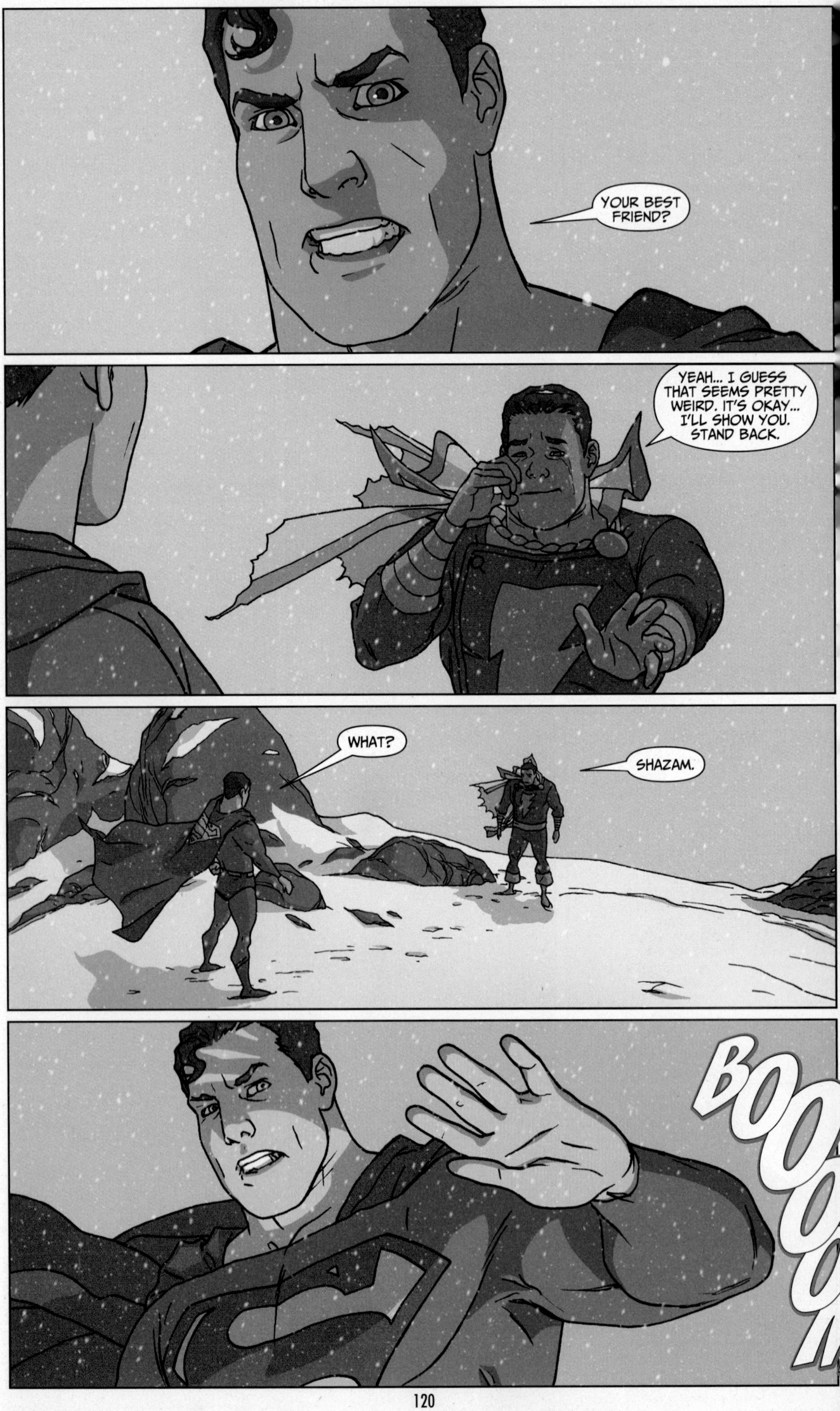
YOUR BEST FRIEND?
YEAH... I GUESS THAT SEEMS PRETTY WEIRD. IT'S OKAY... I'LL SHOW YOU. STAND BACK.
WHAT?
SHAZAM.
BOOOOM

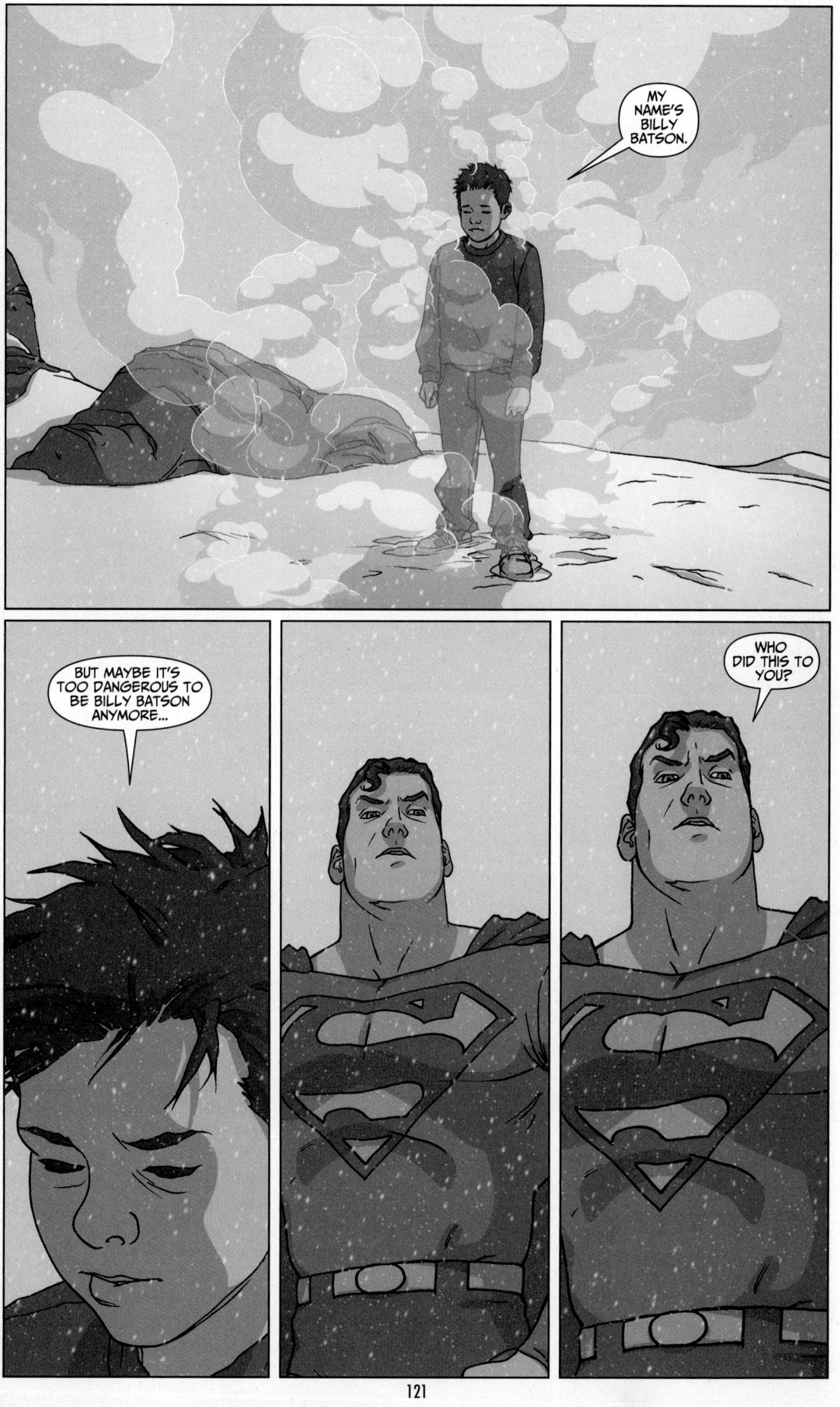
MY NAME'S BILLY BATSON.
BUT MAYBE IT'S TOO DANGEROUS TO BE BILLY BATSON ANYMORE...
WHO DID THIS TO YOU?

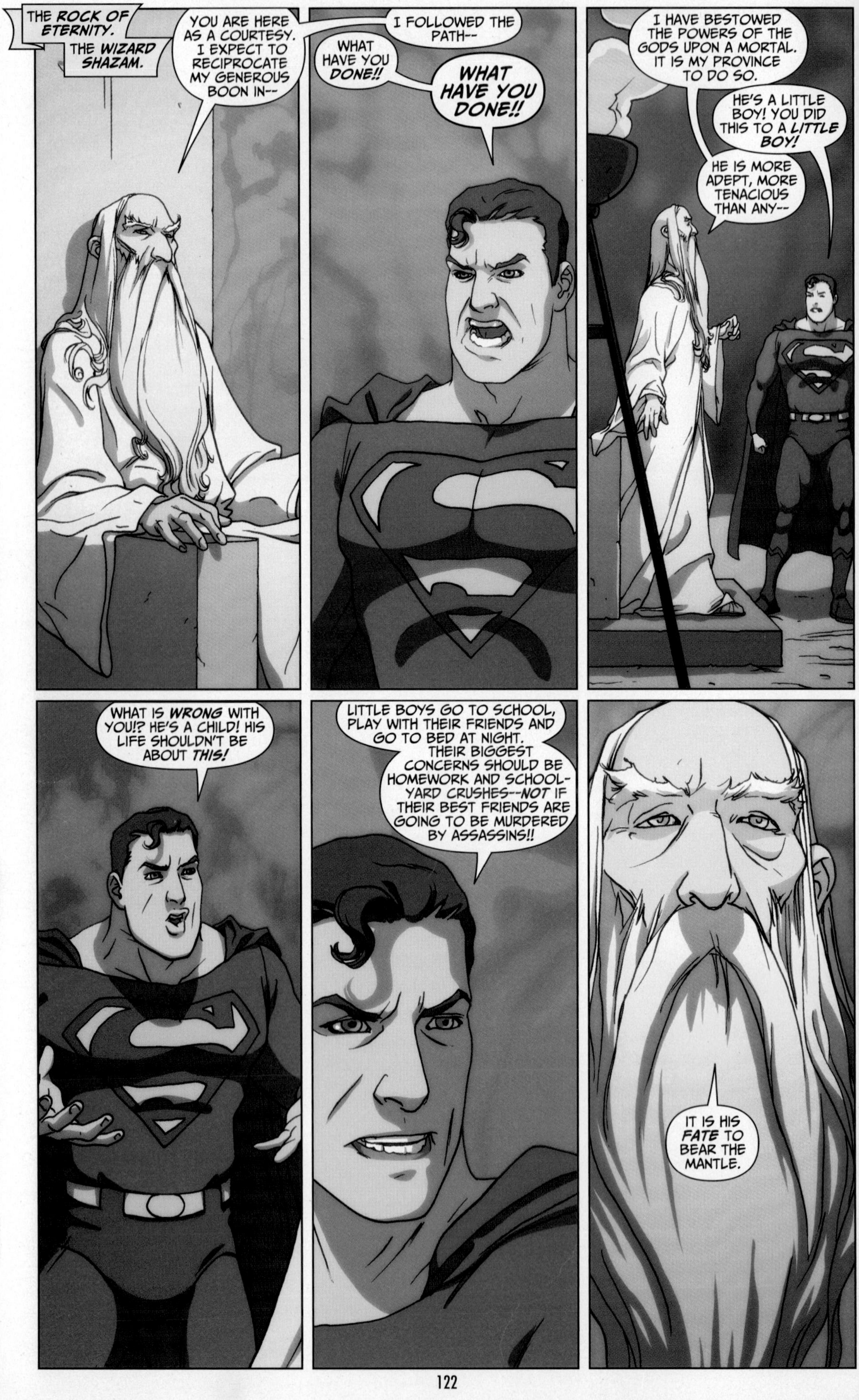
THE ROCK OF ETERNITY.
THE WIZARD SHAZAM.
YOU ARE HERE AS A COURTESY. I EXPECT TO RECIPROCATE MY GENEROUS BOON IN--
I FOLLOWED THE PATH--
WHAT HAVE YOU DONE!!
WHAT HAVE YOU DONE!!
I HAVE BESTOWED THE POWERS OF THE GODS UPON A MORTAL. IT IS MY PROVINCE TO DO SO.
HE'S A LITTLE BOY! YOU DID THIS TO A LITTLE BOY!
HE IS MORE ADEPT, MORE TENACIOUS THAN ANY--
WHAT IS WRONG WITH YOU!? HE'S A CHILD! HIS LIFE SHOULDN'T BE ABOUT THIS!
LITTLE BOYS GO TO SCHOOL, PLAY WITH THEIR FRIENDS AND GO TO BED AT NIGHT. THEIR BIGGEST CONCERNS SHOULD BE HOMEWORK AND SCHOOL-YARD CRUSHES--NOT IF THEIR BEST FRIENDS ARE GOING TO BE MURDERED BY ASSASSINS!!
IT IS HIS FATE TO BEAR THE MANTLE.

DO NOT TALK TO *ME* ABOUT FATE.

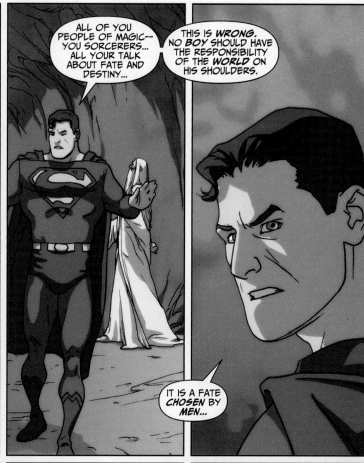

ALL OF YOU PEOPLE OF MAGIC-- YOU SORCERERS... ALL YOUR TALK ABOUT FATE AND DESTINY...

THIS IS *WRONG.* NO *BOY* SHOULD HAVE THE RESPONSIBILITY OF THE *WORLD* ON HIS SHOULDERS.

IT IS A FATE *CHOSEN* BY *MEN*...

HE'S JUST A BOY.

HE IS. A BOY...A BOY WHO COULD USE... GUIDANCE.

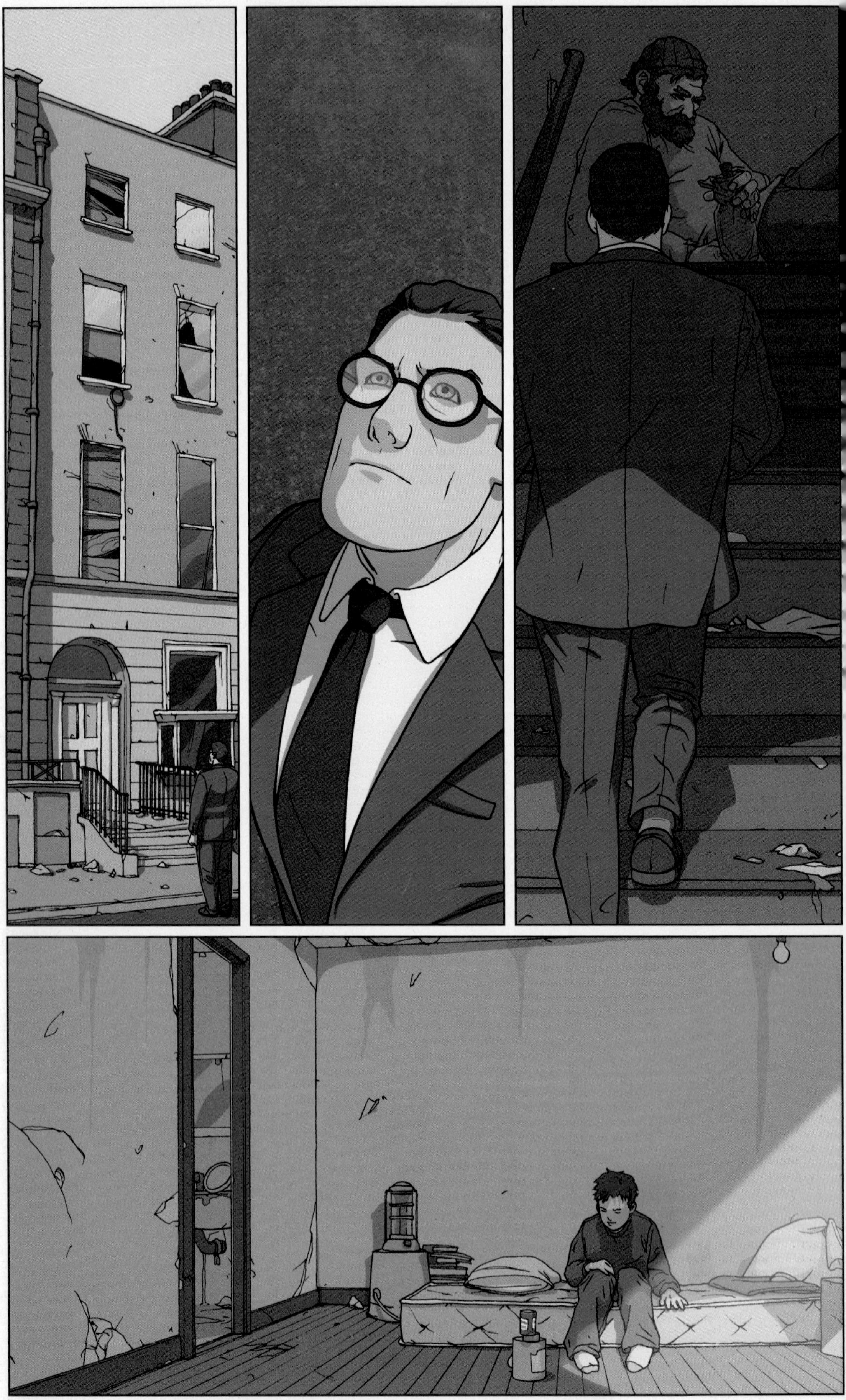

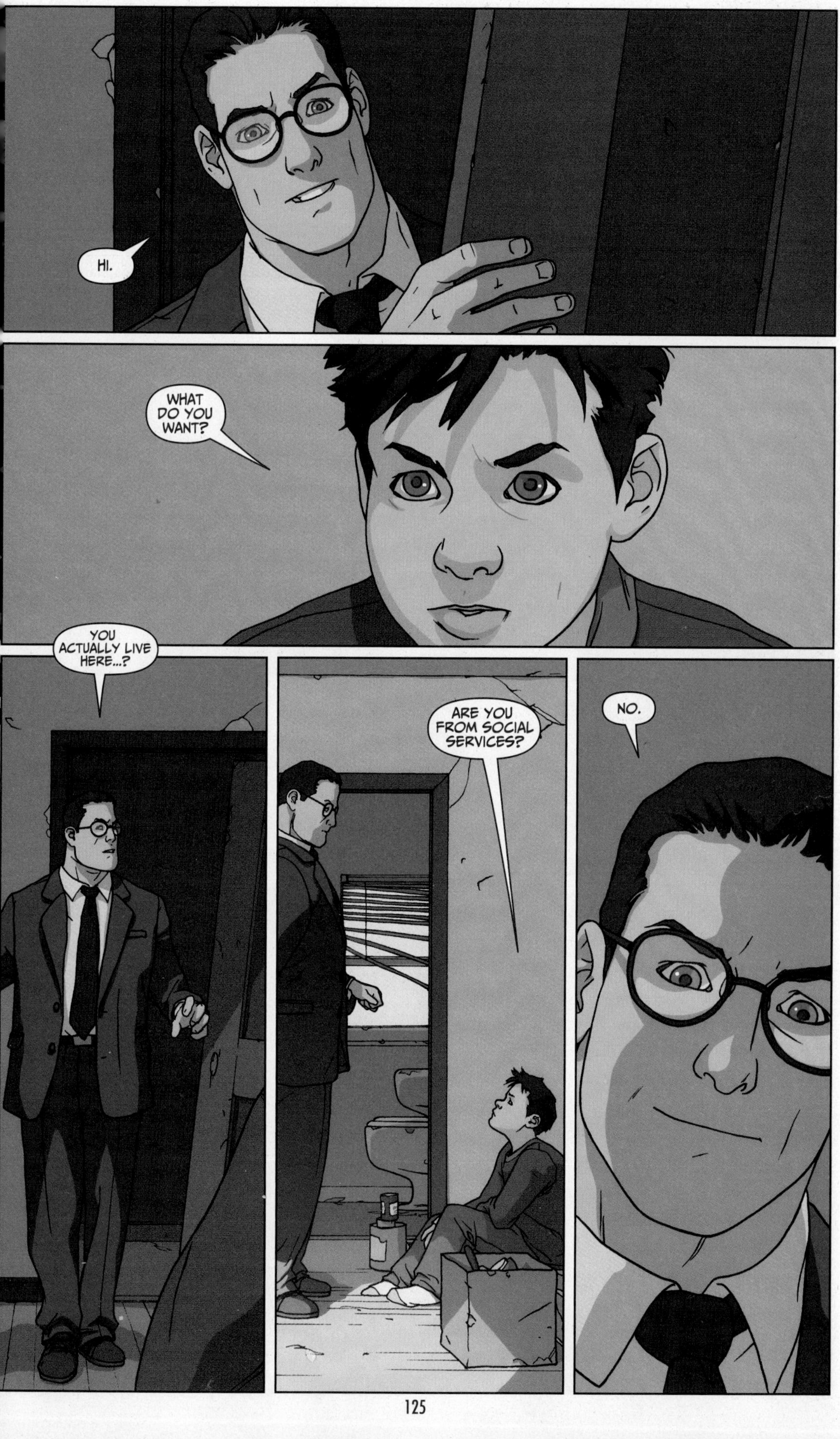
HI.
WHAT DO YOU WANT?
YOU ACTUALLY LIVE HERE...?
ARE YOU FROM SOCIAL SERVICES?
NO.

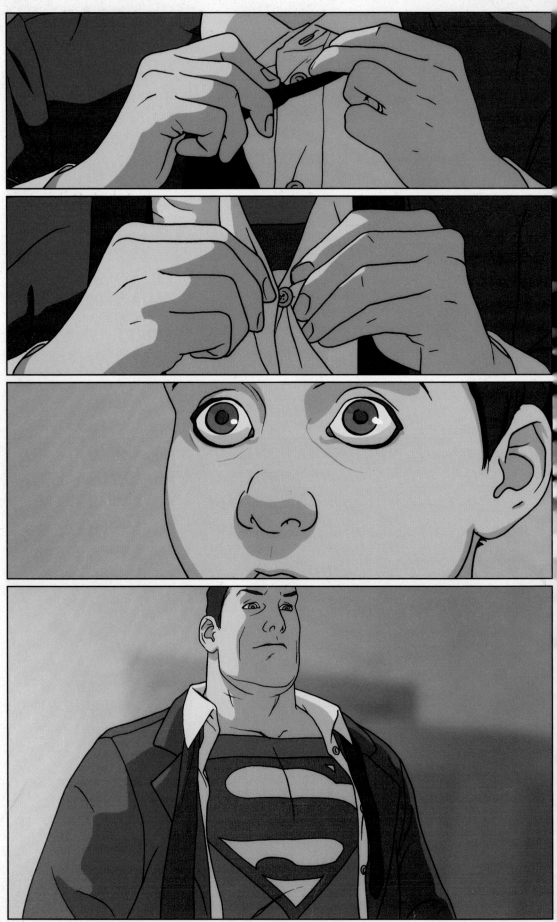

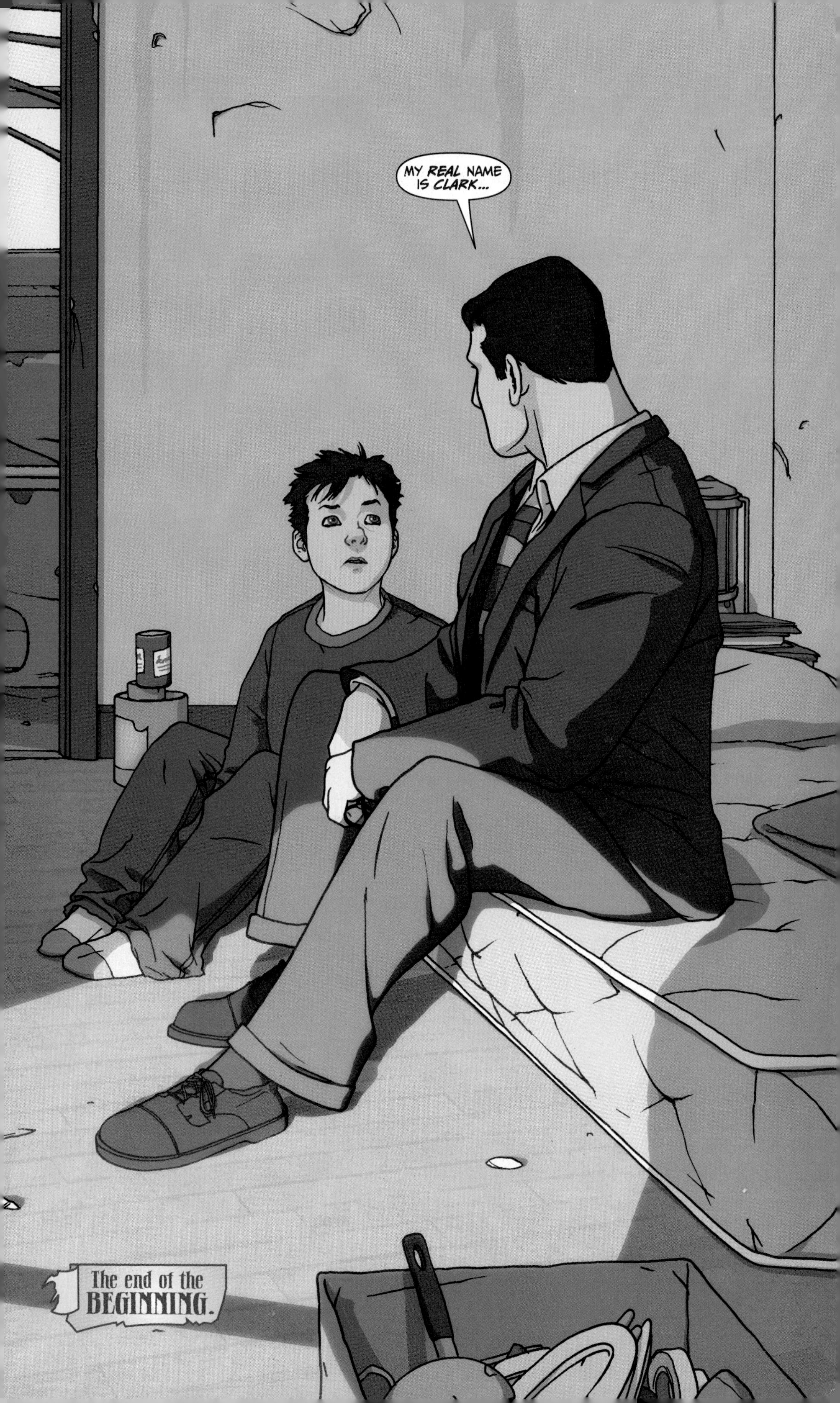
MY REAL NAME IS CLARK...
The end of the BEGINNING.

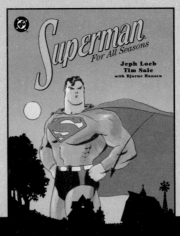
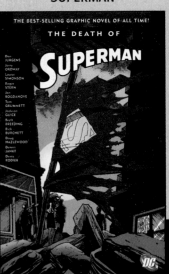